# PERFORMANCE MOTORCYCLES

# PERFORMANCE MOTORCYCLES

## MICK WALKER

CHARTWELL
BOOKS, INC.

**Published by**
**CHARTWELL BOOKS, INC.**
A Division of **BOOK SALES, INC.**
114 Northfield Avenue
Edison, New Jersey 08837

ISBN: 0-7858-1380-2

Editorial and design by
Amber Books Ltd
Bradley's Close
74-77 White Lion Street
London N1 9PF

Editors: Conor Kilgallon/Chris Stone
Design: Graham Curd
Illustrators: Richard Burgess, Mark Franklin, Kevin Jones Associates
Picture research: Lisa Wren

Printed in Italy

## ACKNOWLEDGEMENTS

I would very much like to thank the following people who have helped in producing *Performance Motorcycles* and to say how much I've enjoyed working with the production team at Amber Books on this, my 75th book!
Once again, my good friend Keith Davies of Three Cross Imports for providing material on many of the Italian marques featured in this book, including Moto Guzzi, Cagiva, Laverda and MV Agusta; Luke Plummer, the ever-cheerful Press & PR anchorman of Ducati UK, and Marco Montemaggi, curator of the Ducati museum in Bologna; Chris Willows at BMW GB, Bracknell; Graham Sanderson, formerly of Honda; the Japanese offices of Kawasaki, Suzuki and Yamaha; Bruno Tagliaferri, Triumph's ultra enthusiastic marketing manager; Jim Parker, President of the New Era Racing Club and secretary Brenda Scivyer; Richard Thirkell, organiser of the Lansdowne Classic Race Series; and Ian Kimberley of Harley-Davidson and Buell Specialists, Newmarket, Suffolk.
Finally, thanks to Conor Kilgallon, Lisa Wren and Chris Stone for handling the production side at Amber Books.

# CONTENTS

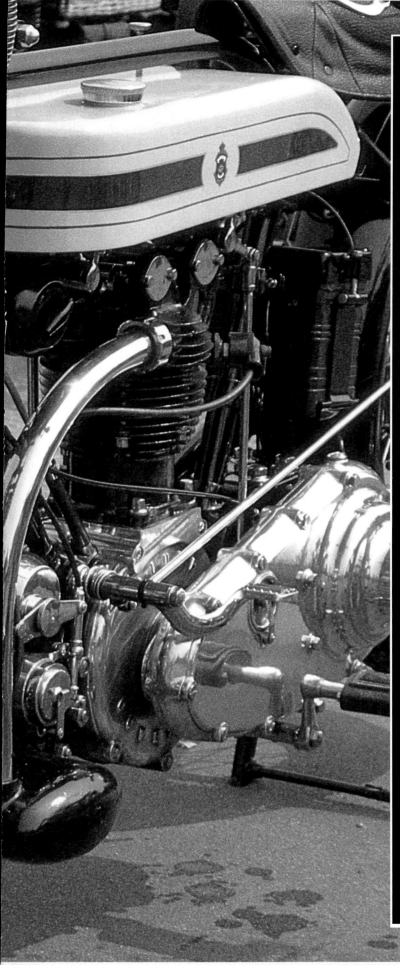

# THE EARLY DAYS

The first motorcycles were primitive affairs lacking any form of suspension brakes or transmission. But thereafter development was breathtaking, with ever more powerful engines, greater stopping power and a host of technical innovations. The purpose of the motorcycle also changed from purely a means of transport to the growth of the performance bike, for both road and track. Until, at the dawn of the 21st century, the performance motorcycle reigns supreme.

Throughout the history of the motorcycle, the 'performance' model in any company's range has been the star turn, the bike which owners adored and others aspired to own. Usually made in smaller numbers and more expensive to purchase than other models, the performance version offered not only extra speed, but also a stunning variety of additional technical innovations, often derived from racing experience. In fact, it would be correct to describe the performance motorcycle as the ultimate in many enthusiasts' eyes. In the veteran and vintage days, the words 'performance motorcycle' meant simply the addition of a tuned engine. From the late 1960s, however, they became the words to describe machines with truly superior speed and improvements in handling, road-holding, braking, and suspension. These machines evolved into the specialised performance motorcycles of today – the Superbikes, Tourers, Super

The 1922 Triumph 499cc Model R sported a 4-valve cylinder head designed by Harry Ricardo. Nicknamed 'the Riccy', it was the hi-tech bike of its day.

Sports Bikes, Retros, Replicas, Miniature Superbikes, and Classics.

Now, in the early years of the 21st century, series production Superbikes such as the Suzuki Hayabusa, Honda Blackbird and Kawasaki ZX-12 are reaching towards an amazing 321km/h (200mph). One could well ask the question: where will it all stop? When the German company Hildebrand and Wolfmüller built the world's first series production motorcycle back in 1894, it needed a huge 1489cc twin-cylinder engine to achieve almost 48km/h (30mph). Speed, of course, is a relative commodity, depending upon technical advances. Yet the modern performance bike remains desirable, even though not everyone wants to travel at great speed – people will always want that special machine.

### RACING DEVELOPS THE BREED

In June 1895, the first official motorised races took place in France, over a course totalling 1200km (745 miles). In all, 21 vehicles were entered, including machines from such well-known automobile manufacturers as Panhard, Peugeot and de Dion-Bouton, and they raced over roads from Paris to Bordeaux and back. Of the three motorcycles entered, the fastest was a five-cylinder, rotary-engined machine, designed by Felix Theodore Millet. The original Millet creation of 1892 had seen the engine mounted in the front wheel; by the 1895 race, however, this had been transferred to the rear wheel. The rigidity of the engine's cylinders acted as a reinforcement for the wheel, which was subjected to intense vibrations from the engine. Millet claimed a maximum speed of 55km/h (34mph).

It is little known internationally that it was the French who pioneered motorcycle racing and, with it, the first real performance motorcycles. They were also the first to exploit commercially motorcycle manufacture between rival manufacturers. Well before the end of the 19th century, several France-based individuals had created organisations to explore the use of the largely untried Otto-cycle engine (pioneered by the German Gottlieb Daimler and his

associate Wilhelm Maybach for two-wheel use in 1885) and thus create a fledgling motorcycle industry. These early French pioneers included the likes of Count de Dion, his mechanic Georges Bouton, Maurice Fournier, Ernest Michaux, and, of course, Felix Theodore Millet. Also, the Russian-born brothers Eugene and Michel Werner had settled in France and become French by adoption.

Unlike elsewhere in Europe, Victorian England was still very much a society dominated by horsepower (the four-legged type!) To protect this lifestyle, there was a vast array of draconian regulations impeding the development of self-propelled vehicles, including a speed limit of 6km/h (3.7mph). It was only in 1896, with the passing of the Emancipation Act, that these restrictions were lifted and the new transport industries began to flourish. Despite this, it was an Englishman, Major (later Colonel) Henry Capel Lofft Holden, who constructed the world's first four-cylinder motorcycles in 1897.

Variable gears were still well over a decade away, so Holden relied instead on sheer power to overcome the inherent inflexibility of direct drive. Like the German pioneers Hildebrand and Wolfmüller, Holden employed long, exposed connecting rods and cranks linked directly to the rear-wheel spindle; however, Holden's engine differed greatly from the Munich product. The four cylinders were placed in horizontal pairs, each like a straight unpinned pipe, closed at both ends. In each pipe was a long piston with a crown at each end. The combustion took place at alternate ends of the cylinders, giving an impulse on each stroke, and total displacement was 1047cc. Substantial gudgeon pins or 'crosshead' pins, as used on a steam railway engine, projected through slots in the cylinder walls to engage with the connecting rods. Automatic inlet valves were employed, but the mechanically operated exhaust valves, lacking any convenient rotary motion in the engine to drive them, were activated via a camshaft chain-driven from the machine's rear wheel.

The four-cylinder Holden engine operated at a mere 420rpm, at which it produced 3bhp, giving a top speed of 39km/h (24mph). Limited production was undertaken by the concern based in Kennington, London, but a change to water-cooling was needed, as early prototypes suffered from overheating. Originally, production had been planned to start in 1898, but it was not until the following year, 1899, that it actually got under way. Unfortunately, water-cooling added to the already considerable weight of the Holden four, so it fared badly against the smaller machines, which offered superior comfort, reliability, and price. Still, three examples were exhibited at the 1901 Stanley Show and one was ridden from London to Petersfield, Hampshire, and back – some 170 km (106 miles) – without any problems; however, that marked the swansong of the world's first 'Superbike'. An 1897 prototype of the Holden survives to the present day in London's Science Museum. Other early four-cylinder motorcycles include the Belgian FN, Austro-Hungarian Laurin & Klement, and the German Dürkopp.

### THE COMPETITIVE EDGE

When France began organising the first speed events and long-distance road races, the other European nation to mount a substantial challenge were the countries of the old Austro-Hungarian empire. At the very end of the 19th century, and into the early years of the 20th century, one of the most important speed events was the classic Paris–Vienna race. The first motorcycles to contest the event from the Austro-Hungarian empire were those from Laurin & Klement. Built at a factory in Mlada Boleslav (now part of the Czech Republic), the first Laurin & Klement machines were built under licence from Werner.

Werner and Laurin & Klement clashed head-on in the 1902 Paris–Vienna race. This extremely gruelling 990km (615-mile), four-day event involved the climbing of the Arlberg Pass, some 1800m (5905ft) above sea level, over largely ill-surfaced roads – and Klement's leading rider, Derny, led for over half

the distance before crashing out. Before this, however, he had done enough to establish both company and country as a leading motorcycle contender. Laurin & Klement (later to become Skoda) were soon joined by Walter and Puch.

## THE BIRTH OF BRITISH RACING

Returning to the UK, the famous Isle of Man TT (Tourist Trophy) was first run in 1907. The race was originally conceived to test the reliability, efficiency, and fuel economy of standard production road-going machines. The Isle of Man was chosen as the venue because, at that time, a blanket 32km/h (20mph) speed limit was in force in the remainder of Great Britain; this meant that the most popular venues for speed events on public roads were therefore

**During the first decade of the 20th century, the Belgian FN four was considered the Superbike of its day. Designed by Paul Kelecom, it had a power output of 9bhp and could achieve 45km/h (28mph). It was sold both in Europe and North America.**

Continental Europe and Ireland. The Isle of Man, however, with its own parliament, was able to close its roads and its authorities were already accustomed to welcoming organisers of speed events and also those with high-performance motorcycles.

One illustration of how the concept of the high-performance motorcycle has changed is to recall that, at the very first TT series, the premier award was for Class 1 (single-cylinder) bikes. Charlie Collier won on a Matchless,

averaging 61.5km/h (38.22mph), while his brother Harry (also on a Matchless) put up the fastest lap of 67.3km/h (41.81mph) before retiring. The Class 2 (twins) race was won by Rem Fowler, riding a Peugeot-engined Norton. By 1909, the two-class system was abandoned in favour of a straight race for singles up to 500cc, and multis up to 750cc. The fuel consumption restrictions were also axed. From then on, the TT became the premier testing ground for high-performance motorcycles until the latter stages of the 20th century, when Grand Prix racing and, later still, WSB (World Superbike) events took over.

Another venue for high-performance motorcycles during the first half of the 20th century was at Brooklands, near Weybridge, Surrey, in the UK. This had the distinction of being the world's first purpose-built motor-racing circuit when it was opened in June 1907. Motorcycles did not feature until the following year; however, once they did, they became an integral part of the Brooklands legend until the circuit finally closed in 1939.

The distinction of the first ever 160km/h (100mph) lap of the Surrey speed bowl went to Bert Le Vack on a 1000cc Zenith V-twin. Noel Pope went on to set the ultimate two-wheel lap at Brooklands in 1939, lapping at 200km/h (124.51mph). It was not until 1909 that official bodies were in place

**The first ever Isle of Man TT took place in May 1907. Rem Fowler won the Class 2 event (for twin-cylinder machines) on this Peugeot-engined Norton, at an average speed of 58.71km/h (36.22mph). He also set the fastest lap of 69.56km/h (42.91mph).**

o record the outright two-wheel speed record. An Englishman, W.E. ('Wee-Wee') Cook, was the first holder of the title, with a speed of 122.18km/h (75.92mph) on a Peugeot-engined 944cc NLG (North London Garages) V-twin on 16 June 1909. From then until the outbreak of World War II in September 1939, numerous men, particularly from the USA, Britain, Germany, and Italy, held the title of 'fastest on two wheels'.

## THE QUEST FOR SPEED

For many, attaining the title of the fastest rider became an obsession. The 1930s in particular saw a host of attempts and new speeds, with the likes of Ernst Henne (BMW), Piero Taruffi (Gilera), Eric Fernihough (Brough Superior), and Joe Wright (AJS) being outstanding. When the war finally ended in 1945, Henne held the record with a speed of

279.43km/h (173.67mph). This was to remain unbroken until the early 1950s.

As in the four-wheel world, Grand Prix races were soon a feature of the motorcycling world. The first of these was the Grand Prix of France, staged in 1904 and won by Laufranchi, riding a 598cc Peugeot V-twin. However, Grand Prix events did not become a regular feature of the calendar until the early 1920s, partly because of World War I from 1914 to 1918. After that conflict, large arms producers made a massive switch to peacetime manufacturing, resulting in the rapid development of new motorcycle models. Many of these were distinct performance motorcycles, produced either as developments of existing machines or specialised high-performance models. This in turn led to a need for bike builders to undertake racing for both technical and publicity purposes. In 1938, the FICM (forerunner

# CARBURETTOR

The carburettor's primary objective is to supply the best mixture of air and fuel to the engine under all conditions of variable load and engine speed. This, especially on a sports or racing engine, is quite a task. In practice, compromises have to be made in order to achieve the best results. Since precise control of the air–fuel mixture is a priority, it is obvious that, in addition to performance, engine reliability and economy are also a direct function of how the carburettor performs.

Motorcycle designers have always had to balance considerations such as maximum speed and acceleration against the goals of economy, smoothness, and reliability, particularly in regard to high-performance models for series production. Even

**The purpose of the carburettor is to supply the best mixture of fuel and air to the engine under all conditions of load and engine speed. The left-hand picture shows the 'carb slide' or 'butterfly' starting its opening phase; in the right-hand picture, it is fully open, giving maximum performance.**

pure competition machines have to be robust enough to finish races and, while fuel consumption is not as important in racing, it does still play a part – too much time is lost if one has to refuel when a fellow competitor does not. Even so, the priorities of just what a carburettor should do have changed somewhat over the years. Since the early 1970s, the trend has shifted towards optimum economy for reasons not only of cost, but also in order to achieve lower pollution levels of unburned hydrocarbons.

While it is theoretically true that an engine can run on mixture ratios of 18 parts air to one part fuel, instability, overheating, and outside environmental temperature limit practical numbers to about 15 parts air to one of fuel. Even then, full-range carburation is still difficult to achieve. It is not only important that carburation of each cylinder of the engine be correct, but also vital that the carburation be balanced between all cylinders throughout the engine's speed and

torque demands. Lack of balance can cause one side of the engine to work harder than the other. This can result in a number of problems, including overheating of one or more cylinders, reduced performance, engine vibration, poor fuel economy, and, in severe cases, even mechanical damage.

A recent development has been the widespread use of the modern high-performance two-stroke sports and racing machines of the Power Jet Carburettor. The Suzuki RGV250 V-twin was one of the very first sports models to use this type of carburettor. Combined with such advances as electronic management systems and power valves (an exhaust valve on a two-stroke and reed valve induction), the Power Jet Carburettor has transformed the modern high-performance two-stroke machine.

**Carburettor types**
Fixed-venturi
Constant-vacuum
Multi-choke

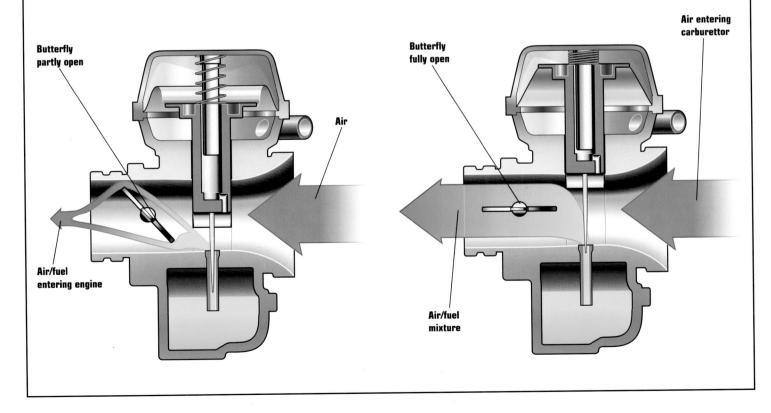

Butterfly partly open

Air

Air/fuel entering engine

Butterfly fully open

Air entering carburettor

Air/fuel mixture

# TWO-STROKE ENGINE EVOLUTION

Like its four-stroke brother, the two-stroke engine has evolved tremendously over more than a century of continuous development. The earlier and most basic two-stroke was the three-port type, with one port each for the inlet, exhaust, and transfer, the latter with a deflector piston being used to guide the gases as they enter the cylinder. This type was employed for many years, but always suffered the blight of piston distortion due to the uneven nature of the piston crown shape.

Piston distortion was partially overcome by the introduction of the flat-topped piston and loop scavenging during the 1920s. In this design, the piston still became hotter on the exhaust side than on the inlet, and thus still suffered from distortion, but the basic shape was improved. Generally known as the piston port induction type, it remains in use today on some machines.

The twin-piston or split-single concept also sought to overcome the problem of piston distortion. This featured two small-diameter, long pistons with a common combustion chamber above, one governing the inlet and exhaust ports, the other the transfer ports. The petrol mixture entered one cylinder via the transfers and pushed the burnt gas ahead of it out of the exhaust in the other. Even so, the problem of uneven heat distribution and distortion remained in the twin-piston type, while the thermal efficiency was lower than that of a conventional single, which reduced any gains in the reduced-charge loss.

It was not until the postwar era that real progress was made. Multiple ports were not new, but the latest development was to have two transfers on each side of the cylinder to do different tasks. Thus their dimensions and angles were arranged to suit their particular tasks, and so was born the five-port engine. Later still came the seven-port design, which had a reed valve in the inlet and a port running directly from the inlet to the cylinder. From this came other designs with reed valves opening directly into the crankcase multiple cylinders, resulting in the incredible horsepower figures seen on today's high-performance machines.

Currently, either disc valve induction or a combination of reed and exhaust valve is used. The Italian Aprilia concern used disc-valve induction and electronically controlled exhaust valves in its range of 125, 250 and 500cc road-racing engines, while the high-performance RS series of sports bikes uses the combination of reed-valve inlet and electronically controlled exhaust valves.

**The Italian Garelli concern was one of the pioneers of the two-stroke engine. This 1926 350cc split-single (using two pistons) utilised a single connecting rod, common combustion chamber, and a long gudgeon pin passing through a slot in the cylinder walls.**

of today's FIM) sports governing body saw fit to institute an official European Championship series; however, the first World Championships did not start until after World War II, in 1949.

## TECHNICAL DEVELOPMENTS

Right from the time of Gottlieb Daimler's first powered two-wheeler of 1885 to feature an internal combustion engine, motorcycle designers and engineers have pushed the envelope of technical development ever forwards. Many advances have been pioneered through use of the motor-cycle in the sporting arena, particularly as far as performance models are concerned. At first, the motorcycle was little more than a pedal cycle with an engine attached. Then came innovations such as suspension, brakes, multi-speed gearboxes, clutches, carburettors, pneumatic tyres, chain or shaft final drive, and multi-cylinder engines.

Although Great Britain as a nation had in many ways been slow to react to the advent of the car and the motor-cycle, its engineers and manufacturers were soon to take over from the French and Germans in both production and racing with the dawn of the 20th century. Several famous British cycle makers entered the motorcycle arena at this time, including Eadie (forerunner to the Royal Enfield concern), Excelsior (not to be confused with the US make of the same name), Matchless, and Raleigh. At first, in addition to Britain's stringent traffic laws, a major problem facing the British was engines; hence many early British motorcycles utilised imported power units. One exception was John Alfred Prestwich (JAP), who built up a large company specialising in supplying proprietary engines for the fledgling British industry from his north London base. JAP's first engine featured the time-honoured ioe (inlet-over-exhaust) valve layout, inherited from the French de Dion-Bouton; however, in 1904, JAP took a quantum leap with its own ohv (overhead-valve) layout.

During the first decade of the 20th century, a flood of now famous British marques made their debut, including

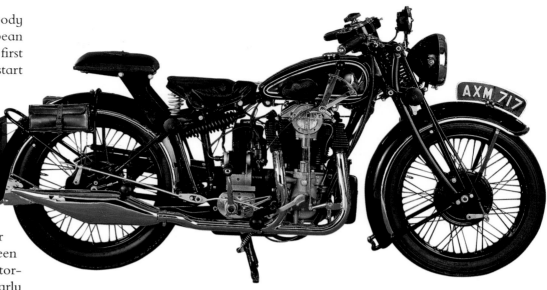

AJS (1909), Ariel (1902), BSA (1906), Douglas (1906), Matchless (1901), Norton (1902), Royal Enfield (1901), Scott (1909), Triumph (1902), and Velocette (1904). Of these, the biggest were BSA (Birmingham Small Arms), Norton (founded by James Landsdowne Norton), and Triumph (formed in Coventry by two German immigrants, Siegfried Bettman and Mauritz Schulte).

The German connection was significant. With its pioneering work carried out in the latter part of the 19th century, Germany was in a good position to exploit the rise in popularity of the internal combustion engine. As in Britain, a whole series of new entrants into the two-wheel motorised revolution appeared in Germany from 1900 up to 1910. The biggest names were Adler (1902), Diamont (1903), Dürkopp (1901), Express (1903), Mars (1903), NSU (1901), Opel (1901), Victoria (1900), and Wanderer (1902). Unlike the British, however, the really major flyers, with the exception of NSU, did not appear until after World War I. DKW, BMW, and Zündapp all began bike production in the war's aftermath.

## AMERICA MAKES UP FOR LOST TIME

Although the USA staged its first motor race (the Chicago–Wankegan) in 1895, none of the vehicles taking part (all classed as motorcycles, irrespective of the number of wheels) was powered by an internal combustion engine. Instead, a weird range of fuels was used, including acetylene, compressed air, city

**The Matchless Silver Hawk was built between 1931 and 1935. It featured a narrow-angle 592cc V4 engine with 50.8 x 73mm bore and stroke dimensions. The single overhead camshaft was driven by shaft and bevels on the offside. Its top speed approached 138km/h (85mph).**

gas, electro-turbine, ether, kerosene, naptha, and even carbonic acid. As for the new technology petrol engine, the stateside reaction was largely sceptical.

One of the first Americans to embrace the combustion engine was Hiram Maxim, an engineer working for Colonel Albert Pope, one of the USA's leading pedal-cycle manufacturers. Even though he did not convince his boss to take up his ideas, Pope's own Columbia motorcycle, built at Hartford, Connecticut, in 1900, became the first US production motorcycle. Another American pioneer was George M. Holey, who built his own ioe single in late 1900; subsequently, in the summer of 1901, Holey made history by winning the USA's first pure motorcycle race (the Boston–New York). Thereafter came a tide of stateside motorcycle manufacturers, headed by Indian, Marsh, Mitchell, Royal, and Wagner (1901); Merkel and Yale (1902); thence Curtiss, Harley-Davidson, Rambler, Thiern, Thor and Tribune (1903). It is also worth noting that Glenn Curtiss (later to win fame as an aircraft manufacturer) built a V8 motorcycle in 1908.

On both sides of the Atlantic, the 1920s saw the large capacity V-twin

For many years, Indian (shown above) and Harley-Davidson were locked together in a sales war for the giant American market. Both marques specialised in building big V-twins with engines up to 1200cc in either side- or overhead-valve form.

reign supreme in the performance stakes – certainly for the road-going motorcyclist. In the USA, this meant Harley-Davidson, Excelsior, and Indian; in Great Britain, JAP and Matchless built a series of V-twin motors which powered the likes of Brough Superior, NUT, and Zenith, plus Matchless machines themselves.

## A SUPERIOR V-TWIN

One of the fastest and certainly most exclusive of these V-twins was the legendary Brough Superior. Often referred to as the 'Rolls-Royce of Motorcycles' the Brough Superior was built by George Brough between 1919 and 1939. Even though only 3000 examples were constructed in total, they carved a special place in the hearts of all lovers of performance motorcycles the world over. Based in Nottingham, George

Brough learnt mechanics from his father, William, who had built his own cars and bicycles powered by de Dion engines at the turn of the 20th century. Yet while his father favoured flat-twin engines, George immediately opted for the V-twin format and it was to be seen on the vast majority of his models.

Entering production in 1921, the first Brough Superior was tested by *The Motor Cycle* magazine on 20 January that year, in both solo and sidecar guise. This machine was powered by a

specially tuned 986cc ohv JAP engine, with Sturmey Archer three-speed gearbox, Brampton Biflex forks, and Enfield cush drive hub. Costing £175 in solo specification, it had, for the time, a superb top gear roll-on performance ranging from 13–129km/h (8–80mph), while its quality of finish and styling made it stand out from other machines. A feature of the finish was the superb heavy nickel plating of many components. The oval, bulbous plated tank, which was to become a Brough trademark, was not only a focal point, but also a highly practical feature.

Creator George Brough was ably supported by men such as Ike Webb and Harold 'Oily' Karslake, and together they created a line of motorcycles which are still held in awe today. The most famous of all Broughs was the SS100, a 50-degree angle V-twin introduced at London's Olympia Show in November 1924. It employed an entirely new 1000cc JAP V-twin engine and was sold with a guarantee that it would exceed 160km/h (100mph) on the track. The design was based on the record-breaking exploits of Bert Le Vack and featured a sturdy duplex, steel cradle frame to which were fitted Castle forks (patented by

**Between 1939 and 1945, Harley-Davidson produced around 88,000 motorcycles for military use. By far the most numerous were the 45cu in (750cc) models. These were coded WLA (America) or WLC (Canada). Postwar, many, such as this bike, were 'civilianised' for a transport-starved public.**

# TELESCOPIC FRONT FORKS

Over the years, there have been four main types of front fork: girder, leading-link, trailing line, and telescopic. The latter has eventually become the standard fit on just about every modern machine manufactured today, with only scooters, mopeds and small batch 'specials' using other types.

The concept of the telescopic arrangement, where the wheel axis moves in a straight line parallel to the steering head, is not new. In fact, as early as 1910, the Scott marque was using it. Other manufacturers followed, but it was not until 1935 that telescopic forks of the modern style with hydraulic damping made their debut on two BMW models. Today they come in all sizes – both conventional and the latest upside-down (inverted) type. Some have rebound-only or two-way damping, or no damping (the latter almost exclusively reserved for smaller, commuter-type bikes). There is never a total lack of damping, as the friction generated between the moving parts of the forks provides some, but this is best kept to the bare minimum otherwise it will affect the forks' operation. Today's designers go to considerable lengths to reduce the stiction force in the forks, as this is invariably higher than the friction once the machine is moving. By employing modern materials and coatings, these forces can be minimised.

Telescopic forks comprise a pair of legs to which the wheel is fixed and a pair of tubes (normally referred to as stanchions), which are held in top and bottom yokes (triple clamps in USA). Today, it is almost universal for the springs to be housed within the tubes, together with the damping mechanism. The tubes are normally hard-chromed for longer life/appearance and each leg will have one or more oil seals. The legs into which the tubes are fitted are manufactured from either aluminium or steel. On really exotic machinery (mainly for racing), magnesium has also been used for fork legs (also referred to as sliders).

As performance has risen, it has become necessary not only to increase the size and strength of the various fork components, but also to brace the legs with either mudguard supports or separate braces themselves. This helps both handling and braking considerably on modern high-performance motorcycles. If your machine is capable of 289km/h (180mph), you also have to be able to stop quickly. Acceleration of such a powerful bike needs forks capable of handling this, but deceleration places even greater forces on the front suspension, particularly when braking hard from three-figure speeds. During the late 1980s, anti-dive devices were seen as a way of combating these forces, but in the end were little

more than a marketing exercise by the Big Four Japanese manufactures. Similarly, replacements for the telescopic fork, such as hub steering, have been offered, but to date none has replaced it.

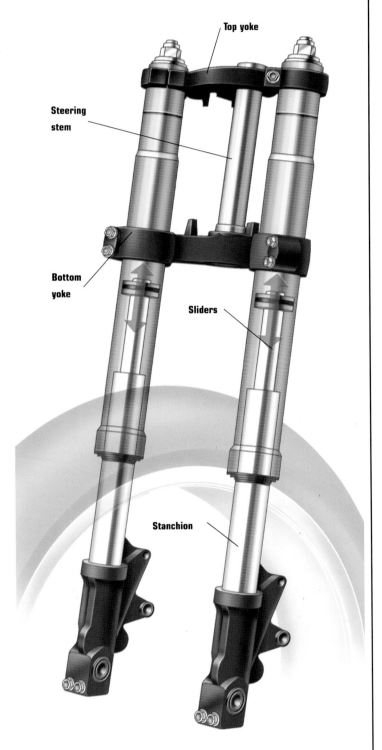

The latest type of telescopic front fork, as shown, features inverted (upside down) layout. This provides increased rigidity and smoother action.

The ultimate speed machine of its era, the magnificent Brough Superior SS100 V-twin. This motorcycle was sold with a guarantee that it could exceed 160km/h (100mph) on the track. Making its debut in late 1924, the Brough Superior was in production until 1939. A 1927 model is shown here.

Brough and Karslake), similar in principle to a Harley-Davidson design.

From the early 1930s, the SS100 adopted an ohv version of the Matchless V-twin and continued to use this engine until production ceased in 1939. In 1932, a machine designed specifically for sidecar usage made its entrance. This employed an 800cc water-cooled four-cylinder engine with the highly unusual feature of twin rear wheels, in addition to shaft final drive. The most unique and glamorous of all Broughs, however, was the Dream, a 997cc flat-four engined model. Displayed on the company's stand at Earls Court, London, in 1938, it sadly never entered production due to the outbreak of war and subsequent closure of the Brough works.

Many famous riders chose Broughs, including men such as Freddie Dixon, Bert Le Vack, Eric Fernihough, and Noel Pope. Lawrence of Arabia owned no fewer than seven examples of the SS100 and it was on one of these that he was to meet his death in 1935.

If the V-twin dominated the 1920s, the era of the high performance, sporting single was the 1930s. Machines such as Norton International and Velocette KSS were at the top of every aspiring speedster's wish list. The first overhead camshaft (ohc) Norton appeared in the

*Norton's famous International overhead cam single was built both before and after World War II. The engine was the work of Arthur Carrol and the machine was available in 348 and 490cc engine sizes. One of the latter, dating from 1952, is illustrated here.*

hands of factory riders Stanley Woods and Alec Bennett during the 1927 Isle of Man TT races, marking the beginning of a glorious period in Norton's long and illustrious history.

## BUILDING A PEDIGREE
During this time, single-cam Nortons gained an astonishing reputation in competition, both nationally and internationally. The name International, chosen for the model that replaced the Walter Moore–designed CSI (Cam Shaft One) in 1931, demonstrated no immodesty at all on the part of the Bracebridge Street Birmingham concern; it simply reflected the outstanding

quality of the bikes and their success. The new engine was the work of Arthur Carrol, who specified dry-sump lubrication and a magneto positioned at the rear of the cylinder. As with CSI, the camshaft was driven, on the offside of the engine, by shafts and bevel gears. The International was offered in both 348cc and 490cc engine sizes.

The first ohc Velocette for street use was the Percy Goodman–designed Model K of 1925. The 129km/h (80mph) sports version, the KSS, debuted in 1929, with a then revolutionary positive-stop, foot-controlled gear change, devised by Harold Willis. Introduced in 1936, the KSS Mark II featured many improvements, including a new aluminium cylinder head with enclosed valve gear. A full racing version, the KTT, was built from the late 1920s to the early 1950s and won the first ever 350cc World Championship in 1949, ridden by Freddie Frith.

**The first overhead cam Velocette for street use arrived in 1925. The 348cc KSS sportster made its debut in 1929, with the then revolutionary positive-stop, foot-controlled gear change. This 1934 machine features rigid frame, girder forks, and Brooklands 'Fishtail' silencer.**

A feature of the period immediately leading up to the outbreak of World War II was the success of multi-cylinder machines in road racing and the influence this had on the entire motorcycle industry. By 1939, there were no fewer than eight main engine types with more than one cylinder, comprising: horizontally opposed twin (BMW and Douglas); vertical twin with pistons in step (Triumph); V-twin (including Brough Superior, Harley-Davidson, Indian, and Matchless); twin 2-stroke (Scott); square-four (Ariel); horizontally opposed four (Zündapp); across-the-frame four (Benelli, Bianchi, and Gilera); and narrow-angle V-four (Matchless). Generally, the USA went for large displacement V-twins, the British Empire (as it was then) for single V-twins and the newly released parallel twin (by Triumph), and Continental Europe the big singles (NSU, Gilera,

and Moto Guzzi, for example) and small capacity two- and four-strokes, while the well-heeled went for BMW's flat twins. As for speed, 129km/h (80mph) was good, 145km/h (90mph) exceptional, and the magic 160km/h (100mph) was the preserve of racing machines or ultra expensive models such as the Brough Superior SS100.

When World War II broke out in September 1939, the high-performance, enthusiast-inspired motorcycle was still something of a rarity; the vast majority of machines being sold were for basic transport needs such as going to work or towing the family sidecar. Despite this, the 1930s and 1940s still saw the emergence of seminal machines. Two representative examples of early multi-cylinder machines which made their mark on performance bike history were Edward Turner's Ariel Square Four and the Triumph Speed Twin.

## ARIEL SQUARE FOUR

Four-cylinder motorcycles were no great innovation in 1930. Examples had already reached production not only in Great Britain, but also in the USA, Germany, Denmark, and Belgium. Even so, the Ariel Square Four made a

huge impact because of its remarkably compact size, neat appearance, low weight, and complete freedom from engine vibration.

In the past, there had been inline fours and V-fours, but the square layout of the Ariel's cylinders was without precedent – nothing like it had ever been put into production before. For much of the 1920s, the Square Four's creator, Edward Turner (designer of the trend-setting Triumph Speed Twin a few years later), had been engaged in the retail motorcycle trade in southeast London. Then, in 1927, he designed an ohc single which brought him to the attention of Jack Sangster, owner of the Ariel concern, in 1928. Thus he was plucked from obscurity and, with no formal training whatsoever, was engaged to work in Ariel's design department. Evidence that he impressed everyone at Ariel is clear – within months he was given the job of designing the most prestigious model in the company's entire history, the Square Four.

The word 'Superbike' had not been coined when the Square Four was publicly unveiled at London's Olympia Motorcycle Show in November 1930. The original model had an engine size

**Making its debut in 498cc guise in November 1930, the Ariel Square Four was, as its name suggests, the first ever motorcycle to feature a square-four cylinder configuration. In 1932, the engine was enlarged to 601cc, then, in 1937, to 995cc (as shown), as the 4G model.**

## SQUARE FOUR 4G MK II (1953-1959)

**Engine:** 4-stroke, square four, ohv, 2-valves-per-cylinder air-cooled

**Bore and stroke:** 65 x 75mm

**Displacement:** 995cc

**Compression ratio:** 6.7:1 (7.2 optional from 1954)

**Carburation:** Single (SU type MC2 fitted from 1954)

**Ignition:** Coil

**Lubrication:** Wet sump

**Gearbox:** 4-speed

**Clutch:** Wet, multi-plate

**Frame:** All-steel construction, single front downtube, branching into duplex tubes under engine

**Suspension:**
*Front:* telescopic forks
*Rear:* plunger, undamped

**Brakes:** Drum front and rear; front aluminium full-width type

**Tyres:**
*Front:* 3.25 x 19in
*Rear:* 4.00 x 18in

**Dry weight:** 197kg (435lb)

**Power:** 40bhp at 5600 rpm (with optional 42bhp at 5800 rpm) 7.2:1 compression ratio

**Top speed:** 164km/h (102mph); higher compression version 167.3km/h (104mph)

of 498cc. Besides its then unique four-cylinder layout, it had a chain-driven, single overhead cam (sohc) and over-hung crankshaft flywheels for three of the four cylinders (this configuration was used for the first production models which went on sale early in 1931; on the original four working prototypes, there were four overhung flywheels). As for the crankshafts themselves, there were two and both were similar in concept, each having a large helical gear cut on the centre flywheel. This expensive

gear-cutting method was changed to spur gears from the 200th engine.

Unusually for a British motorcycle, the Square Four's crankcases were split horizontally, with the engine's main bearings being clamped in the top section. Outboard of each bearing went a flywheel and these carried the crankpin and roller big-end assembly. The fourth crankpin (except on the prototype engines) was extended and joined its outer web in conventional fashion. The cylinder head was cast in

iron and separate to the one-piece cylinder block of the same material. A single Amal carburettor was fitted, mounted between the two forward-facing exhaust header pipes, with an induction passage interconnected between all four cylinders. A magneto was mounted at the back of the two rear cylinders. The compactness of the engine, carburettor, magneto, and transmission (a four-speed hand-operated Burman-made gearbox) is proved by the fact that the existing 500cc Ariel Sloper single frame and cylinder parts were employed.

The 500 Square Four continued into 1932, when it was joined by a larger version with a capacity of 601cc; this was achieved simply by increasing the cylinder bore size to 56mm (2.2in). With the effects of the Great Depression still being felt, Ariel only built the smaller engined model to special order in 1933; this meant that the 500 had effectively taken over. It is worth noting that the engine of the 500 retained ohc, but had straight, instead of helical, coupling gears. A modification to the lubrication system saw the method of oil storage transferred from the rear of the engine to a sump under the unit; this allowed a shorter engine length. Ariel made use of this latter change to use the shorter frame from its 500cc vertical single-cylinder model.

Only minor changes were then made until the 1937 model emerged. A new version should have debuted a year earlier, but its appearance was delayed when Edward Turner, having begun its design, left to work for Triumph. The new Square Four, code-named 4G, was a major redesign, with not only a larger 995cc displacement, but also ohv instead of ohc, dry sump instead of wet sump lubrication, and plain bearing big-ends. In place of the overhung big-ends, there were two forged crankshafts –

both essentially the same and each with a central flange carrying a separate flywheel. The connecting rods were forged in RR56 aluminium and featured split white metal big-ends. The carburettor was now mounted between the two rear cylinders; the gearbox (still a Burman) featured foot-change for the first time; and the crankcases now split vertically instead of horizontally. With a top speed of 160km/h (100mph), the result was a fast, smooth motor-cycle, which the Ariel advertising men referred to as 'Whispering Wildfire'. At the time, only specially prepared racing machines and the ultra-expensive Brough and HRD V-twins could touch

the magic ton; the 4G 1-litre (0.21 gallon) Square Four's inclusion in these ranks made it a serious performance motorcycle of the pre–World War II era.

Before production stopped for the war, in 1939, Ariel had introduced the Frank Anstey–designed plunger rear suspension to the Square Four. Although this lasted until the final models were built in 1959, it was not only over-complex, but also undamped. Several postwar machines were privately con-verted to swinging-arm rear suspension, but never as a production feature. In 1939, Ariel also built a small number of 599cc ohv Square Fours by reducing the 1-litre (0.21 gallon) engine bores to

50.4mm (2in). From the middle of 1946, telescopic front forks replaced the previous girder type; the bike then remained little changed until 1949, when Ariel gave the Square Four an all-alloy engine, thus reducing the machine's weight by 14.9kg (33lb).

The last major redesign came in 1953, with the introduction of the four-pipe Mark II with revised cylinder head and block, plus separate exhaust manifolds and revised styling. A *Motor Cycling* test with a large, heavy double-adult sidecar achieved almost 128km/h (80mph) – a stunning figure for a sidecar machine. The year 1956 brought a change of appearance, with

## SQUARE FOUR EVOLUTION

**1930**
Prototype with 498cc engine shown: unique square-four cylinder configuration, ohc, air-cooled, horizontally split crankcases, iron head and cylinder blocks. Overhung cranks on all four cylinders.

**1931**
Enters production as 500 Square Four. Overhung cranks for three of the cylinders only. Front-mounted single Amal carb; duplex frame from existing 500 Sloper single.

**1932**
Joined by larger 601cc model, achieved by simply increasing bore size to 56mm (2.2in). Both 500 and 600 feature increased engine finning.

**1933**
Square Four range slimmed down to 600 only, with 500 now available only to special order.

**1937**
New, larger model 4G introduced. This featured 995cc ohv, vertically split crankcases, dry-sump lubrication and plain bearing big-ends. In place of overhung big-ends, there were two forged crankshafts, essentially the same and each having a central flange carrying a separate flywheel. Rear-mounted carb and foot-change gearbox.

**1939**
4G model continued; smaller 599cc version introduced by decreasing bore sizes to 50.4mm (1.98in). Later model offered in 1939 only. Frank

Anstey–designed plunger rear suspension optional on 1-litre (0.21-gallon) model.

**1940–mid-1945**
No production because of World War II.

**Mid-1945**
4G model reintroduced, with girder forks and plunger rear end.

**Mid-1946**
Telescopic front forks introduced, together with revised front brake.

**1949**
Aluminium head and barrel castings, together with other weight-saving measures, see weight decrease by 14.9kg (33lb). Magneto ignition replaced by coil/battery with car-type four-cylinder distributor.

**1953**
Four-pipe 4G Mark II introduced with revised cylinder head and block, plus separate exhaust manifolds and revised styling.

**1956**
Introduction of cowled headlamp and full-width light alloy front brake. Increased oil-tank capacity and duplex, endless timing chain.

**1957–1959**
Minimal changes carried out until production of Square Four ceases in 1959 due to slowdown in motorcycle sales worldwide.

a cowled-in headlamp and a full-width, light alloy, front drum brake. Other changes introduced around the same time were an increase in oil-tank capacity and a duplex endless timing chain featuring an improved tensioner device. Minimal changes were made from then until production ceased in 1959. So passed into history a true British motorcycling legend, the famous 'Squariel', which had run for almost three decades from the darkest days of the Great Depression to the relative affluence of the late 1950s.

### SPEED TWIN – THE TREND SETTER

It was when Edward Turner transferred to Triumph in 1936 – after Sangster purchased the company – and was appointed chief designer and general manager that his fame really blossomed.

**The Ariel Square Four was designed by Edward Turner (who was later to design the legendary Triumph Speed Twin). Originally built with overhead cam in 498 and 601cc engine sizes, the definitive 995cc overhead-valve version Ariel Square Four was put onto the market in 1937.**

First came new ohv singles; however, in 1937, there arrived the motorcycle which was to change the face of motorcycling itself, the legendary Speed Twin. At first, Turner had planned an overhead camshaft layout, but this was soon abandoned in favour of a twin-cam pushrod unit pleasingly symmetrical with a gear-driven cam fore and aft of the cylinder barrels – somewhat akin to the layout of the Riley car engine which Turner drove at the time. Turner also believed in utilising existing components

## SPEED TWIN EVOLUTION

**1937**
Speed Twin launched.

**1938**
Enters production with six-stud barrel, magdyno, girder forks and rigid frame. Model 5T. 498.76cc.

**1939**
Eight-stud barrel. New T100 performance version launched.

**1940–1945**
Production halted due to war.

**1946**
5T Speed Twin and T100 fitted with telescopic front forks; 482mm (19in) front wheel. Speedo drive from rear wheel. Smaller 3T (350cc) introduced.

**1947–1948**
Optional sprung hub available. Tank top instruments. Speedo drive from gearbox when sprung hub specified.

**1949**
Headlamp nacelle introduced. Tank top instrument layout axed; parcel

grid offered as option. Oil pressure button on timing chest; speedo drive from gearbox standardised. TR5 Trophy on–off road model introduced.

**1950**
Gearbox redesign, Mark 2 version of Turner-designed sprung hub. Larger 6T (650cc) Thunderbird introduced.

**1951**
T100 and TR5 – new head and barrel in aluminium; racing kit for T100 (two carburettors, open exhausts, remote float chamber, larger oil tank, and revised controls). All models equipped with new front brake with cast-iron drum. Parcel grid standardised. 3T dropped.

**1953**
5T Speed Twin fitted with alternator in place of magneto. New T100C model to replace race kit for T100; dropped at end of year.

**1954**
High-performance version of 6T, the T110, introduced with 203.2mm (8in) front brake and swinging-arm

rear suspension. T100 now with swinging arm and 203.2mm (8in) front brake.

**1955**
All models now have swinging-arm frame; introduction of larger main bearings and shell-type big-ends. T100 and TR5 model with higher compression ratios.

**1956**
T110 model given light alloy head. Ventilated front brake. TR6 on–off road model added.

**1957**
5T, 6T and TR5 given full-width front brake hubs. T100 twin inlet port head. TR6 203.2mm (8in) front brake. First unit construction model, the 3TA Twenty One, introduced, with distributor ignition and fully enclosed (bathtub) rear end; deeply valanced front mudguard.

**1958**
All 500 and 650 models given 'Slickshift' gearboxes. T100 and T110 given 203.2mm (8in) full-

to maximise production–cost savings, so the 498.76cc vertical twin had identical bore and stroke dimensions to the 250 single from the same factory. This meant that production could be rationalised, with pistons, small ends, piston rings, and circlips being common parts.

An iron head and cylinder barrel were specified, the latter with a six-stud base flange, which was dropped in favour of an eight-stud unit in 1939 after some suffered cracking. Ball race main bearings supported the crankshaft, which was flanged at its inner end for bolting to a central flywheel. The connecting rods were of forged RR56 aluminium alloy, with inserted steel caps lined white metal big-end shells. Full-skirt pistons gave a compression ratio of 7.2:1. The gear-driven cams were housed in bronze-bushed tunnels

front and rear of the crankcase mouth, with large radius followings in cast-iron guides, while chrome-plated tubes enclosed dural pushrods which operated forged rockers in bolt-on alloy rocker boxes. Behind the cylinder barrel sat a magdyno gear driven from the inlet cam, while a peg on the end of the shaft drove a double-plunger oil pump.

In prototype, the engine produced 30bhp, while the first production bikes, which appeared in late 1937, generated three or four bhp less – still good enough to give the Speed Twin a maximum speed of 145km/h (90mph). Compared to rival manufacturers' single-cylinder bikes, the Speed Twin was remarkably tractable, more flexible, quicker, and easier to start. To the buying public, the Speed Twin in its amaranth red livery looked small enough to be a twin-port

single and, thanks to the compact engine and transmission, Turner was able to slot the whole assembly in the existing Tiger 90 single frame – the twin actually weighed 2.7kg (5lb) less than the single!

The Speed Twin was destined to influence the evolution of both touring and sporting motorcycles more than any other design, before or since. In fact, the vertical-twin concept held sway until 1969, when Honda brought out its first four-cylinder street bike, the CB750, ushering in the era of the Superbike. Back in 1939, the Speed Twin had been joined by a sportier model, the T100 (also known as the Tiger 100). The T100 designation became synonymous with speed and performance in the 500cc class over the next three decades. With a top speed approaching 160km/h (100mph), the Tiger 100 was

## SPEED TWIN EVOLUTION

width front brake, and T110 a twin-splayed inlet port head. 5T and TR5 models dropped mid-year.

### 1959
5TA Speed Twin unit construction model introduced based on 3TA. All 500 and 650 models acquire new crankshaft. T100 (pre-unit engine) discontinued in June. New high performance T120 650cc with twin carbs introduced.

### 1960
T100A, high-performance version of 5TA, introduced using same cycle parts, including deeply valanced front mudguard and bathtub rear enclosure. 650 models given new frame and front forks. 6T and T110 have same styling as 3TA, 5TA and T100A. TR6 discontinued mid-year.

### 1961
All unit models given modified head angle and floating brake shoes. T100A has higher lift camshaft; model discontinued in August, as is T110. TR6 re-introduced as single carb T120. All 650 models given

modified frame with lower tank rail and floating brake shoes. 6T now with alloy cylinder head and 203.2mm (8in) front brake.

### 1962
5TA and 3TA given new clutch operation, siamezed exhaust pipes with single silencer. The T100SS introduced as replacement for T100A, with half bathtub rear enclosure and sports-type front mudguard, new camshafts, and siamezed exhaust as 3TA/5TA. 6T slickshift gearbox deleted, given siamezed exhaust. T120 heavier crankshaft flywheels, balance factor changed.

### 1963
5TA and 3TA modified with twin exhausts, 3-vane clutch, improved rectifier. T90 sports model intro-duced – as T100SS, but with smaller 350 engine size. Points in timing cover, with T100SS given same modification. New unit construction of 650 models (T120, TR6 and 6T) with new nine-bolt heads. 6T given partial rear enclosure.

### 1964
5TA/3TA given partial rear enclosure as per 6T; points in timing cover. All 650 twins feature new front forks. 6T only 12-volt electrics; T120 only, induction balance pipe.

### 1965
5TA/3TA partial rear enclosure, new front forks. T90/T100SS new forks. All 650 models receive new forks and modified front brake.

### 1966
5TA/3TA frame modifications, partial rear enclosure deleted, 457mm (18in) wheels; 12-volt electrics. T90/T100SS frame modifications and 12-volt electrics. T100T twin-carb model introduced mid-year. 3TA, 5TA and 6T models discontinued mid-year.

The 5TA marked the end of the Speed Twin name, but the lightweight 500 twin concept was carried on by the T100SS (until 1970), T100T (1966–1970), T100R (1970–1973), T100C (1970–1971), and TR5T Adventurer (1972–1973).

The Speed Twin was in many ways both the performance bike and the style icon of its era. In 1949, the now classic headlamp nacelle was introduced. This encased the speedometer, ammeter and ignition/light switch. Note also the adjusting knob for the friction steering damper.

type for the British Army), through 650cc, and ultimately to 750cc. First of the 650s was the 6T Thunderbird, catalogued from 1950 through to 1966. It was introduced in a hail of publicity when, in September 1949, the first three production models were taken to Montlhéry, near Paris. There Jimmy Alves, Len Bayliss, Allan Jefferies, Bob Manns, and Alex Scobie thrashed them round the concrete bowl at an average of 144.8km/h (90mph) for 804km (500 miles), each bike signing off with a lap of more than 160km/h (100mph).

As with the 500, hotter versions of the 650 soon appeared. The first was the Tiger 110 (with pivoted rear fork) — on which Dan Shorey and the teenage sensation Mike Hailwood won the Thruxton 500-mile (804km) endurance

distinguished externally from the Speed Twin by the silver-sheen paintwork, while the engine featured polished conrods and ports, with 8:1 slipper pistons. An aluminium-bronze cylinder head was an optional extra. Ivan Wickstead fitted a supercharger to a Tiger 100 and, before war intervened, set a 500cc class lap record around the Brooklands circuit at 190km/h (118mph).

World War II put a damper on the development of the Speed Twin and Tiger 100, but a special all-alloy variant of the engine, the AAPP, was built to power a generator for use by RAF ground maintenance crews. This development was to influence some of Triumph's sporting postwar models. The Speed Twins and Tiger 100s of 1946 were virtually unchanged from their pre-war brethren, although the engines were not quite as potent, having been modified to cope with low 80 octane 'pool' petrol.

Turner's Speed Twin spawned many descendants during the postwar years, ranging from 350cc (originally a proto-

race in 1958. Then came the famous twin-carb Bonneville. This model was named after Bill Johnson's US Class C speed record of 237km/h (147.32mph), when he rode a souped-up Tiger 110 on the Bonneville Salt Flats in the autumn of 1958. (Class C was for 650cc series production machines.) With 46bhp at 6500rpm as it left the factory, the T120 Bonneville was supremely successful in production-class racing events, especially after Doug Hele brought his engineering expertise to the factory, improving the steering and road holding, and giving the engine a wider spread of power. In 1963 came the change from pre-unit to unit construction, a trend begun in 1957 with the introduction of the 350cc 3TA Twenty One model.

## SPEED TWIN (1938)

**Engine:** 4-stroke ohv vertical twin, air-cooled
**Bore and stroke:** 63 x 80mm (2.5 x 31in)
**Displacement:** 498.76cc
**Carburation:** Amal Type 76 15/16 inch
**Ignition:** Magdyno
**Lubrication:** Dry sump, double plunger pump
**Gearbox:** 4-speed
**Frame:** Full cradle, single front downtube, all-steel construction
**Suspension:**
*Front:* girder forks

*Rear:* rigid
**Brakes:** 117mm (7in) drums front and rear
**Wheels:** Spoked chrome steel rim, 508mm (20in) front, 482.6 (19in) rear
**Tyres:**
*Front:* 76.2 x 508mm (3.0 x 20in),
*Rear:* 88.9 x 482.6mm (3.5 x 19in)
**Dry weight:** 160.12kg (353lb)
**Power:** 26bhp at 6000 rpm (prototype 30bhp)
**Top speed:** 144km/h (90mph)

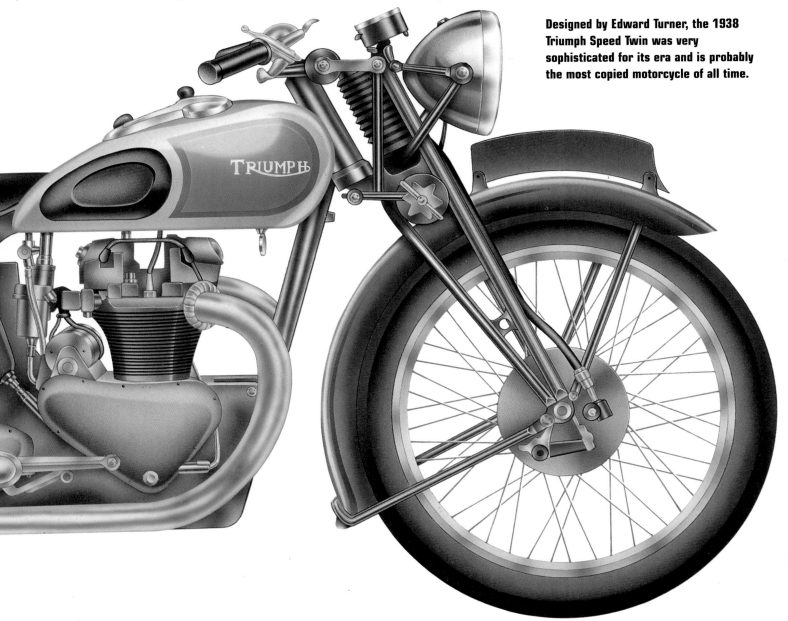

**Designed by Edward Turner, the 1938 Triumph Speed Twin was very sophisticated for its era and is probably the most copied motorcycle of all time.**

# CHAIN FINAL DRIVE

Chains have remained the most common means of transmitting power from the gearbox to the rear wheel since the 1920s, but were first used at the turn of the 20th century. In the beginning, the requisite technology came from the pedal-cycle industry, but it was not long before stronger chains were needed to cope with ever-rising power outputs from the engine. In the very early days, block chain was sometimes used, but this was only suited to lower power applications, as the blocks rubbed the sprocket teeth. A version with rollers also existed, offering improved performance, and, while similar in appearance to the roller-bush chain, had very short outer links. These early forms were soon brushed aside, however, by the roller-type chain which comprises an assembly of fine-tolerance components manufactured to a high quality.

Although the rear final drive is usually, but not always, simplex (duplex is fitted, for example, to the 1980s Benelli 900 Sei), single, duplex and even triplex chains have been used for the primary drive (from the engine sprocket to the clutch sprocket). The gearing of the machine can be altered by fitting alternative teeth sprockets to the gearbox and rear wheel, this either raising or lowering the gearing. By fitting a larger gearbox sprocket or smaller rear-wheel sprocket, the gearing will be raised (higher). Conversely, should one wish to lower (decrease) the gearing, a smaller gearbox or larger rear-wheel sprocket should be fitted. As the rear-wheel sprocket is normally larger by two or three (number of teeth), it is necessary to change only one tooth on the gearbox sprocket compared to two or three teeth more on the rear wheel to achieve the same result.

Worn chain should never be fitted with new sprockets, nor worn sprockets with a new chain; the result will be the same – rapid wear. It is also worth mentioning that chains will either have connecting links or are the endless variety, the latter usually being the case for racing. Endless chains are also used for both primary and camshaft usage. Some modern engines (from the late 1970s) have employed inverted-tooth chain for all, or part, of their primary drive. These are more commonly known as Morse or Hy-Vo chain and are particularly long-lived. This type is usually wider than the conventional roller-chain and is more likely to be found on Japanese multi-cylinder engined bikes. As for the final drive chains, these are produced in various metric sizes including 428, 520 and 530.

**Even though shaft final drive is to be found on several touring bikes, the vast majority of sportsters still use the venerable chain as the most efficient way of transferring power to the rear wheel of a motorcycle.**

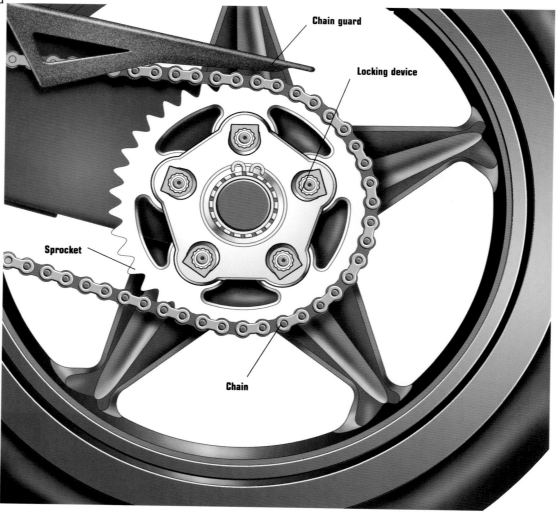

Chain guard

Locking device

Sprocket

Chain

Named after the Bonneville Salt Flats in Utah, the Triumph T120 (and later T140) ohv twin endured from the late 1950s through to the late 1980s. A brand new Bonneville was launched in 2001.

Triumph produced a full racing version of the Bonneville known as the Thruxton. On this came Isle of Man TT success in the production events of 1967 and 1969 (with riders John Hartle and Malcolm Uphill, respectively). Doug Hele was also responsible for the 50bhp 500cc racers on which Gary Nixon and Buddy Elmore dominated the 1967 Daytona 200.

The final 500cc Triumph twin, the TR5T Adventurer, was built in 1972 and 1973, bringing down the curtain on a motorcycle type which had changed the face of the industry. The Edward Turner Speed Twin was a true milestone in the evolution of the performance motorcycle, bringing with it the concept of minimum weight, compactness, and the importance of power-to-weight ratio as never before.

# PLUNGER REAR SUSPENSION

For many years, very few motorcycles had any form of rear suspension, the riders having to rely on the saddle (usually sprung) and rear tyre for a degree of insulation from the rigours of road shocks. Of course, there were exceptions, particularly on racing motorcycles. In this field, there was a slow drift to rear suspension towards the end of the 1930s, following Stanley Wood's two Isle of Man TT victories on rear-sprung Moto Guzzi bikes in the mid-1930s.

Twin-shock rear suspension in combination with a swinging rear fork (otherwise known as swinging arm) became the norm as the 1950s progressed, thanks to the Norton Featherbed frame which had debuted in 1950. However, it was another form of rear suspension, the plunger, which materialised between rigid frame and the swinging arm. The plunger system nearly always featured coil springs as the suspension medium, although rubber was also employed in a small number of cases.

In the Italian manufacturing industry, the heyday of the plunger came during the late 1930s, whereas in Britain it was during the late 1940s. There were, however, examples of plunger-equipped bikes even before the outbreak of World War I. Most followed the same design pattern, with a fixed pillar clamped between the frame supports, a bushed slider incorporating the wheel spindle lugs, and springs top and bottom, plus cover for these.

One of the final performance motorcycles to use plunger rear suspension on a standard production model was Ariel's famous Square Four, which finally ceased production at the end of the 1950s.

# SUPERBIKES

Superbikes are just that, super with a capital 'S'. In performance terms, bikes such as the Suzuki Hayabusa, Honda Blackbird, Yamaha R1 or Ducati 996 can leave a Porsche 911 or Ferrari 550 Maranello trailing in their wake. And it's not just the performance but the sophistication which impresses. State-of-the-art fuel injection systems, 6-pot brake calipers with fully floating discs, advanced suspension and multi-valve technology are examples of a few of the features found on today's crop of Superbikes from the likes of Honda, Yamaha, Ducati and Triumph.

The term 'Superbike' was born at the end of the 1960s, with the launch of the ground-breaking Honda CB750 four. This single motorcycle was responsible for the invention of a whole new market sector within the motorcycle industry; the age of the multi-cylinder bike with a deluxe specification had arrived. Although there had been four-cylinder machines before, it was the specification of the Honda that really changed everything, with modern features such as electric start, overhead camshafts, five-speed gearbox, a hydraulically operated front disc brake, and a myriad of smaller features.

As the 1970s dawned, customers queued up to buy the Honda and the designs that followed – bikes such as the awesome Kawasaki 900 Z1, Suzuki's liquid-cooled three-

**Launched at the end of 1998, the 996 Ducati was essentially a larger displacement, more powerful version of the legendary 916 Superbike which had made its debut in the spring of 1994.**

cylinder GT750 two-stroke, and BMW's R90S flat-twin. Then there was the US Harley-Davidson marque, which joined the bandwagon with its 1000cc XLCH Sportster and 1200cc Super Glide V-twins. Although with smaller-scale production, Italy also waded in with a plethora of interesting and technically innovative models, including Ducati's 750 GT/Sport/Super Sport 90-degree bevel V-twins, the Moto Guzzi V7 Sport, Laverda's 750 SFC parallel twin, and the MV Agusta 750S. The British industry was still there – just – with the BSA and Triumph triples (Rocket 3 and Trident, respectively) and Norton's ohv parallel-twin Commando.

### BIGGER ENGINES

The late 1970s saw a rush to even bigger engines, where maximum cubic capacities ruled supreme. Added to this were several important technical advances, such as more powerful brakes (including triple discs); a Japanese move to double, instead of single, overhead camshafts; and designs with six-speed gearboxes.

The new Superbikes of the era saw the arrival of the Honda CB900 (following an earlier move from single to double overhead camshafts) while Kawasaki came up with the one-litre (0.21-gallon) Z1000. Suzuki joined in with, first, the GS750 of 1977, followed by the mighty GS1000 by the end of the decade. Yamaha, which had previously concentrated on high-performance, small-capacity two-strokes, arrived on the scene with the XS750, soon up-rated to 850cc (both with shaft final drive), before introducing the powerful but heavyweight XS1100 in 1980. BMW, too, joined the displacement race, boring its 900 out to 1000cc, to produce the R100RS which made its debut at the end of 1976. The Italians introduced the 864cc Ducati as the 900SS and finally, in 1979, the Mike Hailwood Replica (following Mike Hailwood's famous 1978 comeback TT victory). Moto Guzzi brought out the Le Mans to great critical acclaim in 1976, using an 844cc version of the early 750cc V-twin motor; while MV Agusta launched

the America and Monza, both with oversize engines. But it was Laverda that really set tongues wagging, when its new three-cylinder model, the Jota, became the first production motorcycle to crack 225.3km/h (140mph) in 1976. By now Triumph and BSA had all but disappeared, but this did not stop Norton increasing the size of its venerable ohv parallel-twin engine to 829cc.

### THE 1980s AND 1990s

A worldwide recession took place at the beginning of the 1980s. This badly affected the motorcycle industry, with many smaller manufacturers – and dealers – going into bankruptcy. It did not, however, slow the development of the Superbike. In fact, if anything, the

**Towards the end of 1996, the reborn British Triumph marque introduced the all-new T595, a Superbike to match anything in the world. It used a 955cc three-cylinder engine, which produced 128bhp, and featured a unique oval-section twin-spar chassis and singled-sided swinging arm.**

recession increased development, as bike builders in Japan and Europe fought hard for remaining sales.

Technically, the 1980s saw the introduction of the widespread use of liquid-cooled engines, six-speed gearboxes, improved suspension (including monoshock at the rear), and more powerful brakes (some, for the first time in production bikes, with four-piston calipers). Some technical innovations such as turbo-charging and Wankel engines, plus 406mm (16in) wheels and anti-dive front forks, did not go any further. Others – including fuel injection, cast alloy wheels, electronic ignition, and streamlining – were to become important, successful advances which are very much a part of the modern Superbike at the beginning of the 21st century.

The most important Superbikes of the 1980s included the Kawasaki GPZ 900R, Suzuki GSX-R1100, Yamaha GZR1000 Genesis, Honda CBR1000, BMW K100RS, Ducati 851, and Moto Guzzi Le Mans 1000. From this list, it is clear that the decade belonged to the Japanese, with only Ducati and BMW producing anything really new in continental Europe. The British had all but disappeared from the scene, while the Americans – in other words, Harley-Davidson – were putting their efforts into the lifestyle cruiser-type bike market, rather than trying to build anything more aggressive.

It was really at the beginning of the 1990s that the current crop of Superbikes began. Unlike the 1980s, the new decade was to witness a worldwide rather than a Japanese-dominated market. Even the British and Americans took part!

Harley-Davidson, in particular, joined the fun. Erik Buell had begun building oddball racing specials in the early 1980s – including a four-cylinder two-stroke 750cc capable of around 290km/h (180mph). After this was banned by the authorities, he chose to build his first Harley-Davidson V-twin engined device, the RR1000 for Battle of the Twins racing. Unlike Harley-Davidson itself, Buell's machines have an innovative approach to chassis layout, employing a monoshock lightweight chassis with advanced suspension and state-of-the-art braking equipment.

Erik Buell's approach was in fact so successful that, in 1993, Harley-Davidson bought into his operation, with the result that development funds and Harley marketing expertise have enabled the Buell-Harley venture to grow at a tremendous rate. This in turn has provided the huge American Harley-Davidson company with an official performance division, although Buell's machines are really a combination of Sports Bikes, Sports/ Tourers, and Street Fighter machines. The 25,000th Buell rolled off the production line in 2000.

In the UK, the old Triumph company and its Meriden factory finally ceased to exist in the early 1980s; Triumph had been in terminal decline well before that thanks to the BSA Group crash of a decade earlier. However, the famous name still had its legions of fans all around the globe – notably in the USA. It was in the dark days of closure in 1983 that British businessman John Bloor moved to purchase the Triumph name. For the remainder of the 1980s, he kept the press at bay while – escaping the notice of almost everyone – he set up a brand-new organisation and planned a new factory on a greenfield site at Hinckley in Leicestershire.

### TRIUMPH – A BRITISH RETURN

The Hinckley Triumphs owed nothing to the old Meriden ones, except the legendary name. In fact, much of the design and engineering followed latest Japanese industry practice. Then, in May 1991, amid a blaze of headlines, Bloor launched his first model, the 1200 Trophy Superbike. A feature of the Bloor era, certainly in the first half of the 1990s, has been to follow a modular approach. This meant that the Trophy used a four-cylinder engine, whereas the next model to appear very shortly after the 1200 was a three-cylinder 900cc bike, the Trident. Even though the new bikes were really new

# CASSETTE GEARBOX

The removable cassette gearbox is not a new concept – it was first used in racing motorcycles not long after the end of World War II. At this time, it was useful because it allowed the rider or mechanic (quite often the same person at that time) to effect gearbox repairs without having to split the crankcases on unit construction motors. The early dohc MV Agusta single was one of the first such machines to employ the removable cassette gearbox as a feature.

In the 1980s, Honda incorporated this gearbox on its RS250 V-twin over-the-counter racer. By now its purpose was to allow the rapid change of ratios needed to keep the two-stroke in the correct power band for differing circuits and weather conditions. The reborn MV Agusta marque (now owned by the Cagiva empire) was the first to fit the cassette gearbox as a standard fitment on a series production street motorcycle: the 1998 MV Agusta 750F4.

It was adopted for the first time on a mass-produced series production four-cylinder roadster, following extended experience by Cagiva's racing department during their years contesting the 500cc World Championship series. The engineering team who created the F4 produced a complete set of gears which were specially designed, together with the gearbox itself, to allow owners to optimise the gear ratios best suited to their particular needs and depending on the prevailing track or road conditions. The era of Grand Prix technology had arrived in yet another area of the performance road bike.

they did cleverly cash in on well-known Triumph model names of the past.

Also clever was the fact that the first models built at the new facilities at Hinckley shared almost all their component parts, including frames, tanks, running gear, and the majority of the engine bits. Engine capacities were altered by using three- and four-cylinder versions with 55mm (2.16in) and 65mm (2.56in) strokes, resulting in 750 and 900 triples and 1000 and 1200cc fours. This allowed Bloor's engineering team to cover various displacement sizes with the minimum cost outlay, and also produce all its motorcycles on the same production lines.

In October 1996, the best-selling newspaper *Motor Cycle News* bore the headline: 'New Brit Superbike Hits the Bullseye'. This was in response to the public debut of Triumph's T595 – an all-new machine and without doubt its most impressive piece of kit since the first Bloor model, the 1200 Trophy, was introduced in 1991. The T595 (and the unfaired T509) represented a clean

break from the firm's policy of building a modular range of models, as they shared virtually nothing with their older brothers. In truth, the newcomers came in response to best sellers such as Honda's Fireblade and Ducati's 916.

The T595 and T509 shared a unique oval-section twin-spar chassis, single-sided swinging arm, and the most advanced fuel injection (Sagem) ever fitted to a motorcycle. In the new across-the-frame three-cylinder engines (the T595 in 955cc and the T509 in 886cc), the Triumph company employed high-tech casting techniques and materials more advanced than those used by even the Japanese. The earlier Bloor 900 triple was used as a basis for the new power plant, but only the

**For 1999, the T595 was replaced by the 955i, which was really a refinement of the older model rather than a new bike. Nevertheless, it has kept the Triumph marque at the forefront of Superbike technology, thanks to its advanced Segram digital fuel injection and ignition systems.**

original connecting-rods remained. Car makers Lotus acted as consultants on certain aspects of the engine design, notably with regard to gas flow and combustion-chamber shape. The fully faired T595 produced 128bhp; the naked, twin headlamp T509, 106bhp. *Bike* magazine recorded a speed of 264km/h (164mph) for the T595.

For the 1999 model year, the T595 was replaced by the 955i, which was really a refinement of the T595, rather than a new bike.

## SPECIALIST MANUFACTURERS

From the time Honda ushered in the era of the modern Superbike with its trend-setting CB750 in 1969, the world's motorcycle manufacturers have poured out a never-ending stream of desirable and often highly innovative bikes, the likes of which could never have been imagined by motorcycle enthusiasts in previous decades.

During the 1960s, an entire industry sprang up around the cult of the café racer, where not only owners of bikes such as the BSA Gold Star and Triumph Bonneville kitted out their mounts with clip-ons, rear-sets, aluminium tanks, and racing seats, but in addition various specials were built, most notably the Triton (Triumph engine, Norton frame). With the virtual demise of the British industry at the beginning of the 1970s, however, a new small-scale industry sprang up catering to those who wanted a special chassis built around – usually – a Japanese four-cylinder engine.

Among the names which flourished in this second coming of the café racer were the likes of Paul Dunstall, Colin Seeley, the Rickman brothers Don and Derek, Fritz Egli, Dave Degans (trading as Dresda), and the Italian firm Bimota. Certainly, during the early to mid-1970s, Japanese Superbikes did not have the best handling, the result being that bikes such as the Honda CB750 and Kawasaki 900 Z1 were soon prime targets for what was to become known as the era of the Specialist Superbike. These bikes proved popular until the Japanese finally got their big bikes to handle from the mid-1980s onwards.

An illustration of Kawasaki's 1994 ZX-9R, with liquid-cooled dohc across-the-frame 899 (73 x 53.7mm) four cylinder engine. This original version of the machine was replaced in 1998 by a new, much lighter model, cut by a massive 34kg (77lb) to a dry weight of 183kg (403lb).

Even so, a small band of specialists still remain today, including names such as Bimota, Egli, Segale, Harris, Niko Bakker, Magni, and Moko.

### HONDA CBR1000

'You meet the nicest people on a Honda', or so the 1960s advertising slogan went, but perhaps Honda took this a step too far during the 1980s when it left the big performance motorcycle missiles to Kawasaki (ZX10), Suzuki (GSX-R1100), and Yamaha (FZR1000

## KAWASAKI ZX-9R (1994)

**Engine:** 4-valves-per-cylinder, 4-stroke double overhead cam, across-the-frame four, water-cooled, unit construction 4-cyclinder
**Bore and stroke:** 73 x 53.7mm (2.9 x 2.1in)
**Displacement:** 899cc
**Compression ratio:** 11.5:1
**Carburation:** 4 x Keihin CVKD 40
**Ignition:** Electronic
**Lubrication:** Wet sump
**Gearbox:** 6-speed
**Clutch:** Wet, multi-plate
**Frame:** Box section, aluminium
**Suspension:**
  *Front:* Telescopic, 41mm
  stanchion
  *Rear:* Uni-Trak, single shock
**Brakes:**
  *Front:* 2 x 320mm (12.6in) semi-floating discs, with 4-piston calipers
  *Rear:* Single 240mm (9.4in) solid disc
**Wheels:** Spoked chrome steel rim, 508mm (20in) front, 482.6mm (19in) rear
**Tyres:**
  *Front:* 130/60 ZR17
  *Rear:* 170/60 ZR17
**Dry weight:** 215kg (474lb)
**Power:** 125bhp at 11,500 rpm
**Top speed:** 275km/h (170mph)

# MULTI-VALVE TECHNOLOGY

Multi-valve technology has been around for a long time. British bikes such as the Rudge had it back in the 1920s and 1930s. What is different now is that,

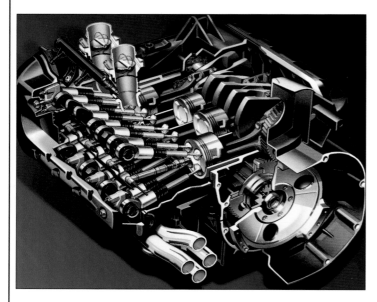

**Multi-valve technology is an integral part of the modern-day Superbike. By the late 1980s, all the Japanese marques had taken it on board, using four or five valves per cylinder. BMW also used it on the 1989 K1 (above).**

as in the four-wheel world, this technology has been developed alongside features such as electronic ignition, fuel injection, and much-improved lubrication. This means that, for the first time, its full advantages can be felt.

Honda pioneered the widespread use of four valves per cylinder, first on its all-conquering Grand Prix racers of the 1960s, before introducing it to many of its production roadsters during the late 1970s and early 1980s. For a short time, Honda also used three-valves during this period. Yamaha took things a stage further, when it introduced the FZ 750 Super Sport dohc four in 1985. Th FZ 750 Super Sport was the first production motorcycle in the world to employ five valves per cylinder.

By the late 1980s, not only had all the Japanese taken on board multi-valve technology (all except Yamaha using four valves per cylinder), but the leading European factories, led by BMW and Ducati, had also embraced the concept. BMW's first model using this technology was the K1 in 1989, while Ducati got there a year earlier with its ground-breaking 851 Superbike; Moto Guzzi was another European marque to pioneer four valves. Since that time, almost every serious performance motorcycle has featured either four or five valves per cylinder, while power figures and engine revolutions have escalated dramatically.

EXUP). As for Honda, it had its range of V-4s (VFR, RC30 etc.) or the more conventional across-the-frame four-cylinder CBR1000. This latter machine was actually a very fine bike and was offered between 1987 and 1999. It began life as a sports bike and ended it as a sports/tourer, but actually it was really a Superbike in the true form.

There was plenty of performance from the 125bhp across-the-frame 16-valve dohc engine. *Bike* magazine achieved a 244.6km/h (152mph) in a 1995 road test (electronically timed). Compared with the Triumph Trophy 1200, Kawasaki ZZ-R1100, and Yamaha FJ1200 in the four-bike test shoot-out, *Bike* concluded: 'The CBR is almost certainly the best, most relevant, most practical all-round bike here.' The only problem as far as the testers were concerned was that it was 35.4km/h (22mph) slower than the Kawasaki! Sometimes, however, speed is not the be all and end all.

During the 1990s, Honda's line-up eventually became the CBR900RR Fire Blade (Sports Bike), the CBR1100 XX Blackbird (Performance Bike), and the CBR1000 (Sport/Tourer). All three were very fine motorcycles in their own right.

## AN IMPROVING OUTLOOK

Like Honda, Kawasaki has had more than one Superbike presence in the past decade – the ZZ-R1100, ZX-9R (and now ZX-12R), and the GPZ1100 (late 1990s, but now discontinued). The ZX Ninja family has been released onto the market in stages. First, in 1994, came the ZX-9R; in 1995, it was the ZX-6R; then the ZX-7R in 1996; and finally, in late 1999, the ZX-12R.

The number '900' is a magical one for Kawasaki, as it has sired machines which have redefined performance motorcycling history, such as the Z1 and GPZ900R. It had been 20 years since the former and 10 years since the latter appeared and, in 1994, 'Big K'

fully expected its new ZX-9R Ninja to prove just as ground-breaking.

Unfortunately, Kawasaki was to be disappointed. Instead, in its first manifestation, the ZX-9R turned out to be more of a mixture of two existing machines, the ZZ-R1100 and ZX-R750. Compromises between the two meant the failure of more than one feature. The 899cc displacement was largely achieved by starting with the existing ZX-R750 (which had been launched in 1989); this was bored and stroked to provide the extra capacity, but with a lower bore/stroke ratio.

One area where much time was spent centred on the combustion chamber. Despite the effort, the first series of the ZX-9R never quite made it, dogged as it was by more than its fair share of engine vibrations, which also coincided with top gear road-cruising speeds. Weight was another problem: the ZX-9R was 215kg (474lb) compared with the ZX-R750 figure of 195kg (430lb).

The spring 1996 issue of *What Bike?* summed up the pros and cons of the original ZX-9R: 'Kawasaki's attempt to outdo the Fireblade, the ZX-9R's too heavy and too softly suspended to beat it in the bends. It's more comfy though, and the engine's close to ZZ-R1100 levels of performance. The front brakes are eyeball-popping, but as a package the Blade is better.'

## AN IMPROVING OUTLOOK

Kawasaki got the message and, for the 1998 model year, it introduced an all-new ZX-9R in which only the name and the tyre sizes remained the same; the engine, frame, swinging arm, wheels, brakes, exhaust, instruments, and bodywork were all new. There was also a lot less weight – down a massive 35kg (77lb) to 183kg (403lb) dry! This was the basis for the even more powerful and faster 1199cc ZX-12R, which debuted for the 2000 model year. With a massive 158bhp at 9500rpm and an electronically timed 293km/h (182mph), it almost matched Suzuki's all-conquering speed missile, the Hayabusa, but lost out to the Suzuki a little on acceleration. In its

favour, the ZX-12R had a much more sportier feel to it and handled better, with brakes which pulled up the Kawasaki much faster than either the Hayabusa or Honda Blackbird.

Even so, the ZX-12R has found the going pretty tough in the face of massive competition from its Japanese rivals. Honda has kept up the front by continuously updating its Fire Blade and Suzuki's Hayabusa has the advantage of being seen as the faster, while the Yamaha R1 has not only won races by the score, but also triumphed in the showroom. The Superbike war has never been hotter.

During the 1990s, Honda could boast of its Fireblade and Ducati its 916; however, in the battle for the title 'World's fastest production bike', for much of that decade this meant Kawasaki's awesome ZZ-R1100 (ZX-11 in the USA). When the ZZ-R1100 was first announced towards the end of 1989, it created a major stir throughout the motorcycling world. Here was a bike that not only set new standards for the sports/touring class, but was also the fastest production roadster ever. It would have been an easy task for Kawasaki to

have created a new flagship by simply taking the top-selling ZX-10, boring it out a bit, adding a couple of styling changes, and selling it at a higher price. Fortunately, this did not happen.

### KAWASAKI ZZ-R1100

The ZZ-R1100 engine's bore size had been increased from 74mm to 76mm (2.9in to 3in) compared to the ZX-10, giving a displacement of 1052cc (an increase of 55cc). The whole cylinder block was tilted forwards 17 degrees (two degrees more than the ZX-10) to allow as large a fuel-tank capacity as possible. Although on paper the engine may have appeared to have been simply an over-bored ZX-10, in reality there were a great many changes, primarily aimed at increasing volumetric efficiency. Formula 1 race-car technology was introduced in the form

**Making its debut in 2000, the ZX-12R is now Kawasaki's fastest machine. With a massive 158bhp on tap, it has been timed at 293km/h (182mph), making it one of the fastest motorcycles ever. It is on a par with Honda's CBR1100XX Super Blackbird and Suzuki's GSX1300 Hayabusa.**

Named after the US Mach 3 spy plane, Honda's CBR1100XX Super Blackbird arrived in 1997 and was the world's fastest production machine thanks to a 164bhp engine which can propel it to 300 km/h (187mph). The cutaway above shows the engine, radiator, fuel, and exhaust system.

of a new, forced-induction system; this drew incoming air from an inlet port at the front of the fairing located below the headlamp, and this was fed via a sealed duct straight to the airbox. The fact that it was sealed (unlike any other production motorcycle at the time) meant that there was no chance for the induction air to be heated by the radiator or engine. The air duct had

## HONDA CBR1100XX BLACKBIRD (1997)

**Engine:** 4-stroke, dohc, 4-valves-per-cylinder, across-the-frame four, water-cooled
**Bore and stroke:** 79 x 58mm (3.1 x 2.3 in)
**Displacement:** 1137cc
**Compression ratio:** 11:1
**Carburation:** 4 x Keihin CVKD 42
**Ignition:** Computerised/electronic
**Lubrication:** Wet sump
**Gearbox:** 6-speed
**Clutch:** Wet, multi-plate
**Frame:** Triple box section, aluminium
**Suspension:**
  *Front:* Telescopic, 43mm
cartridge-type
  *Rear:* Pro-link, single shock
**Brakes:**
  *Front:* 2 x 310mm (12.2in) discs, with 6-piston calipers
  *Rear:* Single 256mm (10in) disc, with 6-piston calipers
**Tyres:**
  *Front:* 120/70 ZR17
  *Rear:* 180/55 ZR17
**Dry weight:** 223kg (491lb)
**Power:** 164bhp at 10,000 rpm
**Top speed:** 300km/h (187.5mph)

important changes, not the least being that the wall thickness of the double box-section all-aluminium perimeter frame had been increased in thickness and the swinging-arm pivot had been redesigned to give less flexing. The extra wall thickness, plus the new (aluminium) swinging arm with dual box-section construction, increased chassis rigidity, especially torsional rigidity. Dimensional changes were restricted to the castor angle and trail, while the wheelbase was reduced. The whole frame was coated with a specially formulated finish to give not only a longer-lasting gloss, but also superior protection from corrosion.

At the front end, the forks were new, to provide additional stiffness; at the rear, a new, aluminium bodied, remote reservoir, nitrogen-charged shock absorber was used for the by now familiar Uni-Trak rear suspension to provide improved fade resistance. Braking had similarly been improved. Up front, a pair of 310mm (12.2in) – 272mm (10.7in) on the ZX-10 – semi-floating discs was each gripped by a four-piston caliper, while at the rear there was a dual-piston caliper for a single 250mm (9.8in) disc.

From 1993, Kawasaki introduced the updated D1 version. Performance was largely unchanged, but the newcomer sported twin ram-air induction, all new chassis, and a larger 24-litre (five-gallon) fuel tank. Mike Grainger, a Kawasaki dealer based in Plymouth, UK, set a new European bike speed record in March 1996 when he averaged 336.36km/h (209.05mph) over 400m (1312ft) on a turbo-charged ZZ-R1100 at Elvington airfield, North Yorkshire, UK.

### HONDA CBR1100 XX SUPER BLACKBIRD

In September 1996, Honda threw down the gauntlet by introducing its new CBR1100 XX Super Blackbird, named after the US Mach 3 spy plane. It claimed the bike was even faster than Kawasaki's ZZ-R.

The 1990s had seen a proliferation of high-powered, big-bore Superbikes that promised ever more breathtaking performance. However, although it had largely dominated the 600 and 900cc categories with its CBR and Fire Blade models, respectively, Honda's

**To provide years of reliable service over high mileages the Honda CBR1100XX Super Blackbird engine has a massively strong bottom end. This contains components such as the crank shaft, gearbox and clutch assemblies. The crank case doubles up as an oil container.**

also been so shaped that any rainwater would lie at the bottom and not be drawn into the carburettors. These latter components (up from 36mm/1.4in on the ZX-10 to 40mm/1.6in) were Keihin CVKD semi-flat-slide instruments, fed by an electric fuel pump, with a duct from the forked induction system to compensate for increased airbox pressure. The original 1990 C1 version of the ZZ-R1100 in unrestricted 147bhp guise gave a maximum speed of around 283km/h (176mph) – all this with a fuel economy some 30 per cent better than a FJ1200 Yamaha!

Although visually similar to the outgoing ZX-10, the ZZ-R's frame nonetheless featured a number of

## GSX1300R HAYABUSA (1999)

**Engine:** Water-cooled, across-the-frame, dohc, 4-cylinder, with 16 valves
**Bore and stroke:** 81 x 63mm (3.1 x 2.4in)
**Displacement:** 1298cc
**Compression ratio:** 11:1
**Carburation:** Electronic fuel injection
**Ignition:** Electronic, digital
**Starter:** Electric
**Gearbox:** 6-speed
**Frame:** Aluminium twin-spar frame and box section, aluminium swinging arm.
**Suspension:**
*Front:* 43mm (1.7in) inverted fork
*Rear:* single shock with aluminium piggyback reservoir
**Brakes:**
*Front:* 2 x 320mm (12.6in) floating discs and 6-piston calipers
*Rear:* Single 240mm (9.44in) disc and 2-piston calliper
**Wheels:** 431mm (17in) 3-spoke aluminium
**Tyres:**
*Front:* 120/70 ZR17
*Rear:* 190/50 ZR17
**Dry weight:** 215kg (97.52lb)
**Power:** 173bhp at 9800rpm
**Top speed:** 297km/h (185mph)

contribution in the litre-plus Superbike class had rested with the by now ageing CBR1000, launched in 1987. Applying lessons learnt in the development of its best-selling CBR600 and CBR900RR (Fire Blade), Honda's engineering squad set out to develop an open-class Super Sports machine that did not simply focus on producing the highest output or fastest terminal speed at the expense of other factors.

The fairing aerodynamics employed by Honda on the Blackbird brought about a new piggyback styled headlamp that positioned the high-beam unit directly over and behind the low beam. This fairing incorporated an isolated air intake to ensure ample quantities of cool fresh air reached the carburettors (fuel injection from 1999 onwards) under all conditions. Also, two intake ducts visible in the nose of the fairing had nothing at all to do with the engine's air intake, but instead directed cooling air to the oil cooler positioned under the steering head.

The Super Blackbird's engine was 85cc bigger than the ZZ-R1100's, with a displacement of 1137cc. Running a compression ratio of 11:1, the liquid-

**Arriving at the end of 1998, Suzuki's mighty GSX1300 Hayabusa used a 1298cc 16-valve four-cylinder engine. It is currently the fastest series production bike in the world. Like the latest Blackbird the Hayabusa uses an electronic fuel injection system.**

cooled 16-valve dohc across-the-frame four put out a class-leading 164bhp at 9500rpm. Gearbox was a six-speeder and there was a quartet of slanted flat-slide 42mm (1.69in) Keihin CV carbs. These were axed from the 1999 model in favour of a more modern integrated fuel injection and ignition system.

Other vital features of the Blackbird's engine included its compact size, a cylinder block which was canted forwards some 20 degrees farther than on the engine powering the CBR1000, a new dual-shaft balancer system, and a 3D map-type ignition system. The latter was a high-accuracy system featuring sensors that monitored throttle angle and engine speed for precise response, optimal performance and acceleration, and smoother power delivery. To harness all that power, a dual-spar diamond configuration for the frame in triple box-section aluminium was selected;

the swinging arm was also aluminium. Backing this up was a set of 43mm (1.7in) cartridge-type front forks with HMAS (Honda Multi Action System), the swinging arm being supported by Honda's well-known Pro-Link rear suspension system.

First introduced on the 1993 CBR1000 and completely revised on the 1996 ST1100 Pan European, Honda's ABS system was specified for the Blackbird. This system engages both sets of brakes when either the front or rear brakes are applied. At the front, dual combined three-piston calipers bite onto 310mm

Suzuki's Hayabusa (meaning 'falcon') is more like a cruise missile than a motorcycle. Its straight-line performance may be unmatched, but it cannot compete with bikes such as the Yamaha R1 through corners. A bonus is that the Hayabusa is a supremely comfortable long distance bike.

(12.2in) dual hydraulically operated discs, while at the rear a single 256mm (10.07in) disc operates with a dual combined three-piston calliper – all featuring sintered metal pads. The 431.8mm (17in) hollow section triple-spoke cast alloy wheels use radial tyres – 120/70 ZR front and 180/55 ZR rear. With a dry weight of 223kg (492lb), Honda claimed the Blackbird could reach 300km/h (187.5mph).

## SUZUKI HAYABUSA

All the Blackbird's features seemed secondary when another Japanese maker, this time Suzuki, stepped in to grab the 'fastest' title with its sensational Hayabusa. Today, Suzuki and the word 'Superbike' mean one thing: the GSX1300 Hayabusa with its mighty state-of-the-art, liquid-cooled, 16-valve four-cylinder engine and 151bhp at

**Below: The Yamaha R1 makes a superb track bike. Its light weight, fearsome acceleration, and superb cornering abilities make it difficult to beat; it was designed by Kunihito Miwa.**

# STATE-OF-THE-ART BRAKING

Since 1980, one area of motorcycle design and development has made more progress than any other – and it is not engines, transmissions, chassis, or suspension. In fact, not one of these has matched the improvements made in braking performance.

Although the first motorcycles to feature disc brakes appeared in the 1950s, it was not until a decade later that the first serious use of them was made. Disc brakes were then largely confined to the race circuit and scooters (the 1962 Lambretta TV Series 3 scooter was the first mass-produced disc-braked two-wheeler to go on sale). As for street bikes, these had to wait a few years, except on limited run (for example, MV's 600). The introduction of Honda's trend-setting CB750 four-cylinder

Superbike in 1969 awoke the public's eyes to the hydraulically operated disc. From then it was a frantic rush, as more and more of the world's bike builders fitted disc brakes. On the Honda, it had been a single disc with a two-piston calliper at the front. Then came a pair of discs on the front wheel, followed by triple discs – two front, one rear (the Ducati 750SS was the first production motorcycle to use the latter in 1974).

Today, triple discs remain, often with four- or even six-piston calipers and floating or fully floating discs.

**The modern braking system is an extremely elaborate and often expensive part of the modern motorcycle. An illustration of its workings is shown below.**

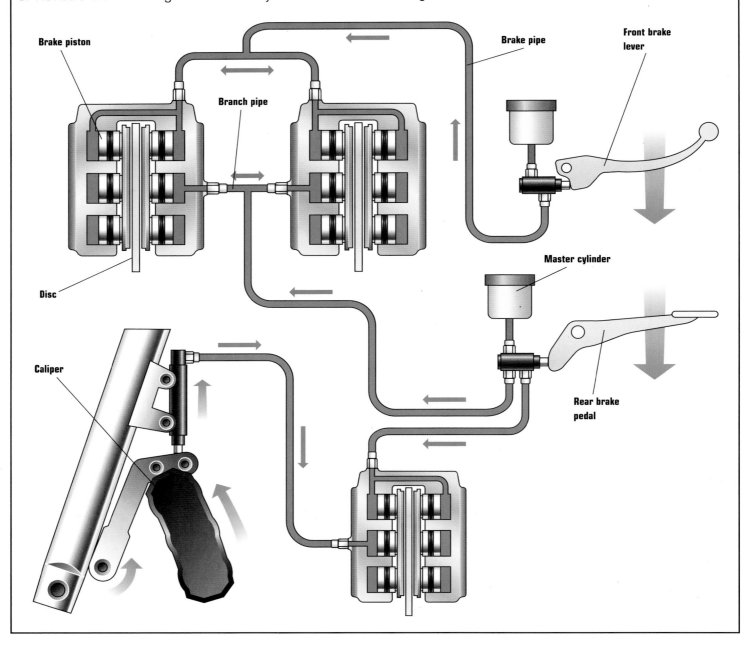

9500rpm. In Japanese, *Hayabusa* means peregrine falcon. The two-wheeled version of the Hayabusa is certainly a savage piece of performance kit, but more akin to a cruise missile than a bird of prey. Perhaps the most amazing thing about Suzuki's 173bhp monster is that there is nothing revolutionary about it. The Japanese company has simply refined and developed some tried and tested four-cylinder technology, giving it more horsepower, using more cubes in a lighter bike with better aerodynamics than any other sports/tourer that has gone before.

The Hayabusa's 1298cc across-the-frame four has its technology based on the latest GSX-R750. The double overhead chain-driven camshafts act directly on bucket tappets with a pair of 33mm (1.3in) inlet valves and a pair of 27.5mm (1.08in) exhaust valves per cylinder. An electronic engine-management system monitors and controls the two-stage fuel injection, the ignition system, the flapper valve on the airbox, and the fuel pump. Ram air ducts are placed close to the centre line of the motorcycle and use the integrated indicators to force more air into them. The exhaust system consists of four stainless-steel header pipes into two impact-moulded aluminium mufflers. A pulsed secondary air system reduces unburned hydrocarbons and there are dual catalysts mounted just downstream of the exhaust collector box which reduce emissions still further, with virtually no effect on overall power output.

## HAYABUSA CHASSIS

For the chassis, inspiration for the twin-spar aluminium frame and box-section swinging arm came from the latest generation of GSX-R750 sportster, but with increased (15 per cent) rigidity. With a wheelbase of 1485mm (58.46in), trail of 98mm (3.85in) and steering-head angle of 24.2 degrees, the antics of the Hayabusa are less sharp than those of the GSX-R750, while the 43mm (1.69in) inverted forks are fully adjustable and offer 120mm (4.72in) of wheel travel. The single rear shock absorber employs an aluminium piggyback reservoir, is fully adjustable,

**The Yamaha R1 makes an equally effective road or track tool. With its performance, handling and braking power right up there with the best. This particular bike is part of the V&M British Superstock squad which has scored many successes at circuits like Brands Hatch and Donington Park.**

and features a 70mm (2.75in) stroke which provides 140mm (5.51in) of travel. Braking is taken care of by twin 320mm (12.59in) floating discs and Tokico-made six-piston calipers up front, with a single 240mm (9.44in) disc and twin-pot calliper at the rear.

As with 'fastest' bikes of the past, tyres presented something of a problem. Specialists at Bridgestone solved this by extending its Battlax BT56 range to manufacture tyres especially for the GSX1300R. Designated BT56F Radial J 120/70 ZR17 (58W) front and BT56R Radial J 190/50 ZR17 (73W) rear, they are the only tyres currently homologated for the Hayabusa.

Suzuki's design team paid a great deal of attention to the Hayabusa's aerodynamics. This is understandable, given that they were (successfully) attempting to create the fastest standard production motorcycle on the planet. Key factors in their mission were: frontal projected area (A) and the coefficient of drag (Cd). At around 200km/h (125mph), reducing the CdA of a motorcycle by 0.01 adds 1km/h (0.62mph) to top speed and is the same as increasing engine power by one or two bhp. At 300km/h (187mph), reducing CdA by the same amount adds 3–4km/h (1.8–2.5mph) and is the equivalent of 4–5bhp. Hence, as speeds increase, aerodynamics become more important than power.

While one might assume that all things can be solved by computers, in aerodynamics wind tunnels still play a vital role. Suzuki extensively tested the Hayabusa and rider in the wind tunnel as a one-piece package. This led to the distinctive vertically arranged twin headlights, integrated indicators, protruding nose, and narrow radiator. Other factors included a front mudguard with extended lower section, a rear belly pan, the faired-in seat hump (tail cowling), the ultra-low screen, and new-shaped mirrors. The visual result may not be to everyone's taste, but the result, according to Suzuki, is a class-leading CdA figure. It is also worth mentioning that the former 'Speed King', Honda's CBR XX Blackbird, has 0.285sq.m (3.06sq.ft) of frontal area, compared to the Hayabusa's 0.270sq.m (2.9sq.ft) figure. (Weight wise, the Blackbird is 223kg/492lb, the Hayabusa 215kg/474lb.) Not only that, but, at 164bhp, the Honda produces a full 9bhp less than the mile-munching Suzuki. Enough said?

Currently, the Hayabusa rules at the top, at least in the speed stakes, although Kawasaki's ZX-12R is pushing it hard. However, for almost a decade-and-a-

**The 998cc R1 scores over the opposition by having a lower weight. The engine sits forward in an aluminium twin-beam which allows a low centre of gravity.**

half, the GSX-R1100 was Suzuki's Superbike, although by the mid-1990s it had been surpassed by several newcomers including Honda's Fireblade and then the Blackbird, Ducati's 916, and even its own GXS-R750, which received a major update itself. All this left the venerable GSX-R in the shade. The final nail in the coffin was another Suzuki, the TL 1000 V-twin.

## YAMAHA

Like Suzuki, Yamaha stayed with the old Superbike order too long, which in its case meant the FZR 1000 EXUP and air-cooled FJ1200 sports/tourer. The FZR's 1002cc 125bhp engine had great power and handling for its day, while the five-valve per cylinder four-cylinder engine with EXUP exhaust valve provided a fantastic spread of smooth power. It was superseded, for the 1996 model year, by the new Thunderace (still 1002cc). This now gave 124bhp and was the bigger brother of the YZF Thundercat 600. Like the Thundercat, the Thunderace was a more comfortable tourer than the single-purpose sportster, and sales struggled.

As for the FJ1200 (itself derived from the FJ1100 of the mid-1980s), this was a 1188cc 125bhp 16-valve air-cooled four, with limited ground clearance, especially when two-up. Originally, the FJ came with anti-dive front forks, but these were ditched in favour of conventional units in early 1988, along with 431mm (17in) wheels in place of 406mm (16in) assemblies, and better brakes. Also, some later models were fitted with ABS brakes. It is generally agreed that, together with Honda's CBR1000, the FJ is one of the most comfortable Superbikes ever.

Yamaha realised that it needed something special to take on the other manufacturers and, good as the Thunderace was, this was not to be the answer. So, in 1998, it launched the R1 and in doing so shot straight to the top of the sales chart. The R1 was that special – it simply grabbed the rider as soon as he turned the ignition key to start the engine. Plenty of other bikes go round corners faster or will accelerate as hard, but none will do it in such style or such a good overall package as the R1. A classic had been born.

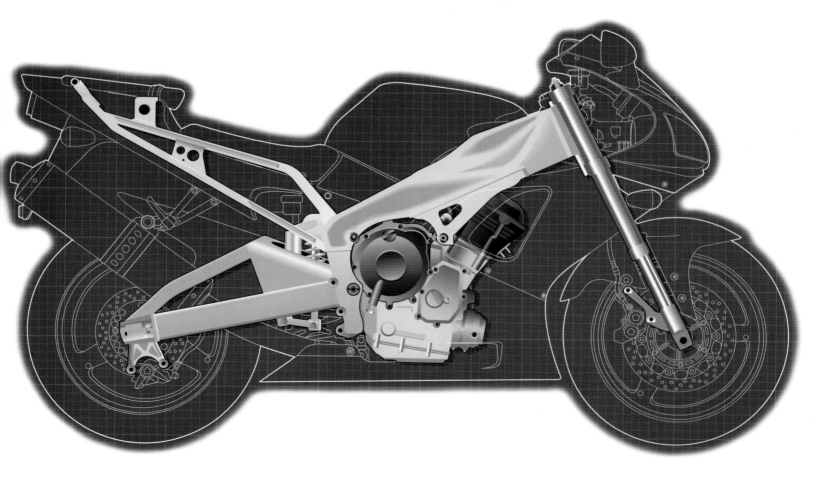

When it was announced at the end of 1997, Yamaha's R1 caused a massive stir – even now, it is still causing ripples in the performance bike pond and remains a 'must have' for many speed freaks. Weighing an amazingly low 177kg (390lb) – less than most Super Sport 600s – the R1 deserved its instant fame, as it was an incredibly able piece of machinery. The R1's project leader in Japan was Kunihito Miwa, who decided in 1995 to set about designing and building the fastest, lightest, and best-handling sports bike ever. The result was to be a testament to just how close Yamaha has come to making every other sports bike obsolete.

## R1 ENGINE

The R1 has an extremely compact 998cc engine which is based on Yamaha's familiar 20-valve technology, but is considerably smaller and lighter than its predecessor, the YZF1000R Thunderace, and employs a one-piece cylinder and crankcase assembly. A more sophisticated EXUP system takes into account rpm, throttle position, and even the speed at which the throttle is being opened, and provides additional grunt. Besides its five-valves-per-cylinder technology, which it has used to considerable effect in its 750cc and above class engines since the introduction of the FZ 750 in 1985, Yamaha's

other major four-stroke development of recent years has been EXUP (Exhaust Ultimate Power Valve). This is a special variable exhaust valve fitted to the exhaust system's collector box, and operated by a computer-controlled servo motor which performs according to engine revolutions. The valve effectively regulates exhaust pipe-end conditions, thereby controlling the exhaust gas-pressure wave produced during inlet and exhaust valve overlap. EXUP has the advantages of improving intake efficiency, reducing fuel consumption, and allowing Yamaha's engineering team to improve low- to

**At the end of 1996, both Honda and Suzuki announced Ducati-type V-twins. Suzuki's offering was the 996cc TL1000S, which was faster than either the Honda Firestorm or the then current Ducati 916. In the handling stakes, however, the Suzuki struggled. This particular machine is taking part in the 1998 Snetterton 8-hour endurance race.**

mid-range torque without having to sacrifice peak rpm performance.

The first Yamaha production model to feature the EXUP system came in the spring of 1987 and was the 'Japan only' FZR400R. This motorcycle had a 399cc Genesis-design, 16-valve, liquid-cooled, across-the-frame, four-cylinder engine featuring narrow-angle valves, straight inlet tracts, and compact combustion chambers for optimum power output, while the cylinder block was inclined forwards at 35 degrees. But perhaps the most amazing thing about the FZR400 was its ability – with the optional race kit fitted, it could rev to an amazing 16,000rpm!

The R1's shorter, more compact engine sits well forwards in the new aluminium twin-beam Delta-box frame, allowing a longer swinging arm (also in aluminium) to improve stability and traction. Wheelbase is an ultra-short 1395mm (54.9in) compared, for instance, with Honda's Fireblade at 1405mm (55.3in). Suspension is multi-adjustable, and the upside-down front forks feature

---

## YZF-R1 (1998)

**Engine:** Water-cooled, across-the-frame, dohc, 4-cylinder, with 20-valves and EXUP

**Bore and stroke:** 74 x 58mm (2.9 x 2.3in)

**Displacement:** 998cc

**Compression ratio:** 11.2:1

**Carburation:** 4 x Mikuni 32mm (1.26in)

**Ignition:** Electronic

**Starter:** Electric

**Gearbox:** Six-speed

**Frame:** Aluminium Delta-box 2, with aluminium swinging arm

**Suspension:**
*Front:* inverted telescopic fork

*Rear:* rising-rate monoshock

**Brakes:**
*Front:* 2 x 320mm (12.6in) floating discs with 4-piston calipers
*Rear:* single 220mm (8.7in) disc and 2-piston calliper

**Wheels:** 3-spoke hollow, aluminium

**Tyres:**
*Front:* 120/70 ZR17 58W
*Rear:* 190/50 ZR17 73W

**Dry weight:** 177kg (390lb)

**Power:** 150bhp at 10,000rpm

**Top speed:** 278.4km/h (173mph)

extra rebound damping at the end of their travel to help keep the front wheel down during hard acceleration. Kunihito Miwa and his team also paid attention to components such as the wheels (a massive 152.4mm/6in rear, with a 190-section tyre) and brakes, which, although based on the Thunderace, had been revamped to reduce weight. Even the dashboard was a distinctive piece of hardware, with a digital display that included a speedometer, clock, and low-fuel warning light, while the massive conventional tachometer dominated the rider's view.

It was riding the R1, however, which really made an impression. This 998cc, fire-breathing rocketship has a unique combination of agility and outright power. Another big bonus is that, like all the five-valve-per-cylinder Yamaha engines, it can also behave like a pussycat, with its smooth power delivery and a chassis that endows it with race-bred handling. But perhaps the best feature – certainly for road riders – is just how tractable the R1 is.

While it can be a little frenzied over 7000rpm, it is at low speeds that it is utterly amazing for a sports bike, driving smoothly from 32.18km/h (20mph) in top gear (around 1000rpm); there is absolutely no hesitation in the power curve all the way up to the 11,750rpm red line.

## A REAL RACER

In many ways, the R1 has been built like a race bike, in respect of its 'minimum weight' design exercise. For example, the braking system is based on the excellent type from the Thunderace/Thundercat. The four-piston calipers have been lightened, however, to reduce unsprung weight, while the three-spoke alloy wheels are hollow and much lighter than conventional ones. Losing weight here really assists the suspension.

While the R1 is no armchair ride, it is still quite comfortable for such a focused speed machine. In many ways, the R1's riding position is very much like that of the Ducati 916/996 in the

**In 2000, Honda launched its new VTR SP-1 (RC51 in the USA). The racing version, in the hands of Colin Edwards, lifted the WSB crown. The production model can reach 275km/h (170mph) and weighs in at 200kg (440lb).**

way the rider leans over the top of the small fairing screen. Again, this is a well thought-out part of the design which helps keep the front down during hard acceleration. Like virtually all modern sports bikes, the R1 is very much about the rider. This is not the bike to have if you are going to carry a pillion passenger regularly.

Even though it won the coveted *Motor Cycle News* Machine of the Year title for both 1998 and 1999, Yamaha still released an updated R1 for 2000. In total, the new-generation R1 had more than 250 changes (most of a minor nature). One of the most notable was the fitment of an all-new fairing which increased aerodynamic efficiency and at the same time helped reduce

Making its debut in 1994, the 916 Ducati was one of the truly great motorcycles of the last decade of the 20th century, combining a powerful Desmo V-twin engine with race breed handling and braking capabilities. The 916 was styled by Massimo Tamburini.

rider fatigue. In addition, by fitting a range of special lightweight parts – including a new titanium muffler – Yamaha were able to shave 2kg (4.4lb) off the weight, taking it down to only 175kg (385lb).

## JAPANESE V-TWINS

At the end of 1996, both Honda and Suzuki announced 'Ducati-type'Vs, with the launch of the Honda VTR1000 Firestorm (996cc) and Suzuki TL1000

**The limited edition UK-only Ducati 996 Fogarty Replica went on sale in 1998 in honour of Fogarty's achievements on the track. It put out 120bhp and could top 267km/h (165mph) from its fuel-injected 90-degree Desmo V-twin engine. Only 202 examples were built.**

(also 996cc). Interestingly, only Suzuki chose to follow Ducati's lead by using fuel injection, although even they did not embrace this fully and adopted a less efficient system. Honda, meanwhile, chose a pair of 48mm flat-slide CV carbs instead. Everyone assumed that, because the two Japanese manufacturers had 'stolen' Ducati's 996cc engine size, bore and stroke dimensions of 98 x

66mm (3.9 x 2.6in), four-valves-per-cylinder, dohc, and the 90-degree V-twin layout, all three engines would perform the same. But out on the road they were each quite different. The Suzuki made the most power (125bhp at 9500rpm), had a four-cylinder-type power rush at the top end, and, in its original TL1000S form, came bottom of the three in the handling department

# SINGLE-SIDED SWINGING ARM

Now utilised by several manufacturers in their own individual fashions, single-sided swinging-arm technology was first pioneered by the French-based ELF racing team during the early 1980s, with much of its funding provided by the massive Japanese Honda company. The brain behind the ELF racing team was André de Cortanze, the same man who had been responsible for cars such as the Le Mans 24 Hours race–winning Alpine Renault A442 and the hugely successful Peugeot 205 Turbo 16 rally car which had won several world championships. So much for his four-wheel credentials, what about those of the two-wheel variety?

The answer has to be that de Cortanze's innovative engineering – perhaps revolutionary would be a more suitable description – did not quite achieve the same level of success, with the exception of the single-sided swinging arm. The first ELFe (the 'e' standing for endurance) debuted in 1980. Much of the machine's construction owed its existence to car-racing technology.

Notably, at the rear of the machine was a giant but exceedingly light cast-magnesium single-sided swinging arm, which enabled a wheel change to be carried out in less than 10 seconds, leaving the chain, sprocket, and brake disc in situ and hence undisturbed.

Although the ELF endurance racing programme was axed at the end of 1983, to be followed by the design and construction of a purebred GP bike, the de Cortanze concept of the single-sided rear suspension was to live on in the motorcycling world and is now used by several manufacturers, including Honda, Ducati, MV Agusta, and Triumph.

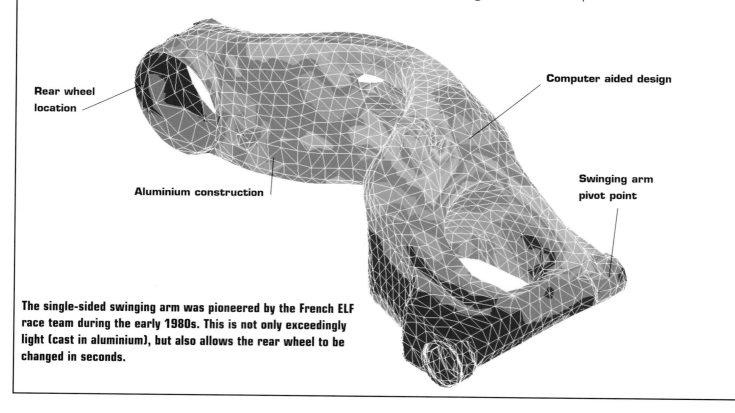

Rear wheel location

Aluminium construction

Computer aided design

Swinging arm pivot point

**The single-sided swinging arm was pioneered by the French ELF race team during the early 1980s. This is not only exceedingly light (cast in aluminium), but also allows the rear wheel to be changed in seconds.**

(Suzuki even had to retro fit a steering damper). The Honda VTR1000 Firestorm produced the least power (110bhp at 9500rpm), but was the most rideable of the trio and the most rider friendly in terms of comfort. As for the Ducati, at the time the other two were launched, only the racing version had a 996cc engine size – the production street bike was still a 916cc, and this was a third more expensive than the Japanese duo. Even so, *Fast Bikes* magazine still put the Ducati on top, even going as far as to say: 'Only the Blade [Honda's CBR900RR Fire Blade] comes close to emulating the 916. Basically, these two here (TL1000 and VTR1000) don't even get a look in.'

In the longer term, both Japanese manufacturers built uprated versions of their V-twins. Suzuki was first with the TL1000R in 1998. It achieved this by giving the engine 10bhp more (now 135bhp), a heavier beam frame, and a GSX-R style job, which included a full fairing. Even so it still was not quite right. Honda took much longer; however, when they launched their VTR SP-1 (RC51 in the USA) for the 2000 model year, they created what *Motor Cycle News* called 'The raciest road bike money can buy'.

They also beat Ducati when the Texan Colin Edwards won the 2000 World Super Bike championship title. The production SP-1 can exceed

273.6km/h (170mph) and weighs in at 200kg (440lb), which, when compared with its WSB championship–winning brother, means 50bhp less and 38kg (84lb) heavier.

## THE GREAT ITALIAN REVIVAL

Just as the Italians had used the Superbike to relaunch their bike industry in the 1970s with such classics as the Ducati 750SS, Moto Guzzi Le Mans, and Laverda Jota, history is now repeating itself with a whole rush of equally stunning pieces of kit, including the Ducati 916/996 series, the MV Agusta F4, the Benelli 900 Tornado, and the Aprilia RSV Mille, to name but a few. But how did all this happen for a second time.

During his 30-plus years as Ducati's design chief, the legendary Ing. Fabio Taglioni achieved many great things. It was he, of course, who created the L-shaped 90-degree V-twin, at first with bevel-driven, and later belt-driven, overhead camshafts, added to the famed desmodromic valve operation. But there were significant areas in which this great man showed virtually no interest at all, especially four valves

**Although it may look the same as the 916, Ducati's 996 offers even more performance. In particular, the 996cc engine provides both more speed and enough extra torque to satisfy even the most demanding rider. Making its debut at the end of 1998 the engine's bore size was increased to 98mm.**

per cylinder, liquid-cooling, and fuel injection. Instead, it was left to Taglioni's successor, Massimo Bordi, to exploit these three important features.

Bordi had joined Ducati in early 1978 and, as events were to prove, was a perfect choice to follow in Taglioni's footsteps. Unlike many who would have simply gone for a totally new approach, Bordi took on board the established design formula and instead studied

## DUCATI 916 (1994)

**Technical specification:** 916 SP (1995)
**Engine:** Water-cooled, dohc, 4-valves-per-cylinder, 90-degree Desmo V-twin
**Bore and stroke:** 94 x 66mm (3.7 x 2.59in)
**Displacement:** 916cc
**Compression ratio:** 11.2:1
**Ignition:** Electronic IAW type
**Fuel system:** Weber-Marelli electronic indirect type
**Gearbox:** 6-speeds
**Frame:** Lattice type, round steel tubing, aluminium single-sided swinging arm
**Suspension:**
  *Front:* inverted fork with 43mm (1.69in) stanchion diameter
  *Rear:* monoshock
**Wheels:** 431mm (17in) cast aluminium, 3-spoke
**Tyres:**
  *Front:* 120/70 ZR 17
  *Rear:* 190/50ZR 17
**Dry weight:** 195kg (430lb)
**Power:** 131bhp at 10,500rpm (crankshaft)
**Top speed:** 270km/h (168mph)

**916 variants**
916 Strada (single seat)
  1994–1996
916 SP 1995
916 Biposto (dual seat)
  1995–1998
916 SPS 1997–1998
916 Senna I 1995
916 Senna II 1997
916 Senna III 1998

ways in which this could be updated to make the best use of modern technology. He shortlisted four main areas: multi-valves, double overhead camshafts, liquid-cooling and fuel injection.

During the early 1980s, at a time when Bordi was carrying out this work, no other mainstream Italian motorcycle manufacturer was actively seeking out this modern technology. In truth, this was also a time of deep financial crisis at Ducati and, if the subsequent Cagiva takeover (from the Italian government) had not occurred, it is more than likely that Bordi's ideas would have remained ideas only. However, with the Cagiva buyout in May 1985 and the resultant vast increase in funding – and enthusiasm – Bordi's concept of a new era V-twin engine was given the go-ahead.

### THE V-TWIN IS REBORN

The first the world saw of this plan was to be in the 1986 French Bol d'Or 24-hour race, when the original prototype of what was to emerge as the 851 had its first real test. Even though a retirement was posted through gearbox problems, it was not before the bike had given extremely positive signs for the future. The first production 851s (851cc) arrived in 1988, a total of 500 examples being built for sale (300 Strada and 200 Kit). These came after pre-production examples had been exhibited at the Milan Show the previous November. The Strada was a fully street-legal machine with quiet silencers; the Kit was basically a semi-racer with open pipes and higher output engine.

The second major happening in 1988 was the debut of a proper racing version which, ridden by Marco Lucchinelli, won the first ever WSB (World Superbike) race held at Donington Park, England, in spring 1988. On the street, the 851 went into mass production for the 1989 model year, while the racing project received an 888cc engine size. Ducati won its first World Super Bike championship in 1990 (Frenchman Raymond Roche) and went on to dominate the class during the 1990s, winning no fewer than eight world titles in that decade,

including a record-breaking four by the British Star, Carl Fogarty.

Meanwhile, the 851 street bike was developed into the 888cc before being totally redesigned as the 916 for the 1994 model year. The 916 eventually gave way to the 996 (996cc), which went on general sale towards the end of 1998. The 916 engine was then used for the ST4 sports/tourer, but even this became a 996 for the 2001 model year.

Whereas Honda's CBR900RR Fire Blade is clinically efficient – like a surgeon's scalpel – Ducati's 916 was simply the most beautiful thing on two wheels when it arrived on the market in the late spring of 1994. For many, the 916 was not merely a Superbike, but *the* Superbike. Judged on style, the 916's creator, Massimo Tamburini, had come up with a motorcycle that was a style icon. The choice of a Ferrari racing red colour scheme only added to the overall effect, as did the 'pillar box' twin-headlight fairing; hi-level, underseat aluminium (Termignoni carbon-fibre on limited edition SP/SPS versions) silencers; single-sided swinging-arm; and a deep-throated booming exhaust note. Not only did the 916 have style in abundance, but it also had a pedigree virtually unmatched in modern motorcycling. Essentially, it was a purebreed racer, with the bare minimum of equipment necessary to make it street-legal: lighting equipment, an electric starter, and a number plate support! It was little more than a production version of very similar motorcycles used by the Bologna-based marque to such great success in the WSB (World Super Bike) racing.

Although uprated and with an increase in displacement, the 916's engine assembly owed many of its features to the models it superseded – the 888 and the earlier still 851 series. All shared the same basic liquid-cooled dohc four-valves-per-cylinder 90-degree Desmo V-twin layout, with the much-acclaimed Weber-Marelli integrated electronic fuel injection and ignition systems. The 916 (like the 851 and 888) had an engine displacement that matched its model code, in the 916's case achieved by

increasing the stroke from the 888 model's 64 to 66mm (2.5 to 2.6in), with the bore remaining unchanged at 94mm (3.7in). Ducati sources stated maximum power at the crankshaft to be 114bhp at 9000 rpm, with a safe maximum rpm of 10,000.

Yet these figures only provided half the story, the newcomer being much stronger throughout the rev range than the model it replaced. This was thanks

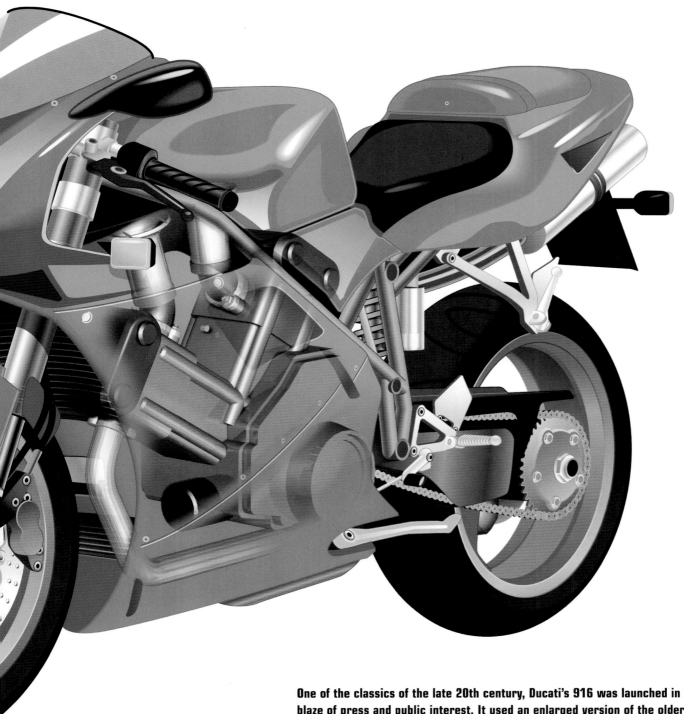

One of the classics of the late 20th century, Ducati's 916 was launched in 1994 in a huge blaze of press and public interest. It used an enlarged version of the older 851/888 four-valves-per-cylinder belt-driven engine with fuel injection and six-speed gearbox.

to the considerable development time and effort expended by not only Massimo Bordi's engineering team at the Ducati headquarters in Bologna, but also Massimo Tamburini and other members of the Cagiva Research Centre (CRC) based in San Marino. This latter group undertook not only the chassis development, but also the vitally important area of intake and exhaust systems. A little realised fact is

that much of the 916's development phase was undertaken by CRC, not Ducati, this coming at a time when Cagiva were the owners of the Ducati marque.

## RAM AIR DUCTS

Another important aspect of the 916 project was the use made of RAM – a ram-effect pressurised airbox. Best described as a force-fed ram-type air

ducting arrangement similar to that used on several large displacement Kawasakis, this is where air is forced into a pressurised sealed container through ducts in the front of the fairing. The 916 also used this airbox as a stressed-frame member; this was manufactured in carbon-fibre on the SP version. This actually ensured that the 916 steel trellis frame was stiffer than Cagiva's 500 Grand Prix racer! As for the chrome-molybdenum steel frame itself, this was entirely new, even though the basic format could be traced back to the 500SL Pantah of the late 1970s. The 916 version benefited more from this than the Pantah, thanks to the advent of CAD (computer-aided design), which calculated the best balance between outright strength with a high resistance to bending loads and maintaining the lowest possible weight.

The superbly crafted single-sided swinging arm utilised the latest construction techniques, including the use of hi-tech chilled aluminium alloy on a 'closed differential' section. A stub axle was fastened to the swinging arm via an eccentric hub to allow easy chain adjustment. There was a single large-diameter nut for speeding up the wheel removal process. The rear suspension (using a Japanese Showa single shock) worked through a newly designed linkage system which increased wheel

**Long awaited, Aprilia's RSV Mille Superbike was launched at the 1997 Milan Show. Its 998cc liquid-cooled 60-degree V-twin engine uses a mixture of chains and gears to drive the double overhead camshafts. Unlike Ducati and the Japanese V-twins the Aprilia uses dry sump lubrication.**

travel to 130mm (5.11in) and employed prompt and precise response. At the 916's front end, a set of 43mm (1.69in) inverted (upside-down) Showa forks provided an excellent combination of strength and suppleness in this vital area.

Another feature of the 916 was its patented adjustable steering headset, which allowed the rider to 'tune in' the steering geometry of his choice, to suit track conditions or personal preferences. Except for specialist, limited-built,

hyper-expensive machines such as Bimota, Ducati thus became the first mainstream motorcycle manufacturer to offer such a feature as standard.

Another guide to the design team's attention to detail were the wheels. The front component, with a 88.9mm (3.5in) rim, used a unique angled valve stem. This may seem trivial, but was actually a significant feature, allowing easy access for a tyre-pressure gauge. The 139mm (5.5in) rear rim was also of a special design, enabling it to function with the sexy single-sided swinging arm.

## A POWERFUL IMPROVEMENT

Due to intricate tuning and balancing of the radical stainless-steel exhaust pipes and updating of the fuel injection monitoring and metering systems, the factory was able to claim that the larger displacement, longer stroke motor of the 916 provided increased power and torque throughout the entire rev range. Other significant improvements over earlier Ducati V-twins had been achieved, notably to the crankcases (a definitive weakness on the 888 engine, particularly under racing conditions) and the valve material itself. The latter improvement had a visible benefit to owners in the form of longer service intervals between valve adjustments. Of all the 916 features, however, the three which grabbed the most attention were the single-sided swinging arm, the

**Besides the standard RSV Mille, Aprilia also offer other versions including the R and SP. These add to the performance, including improved suspension, revised fuel injection, lighter wheels, and extra carbon fibre. The Australian Troy Corser is the Italian factory's No. 1 WSB entry.**

exhaust system which exited through a pair of silencers just underneath the seat, and the ultra-distinctive bodywork, particularly the twin 'pillar-box' head-lamps of the curvaceous fairing.

Above all, it was the 916's ability to transfer all its available power onto the tarmac which made it an overnight classic. This, together with its sculpted lines and sleek looks, gave it the edge over any other Superbike of its era. In 1999, the 916 was replaced by the 996, with yet more power. But, for many, the definitive Ducati will always be the stunning 916. Currently, Ducati's styling designer chief, Pierre Terablanche, is struggling with the new 999 project. The 916/996 will be a hard act to follow.

Before moving on, it is worth looking more closely at one aspect of Ducati's technical involvement which impacted closely on the rest of the biking frater-nity – fuel injection. In 1987, while the Ducati factory was designing and developing its first four-valves-per-cylinder 90-degree liquid-cooled Desmo V-twin – which was to emerge as the 851 of 1988 and subsequently go

**MV Agusta's stunning F4 could just as well have ended up a Cagiva, a Ducati or a Ferrari. The fact that it is an MV is a fitting tribute to a marque which has scored more than 3,000 international race victories by the likes of Surtees, Hailwood, Agostini and Read.**

through an evolution which then saw the 888, 916, 748 and ultimately the 996 – Bordi decided to incorporate the then new (to bikes) Weber-Marelli integrated electronic fuel injection and ignition system. Bordi chose this system for a number of reasons, including Weber-Marelli's location in Bologna, where Ducati is also located; the fact that practically all the components of the Weber-Marelli system were already well proven; 'off-the-shelf' availability (for example, the fuel injectors were the same as fitted to many thousands of Fiat and Lancia cars); and, finally, the Weber system's known reliability and added advantage of being able to meet future emission and fuel requirements.

## THE ELECTRONIC ADVANTAGE

Ducati had, in fact, selected an 'open loop' electronic fuel injection system pioneered in Ferrari Formula 1 cars. This featured a limited number of sensors and in some ways resembled the type used on Kawasaki's GPZ1100. The sensors monitored air temperature and density coolant temperature, engine revolutions, throttle position, and ignition combustion (or detonation). There was no box-like flow meter as employed in the Bosch system found on BMWs, nor a lambda probe, the latter often seen on sophisticated car systems.

In the Weber-Marelli computer memory, a number of 'maps' have been encoded. On the basis of the engine's running conditions, combined with information coming from the sensors, the computer then plots the optimum ignition advance curve, as well as the timing of the injectors. Fuel is supplied at a pressure of $3.05kg/cm2$ (43.5psi) by an electric pump and thence squirted directly into the inlet tracts by a pair of injectors for each cylinder, in a phased mode. There are either one or two injectors on Ducati V-twins, depending upon the year and model.

In comparison, the Bosch system (as used by BMW) employs a 'gate' to measure the weight and flow of air entering the engine unit. The system's 'brain' then decides (subject to load, engine speed, and other factors) just how much fuel the injectors should throw into this measured mass of air for optimum combustion. The Bosch system is highly accurate, but its gate still restricts air flow into the engine and outright performance therefore suffers.

BMW may not be too concerned, as its bikes are aimed at the sports/touring market, whereas the four-valves-per-cylinder Ducati V-twin series is firmly in the sports/racing arena. As such, Bordi appreciated that the Weber-Marelli system with its 'mapped' system did not rely on measuring the air flow directly, but reacted to feedback from the engine. The basis of the Italian system is what is known as the Alpha angle – the degree of opening of the butterfly varying from 90 degrees, with the throttle closed, to 0 degrees flat out.

Using a dynamometer, Weber's designer, Aureliano Lionello, connected the Ducati dohc, four-valves-per-cylinder, liquid-cooled engine to a flow meter and exhaust gas analyser, then tuned the injector system and ignition advance to deliver optimum performance at 16 different angles and 16 different rev bands. The resulting mass of data was then plotted onto graphs referring to possible operating conditions, using a special computer. Aureliano then mapped the Weber system's microchip to conform to the lessons learnt from this data during actual working conditions.

The system's microprocessor also corrects for water, oil, and air temperatures, atmospheric pressure, fuel pressure, and changes in battery voltage; choke function and injection timing and duration are also varied subject to the microchip's map. The programming can be varied to improve engine braking, fuel consumption, and exhaust emissions. Any changes to an engine's specification – a different camshaft, for example – usually requires a reprogrammed chip, so a works racer is harder to reproduce than a standard production engine.

Before Ducati moved to fuel injection, the largest carburettor size had been 42mm (1.65in) on a racer and 40mm (1.6in) on a production roadster. However, even with the original fuel-injected production models (the 851 of the late 1980s), it was able to use massive 50mm (1.7in) inlet tracts, which fed dead straight to the paired inlet valves. There is no doubt that the use of the computerised fuel injection and ignition systems has played a vital role in Ducati success on both road and track, combining as it does the old world virtues of a 90-degree angle V-twin with modern technology.

## APRILIA

Strongly rumoured to have been the only Italian bike manufacturer never to have made a loss, Aprilia is a company which has exploded from almost nothing two decades ago to a

world leader in its field. This dynamic firm has taken on and beaten the mighty Japanese factories on the GP circuits and is now showing that it intends to do just the same in the showrooms. Behind its track successes, Aprilia has grown fast, from £57 million turnover in 1992 to £385 million in 1999 – and it is still growing. With the launch, in late 1997, of its first Superbike, the RSV Mille Aprilia finally had a full range of mopeds, scooters, and motorcycles from 50cc upwards. In the year 2000, it swallowed up two famous Italian brand names, Moto Guzzi and Laverda, to add to its growing portfolio.

The RSV project actually began life in the late 1980s, when Aprilia decided to invest some 60 billion lire, with the aim of expanding its model range to some 25 different models, up to and including a Superbike. At first Aprilia were keen on a 750; then, by 1993, a '900' was mentioned; before finally, in 1995, a 1-litre (0.21-gallon) was chosen. This decision was helped by the fact that this capacity would also make full use of the existing World Super Bike rules, which at that time saw fours limited to 750cc, three cylinders to 900cc and twins 1000cc.

That same year, a prototype engine for Aprilia's Superbike entry was displayed at the Bologna Show. Some people questioned Aprilia's choice of a 60-degree layout for its V-twin; the majority of manufacturers followed

Ducati's 90-degree format and it was widely believed that having a narrower angle would prove a disadvantage. Interviewed in 1998, Georgio Del Ton, Aprilia's head of engine development, said: 'With everyone else jumping on the 90-degree bandwagon (Honda and Suzuki, for example), we felt it necessary to establish our own identity. We compared both layouts very carefully. The 90-degree engine has many advantages, but we felt there were too many compromises with its design when building a lightweight, compact, sporting motorcycle. For example, we were able to keep the RSV's wheelbase in check without resorting to trick alternative rear shocks and side-mounted radiators. It also allowed us to keep fuel injection components close together (thus eliminating bulky and over-complex throttle linkages), which is critical to allowing straight, short inlet tracks for the cylinder heads.'

Another departure from the Ducati formula was the employment of a dry, rather than a wet, sump lubrication system. Del Ton and his team (working closely with their Austrian engine builders, Rotax) chose a dry sump because this layout had the advantage of drastically reducing the size of the oil container area below the crankshaft, thus allowing the engine unit to be positioned much lower in the frame. Scavenged oil was stored instead

## ADJUSTABLE STEERING GEOMETRY

Massimo Tamburini was a co-founder of the famous Bimota company, which was formed on 1 January 1973. The marque took its name from the three partners who set it up: Bianchi, Morri, and Tamburini. At first, Bimota built frame kits, particularly for racing customers. Then, in January 1977, at the Bologna Show, Bimota introduced its first Superbike, the SB2 (Suzuki Bimota Two, the first Suzuki-Bimota having been a racer). Powered by one of Suzuki's new GS750 dohc across-the-frame air-cooled four-cylinder engines, the SB2 was nothing if not unorthodox, with features such as a space frame; a single, vertically mounted rear shock absorber; a fuel tank located under the engine; and adjustable steering geometry.

These features were the work of Tamburini (who was later to design Ducati's 916 and the MV Agusta F4 of the 1990s). At the time, variable steering geometry was a Bimota exclusive, with the fork legs and steering column at slightly different angles. By featuring eccentric upper and lower steering-head bearings, the bike's trail could be changed to suit the rider's requirements for either fast or twisty conditions. In Bimota's KB1 (introduced at the 1977 Milan Show), the steering column was inclined at 24 degrees and the fork legs at 28 degrees, while the trail could be varied between 99 and 119.4mm (3.9 and 4.7in). Adjustable steering geometry has made a return, in revised form, on both the Ducati 916/996 series and the MV Agusta F4.

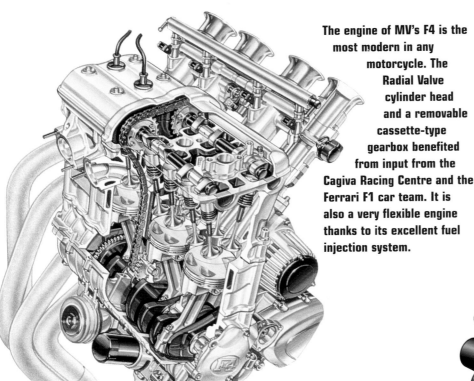

The engine of MV's F4 is the most modern in any motorcycle. The Radial Valve cylinder head and a removable cassette-type gearbox benefited from input from the Cagiva Racing Centre and the Ferrari F1 car team. It is also a very flexible engine thanks to its excellent fuel injection system.

powerful spread of light on main beam, making riding at night a pleasure rather than a chore.

In its standard form, the RSV produces 128bhp at 9500rpm, giving a maximum speed of 264km/h (165mph); the more expensive, limited production SP variant is capable of 290km/h (180mph) with optional race kit.

### THE MV AGUSTA F4

Aprilia and Ducati both have V-twins Superbikes which can challenge the rest of the world on both road and track, but what of the rest of the

within a separate oil tank located within the nearside of the engine. To quell the extra vibrations from the 60-degree layout of the cylinders, Aprilia's development team fitted dual counter balancers, one in front of the crankshaft and the other between the two overhead camshafts in the rear cylinder head. With ultra-short stroke measurements of 97 x 67.5mm (3.8 x 2.7in), the RSV engine displaced 997.62cc.

When the big Aprilia V-twin finally went on sale during 1998, it soon silenced its detractors by proving to be a lot better than the critics had ever imagined. The 1999 *What Bike?* annual had this to say about what was probably Aprilia's most important model ever: 'The Ducati 996 is an incredible track machine but can't rival the Aprilia's rideability and comfort. The Suzuki TL1000R has a shade more power, but is heavier and lacks the low down drive of the Aprilia. The Mille's combination of real world performance and all-day comfort scores highly.'

As Ducati had shown from its first production four-valves-per-cylinder 851 model in 1988, Aprilia's decision to use electronic fuel injection and

ignition systems shows these features as absolute must-haves for the modern, high-performance, high-efficiency V-twin engine. When designing the chassis, Aprilia's engineering team was able to draw on the factory's considerable Grand Prix racing experience. Particular care was taken with the torsional stiffness (including an industry-best figure of 650kg (1432lb), bending resistance and road performance. The design itself was of the inclined double-beam type manufactured in aluminium alloy; the swinging arm (with a single German Boge hydraulic rear shock) was also of aluminium alloy.

Other details of the RSV specification included: inverted 43mm (1.7in) Showa front forks; Brembo braking two 320mm (12.6in) stainless-steel discs at the front with four-piston calipers; and a single 220mm (8.7in) stainless rear disc with a two-piston calliper. A distinctive styling feature was the headlamp – a triple assembly, providing a particularly

Italian industry? The other success story is the MV Agusta rebirth, thanks to Claudio Castiglioni and Cagiva. Seen by many as the ultimate in prestige motorcycles, the MV Agusta F4 was launched in 1998 to a fanfare of press and public acclaim, its style and glamour even outdoing Ducati's super sexy 916. It also had the name – MV Agusta denotes something very, very special in the motorcycle world, having won more Grand Prix races and world titles than any other marque in history. The F4's evolution was also one of considerable interest, as it might never have been marketed as an MV at all. Instead, it could just as well be a Cagiva, a Ducati, or even a Ferrari! The fact that it was an MV represents a fitting end to one of the strangest true-life motorcycling projects of all time.

The F4 saga is really the result of dinner-time discussions between two men – Claudio Castiglioni (the Cagiva boss) and Massimo Tamburini (designer of Ducati's 916) – with the added intervention of Piero Ferrari, son of Enzo Ferrari, and Ferrari's owners Fiat. First rumours concerning a brand-new Cagiva-masterminded Superbike came at the beginning of the 1990s. Photographs of the new engine, an across-the-frame four, were first released at a Ferrari press conference in 1993 – by mistake. The Cagiva Group

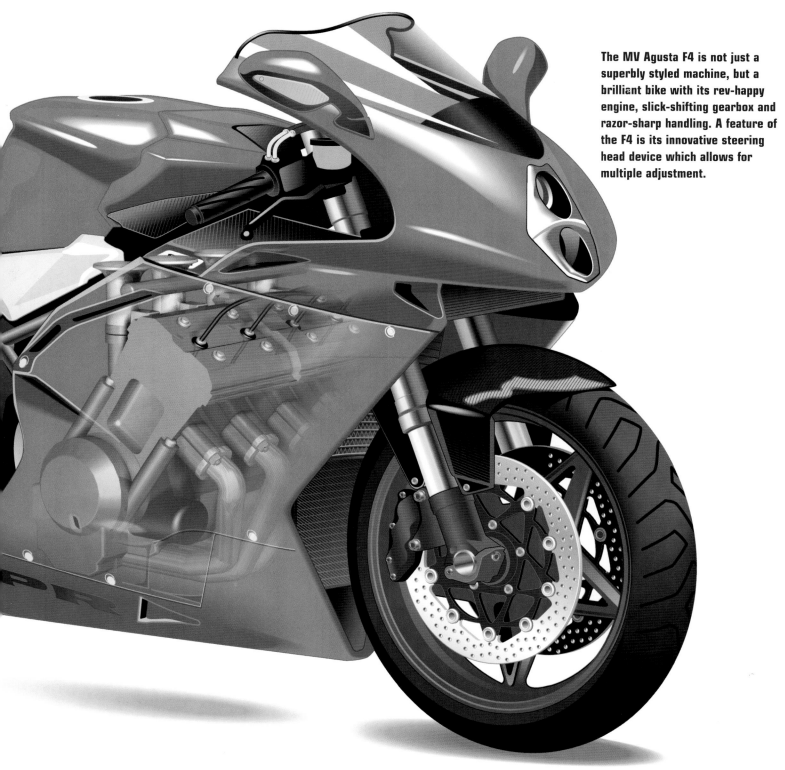

**The MV Agusta F4 is not just a superbly styled machine, but a brilliant bike with its rev-happy engine, slick-shifting gearbox and razor-sharp handling. A feature of the F4 is its innovative steering head device which allows for multiple adjustment.**

**The four-pipe underseat exhaust of the MV Agusta F4 is a trademark of the bike's designer, Massimo Tamburini, and is a progression of the layout conceived for the Ducati 916, another Tamburini masterpiece. The noise this emits is a fierce howl at peak rpm.**

had kept the engine behind closed doors, even keeping it out of sight when a fully finished prototype was photographed on the road in Italy. However, when Ferrari Engineering featured a colour picture of the power unit at the launch of its new 465 GT car, Castiglioni was forced to confirm that the engine was being developed in conjunction with Ferrari. At the same time both Claudio Castiglioni and Piero Ferrari had to admit that they had test ridden the machine.

Castiglioni said at the time of the 1993 press conference that producing target power was 'no problem'. The photograph revealed that the straight four, topped by a bank of fuel injectors, was similar to half a Ferrari V8. It featured several interesting innovations, including a radial-valve cylinder head and cassette-type gearbox. There is no doubt that Cagiva's financial problems (it ended up selling Ducati) of the mid-1990s held up development of the F4

project, as it did with the Ducati 916. However, after the sale of Ducati to the American financial group TPG, Cagiva was able to build the F4 without the combined worries of what it would do to Ducati sales and the easing of its financial position.

While Cagiva still owned Ducati, the F4 was badged as a Cagiva (but only during the development stage). By the time the F4 was finally ready, early in 1998, it was to be badged an MV, the Castiglioni family having purchased the MV Agusta name during the early 1980s. This was very much as John Bloor had done in England when he bought the Triumph name and subsequently used it on a new line of bikes.

## A MASTERPIECE OF ENGINEERING

The F4's frame is made up of a 'mixed' steel and aluminium structure, the section being composed of a trellis in round, chrome-molybdenum steel tubes which wrap around the engine, connected at the rear to light-alloy plates that provide a pivot point for the swinging arm. A special feature is that the trellis/plate connecting points can be separated to allow the division of the F4 into two distinct sections: the front end with the steel cage connected to it and the rear part with the swinging

arm pivot-points and the rear end, leaving the engine free from any superstructures. The advantage of this is simple, not only for the purposes of assembly, but also for servicing operations over the life of the motorcycle.

The F4's engineering team invested considerable time and effort into the single-sided swinging arm. Cast in light alloy, it is a work of art in itself; on the 'gold' F4, there are a pair of buttons just forward of the rear wheel sprocket to allow the rider to adjust the ride height of the machine. Suspension was taken care of by specially built

## F4 SERIE ORO (2000)

**Engine:** Water-cooled, dohc, 16-valve across-the-frame four, with radial valve cylinder head
**Bore and stroke:** 73.8 x 43.8mm (2.9 x 1.7in)
**Displacement:** 749.4cc
**Compression ratio:** 12:1
**Ignition:** Electronic, digitally controlled
**Fuel system:** Weber-Marelli fuel injection
**Gearbox:** 6-speeds
**Frame:** Chrome-molybdenum steel tubular trellis frame, with patented adjustable steering system, swinging arm in magnesium alloy (aluminium alloy on F4S)
**Suspension:**
*Front:* 49mm (1.9in) inverted hydraulic front fork
*Rear:* single shock absorber with adjustable rebound, compression damping and spring pre-load
**Wheels:** 5-spoke magnesium alloy (aluminium alloy on F4S)
**Tyres:**
*Front:* 120/65 ZR 17
*Rear:* 190/60 ZR 17
**Dry weight:** 180kg (397lb)
**Power:** 126bhp at 12,200rpm
**Top speed:** 275km/h (171mph)

49mm (19.29in) stanchion inverted Showa-made front forks and, at the rear, a 'floating' monoshock unit based on a single air/oil shock absorber which can be adjusted for compression, rebound and spring pre-load.

A feature of the F4 is its adjustable steering-head angle device. Massimo Tamburini had, with both Bimota and Ducati, done previous work on adjustable steering head angles. On the F4, this device allowed, with simple adjustment, different angles to be obtained to suit individual riders' needs. The Öhlins hydraulic steering damper is mounted across the frame as on the Ducati 916 series – a Tamburini trademark. The rear wheel is supported by a spindle and the job of the single central nut in terms of its functional concept and size are the same for all current F1 racing cars. The whole unit is supported by an eccentric hub that

offers the means of adjusting chain tension. Not only does the F4 feature six-piston calipers at the front, but also these feature pistons of different diameters, derived from Cagiva's GP experiences. At the rear, unusually, the single disc has a four-piston calliper which is claimed to out-perform all others currently on the market.

The F4's engine is probably the most modern of any motorcycle in existence. Features such as the Radial Valve cylinder head – a first on a modern high-performance motorcycle – allow each cylinder to have four radial valves, with direct control of the valves by means of tappets and tapered cams. Nothing was spared in the search for performance. In order to attain a highly compact combustion chamber, and the smallest angle between the valves in its class (22 degrees), without running up against a decrease in the resistance of

the middle zone of the driving shaft, a specially designed transmission system was adopted to control the timing chain. In this way, the toothed wheels on the camshafts could be reduced in diameter, allowing for the most compact head and cover unit in four-cylinder engines of the same displacement. A removable (cassette-type) gearbox with six ratios was adopted for the first time on a mass-produced four-cylinder street bike, following the experience of the Cagiva Racing Department during its years of 500cc World Championship activity (which ended in 1994).

**The MV Agusta F4 uses a 749.4cc water-cooled, dohc, 16-valve across-the-frame four, with an electronically controlled digital ignition and fuel injection system. Top speed is 275 km/h (171mph), even so it can be truly described as gentleman's machine thanks to its sophisticated design.**

Due to the availability of a complete set of specially designed gears, it is possible for both the road user and the racer to optimise the gear ratios best suited at the time, depending upon track or road conditions. The F4 is as good in practical riding terms as it is from the styling and technical perspective. This is a bike which has been designed and built by motorcyclists. Everything is in exactly the right place and it all works.

In many ways, the F4 is best described as a gentleman's machine. While it does not have the armchair comfort of a Honda Gold Wing or even a sports/ tourer such as the CBR1000, by single-purpose sports bike standards, it is

**The fairing of MV Agusta's F4 sports air vents (one either side) for the ram-air system and sealed airbox, the design following work carried out on the Cagiva 500cc four-cylinder Grand Prix racer. Also note the Showa inverted front forks and sharp styling lines.**

comfortable. As for attention to detail, this can only be described as breath-taking. Compared with the standard (regular) F4S, the Serie Oro has a number of extras: magnesium alloy (instead of aluminium alloy) for the swinging arm and rear sub-frame assemblies (with gold finish instead of a grey finish); carbon-fibre bodywork (instead of heavier fibreglass); aluminium floating disc flanges for the front brakes (instead of steel); and magnesium wheels (instead of aluminium alloy).

Whether you choose the F4S or Serie Oro, you will be guaranteed a top performer and a unique piece of motorcycling Superbike heritage that's set to become a future classic.

## OTHER ITALIAN MARQUES

Marques such as Benelli, Bimota, Laverda, Gilera, and Moto Guzzi are all big names in Italian motorcycling history. Bimota, much the smaller of the five, has, like the others, been hit by

financial and/or ownership problems over the past decade. It is currently owned by Francesco Tognon, the man who had earlier saved Laverda. Bimota has never really recovered since the Japanese learnt how to make frames to match the power of their engines during the mid-1980s. At present, it offers models with both Suzuki and Yamaha engines, and up until very recently from Ducati. However, in the past, both Honda and Kawasaki power units have been employed. During the late 1990s, Bimota produced its own engine – a 500cc two-stroke V-twin of extremely modern design – but it unfortunately suffered a host of problems which often meant customers being refunded and the bike returned to the factory.

Laverda built the world's first 225.3km/h (140mph) Superbike, the Jota, in 1976. For a decade afterwards, the Laverda name was associated with speed, power, and prestige. But a series of management errors – including an

ill-fated V6 project – saw Laverda become bankrupt in the late 1980s. In 1992, local businessman and bike enthusiast Francesco Tognon stepped in and re-launched the marque in a brand-new factory. However, the long-promised 'new' Jota 900/1000cc triple never arrived. With Laverda relying on sales of a dohc twin-cylinder engine based on the old Alpino, more financial problems occurred at the end of the 1990s. In 2000, Aprilia stepped in and bought the ailing company.

What of the famous long-established Moto Guzzi marque? Like Laverda, it had been a major player in the Superbike stakes during the golden age of the 1970s (with bikes such as the V7 Sport and the Le Mans), but it declined thereafter. After De Tomaso sold out in the early 1990s, the factory's ownership was always open to question. There was never any money to develop the new ideas put forwards. Even a move to Modena did not eventuate. Like Laverda, Moto Guzzi was swallowed up by Aprilia during the year 2000.

### BENELLI AND GILERA

Will Moto Guzzi or, for that matter Laverda, build Superbikes in the future? This will depend upon Aprilia. Certainly, as far as Guzzi is concerned, it seems more likely that its bikes will either be like the California cruiser or the V11 Sport retro. This leaves just two famous names from the past, Benelli and Gilera. The former has seen its upheavals. First De Tomaso (who had also owned Guzzi) unloaded the company at the end of the 1980s. Then came a period of 50cc-only production. A new management team then put Benelli back on the map and into profitability with a range of ultra-modern scooters during the latter half of the 1990s. Finally came news of an exciting new Superbike entry, the 900cc three-cylinder Tornado.

The Tornado was a famous Benelli model name from the early 1970s, but, whereas that bike used a 650 ohv parallel twin engine, the new Tornado had almost a third more cubic capacity and an extra cylinder to boot. Although the first production Tornado

**One of the famous Italian racing marques making a return with a Superbike is Benelli. Its first model was the 900 Tornado, which used a three-cylinder, 12-valve engine. The Tornado name comes from a famous Benelli model from the classic era.**

features an 898.4cc engine size, Benelli plans an entire family of models of various displacements. The cylinders are vertical and the 12 valves (four per cylinder) are inclined 15 degrees and driven by a chain on the nearside (left) of the cylinder block. The frame is in two sections: a chrome-molybdenum steel front and aluminium rear, with the rear providing attachment for the single, vertically mounted shock absorber. The steering head is adjustable and there are 431.8mm (17in) five-spoke racing quality aluminium wheels, a wet multi-plate clutch, and six-speed cassette-type gearbox. Weighing in at 185kg (408lb), the 900 Tornado has a claimed top speed of 280km/h (174mph).

Another Italian Superbike entry on the cards is a new four-cylinder Gilera, but again it is the victim of financial changes within its parent company, Piaggio. In the 1950s, together with

MV Agusta, Gilera won a clutch of 500cc Blue Riband Grand Prix races and world championship titles.

For the past 30-plus years, ever since Honda took the motorcycle industry by the scruff of the neck with the introduction of its superb CB750 four, the word 'Superbike' has meant just that. It is a category which is seen as the ultimate in series production motorcycle design and manufacture. It is all about power and prestige. The great marques such as Triumph, Suzuki, Yamaha, Kawasaki, Aprilia, MV Agusta, Ducati, and, of course, Honda are important players. BMW and Harley-Davidson do make Superbikes – they just happen to be in the sports/touring and cruiser sectors.

Considering the awesome speeds of which bikes such as the Suzuki Hayabusa, Kawasaki ZX-12R, and Honda Blackbird are capable, one can only guess where the Superbike will go from here. Perhaps the MV Agusta F4 points the way forwards as a styling icon – an object of desire in which out-right performance is secondary to considerations such as artistry, a prestige name, and innovative engineering.

# SUPER SPORTS BIKES

Currently the most popular class in the biking world, Super Sports refer to 600 multi cylinders or 750 twins. This is because they combine performance aplenty with relatively light weight and a lower purchase price than a Superbike. The first of the genre was the Kawasaki GPZ600R back in 1985. Since then the Japanese manufacturers have fought a bitter sales battle in this sector for the number one spot – with Honda and its long-running CBR series usually coming out on top.

The most common Super Sports bikes are to be found in the 600cc category, dominated by the big four Japanese makers – Honda, Kawasaki, Suzuki, and Yamaha – and most recently joined by an exciting new entry from the reborn British Triumph marque. But the top seller remains Honda's legendary CBR600, followed by the Yamaha R6, Kawasaki ZX-6, and Suzuki GSX-R models.

## KAWASAKI SETS THE BALL ROLLING
In 1984 Kawasaki set the motorcycling world alight with its ground-breaking GPZ900R, which at the time represented the cutting edge of big-bike technology – an unbeatable combination of speed, handling, braking, and

With the arrival of its R6 in 1999, Yamaha shot to the forefront of the Super Sports 600 ranks with a combination of low weight and searing performance.

rider comfort in a single package. The GPZ900R was also the first Superbike with a liquid-cooled across-the-frame 16-valve, dohc, four-cylinder engine. The huge sales success of the GPZ convinced Kawasaki that it had struck on a winning formula. As many riders did not want, or could not afford, such a machine, Kawasaki's management team came up with the idea of down-sizing the same concept. In the process, it effectively created a brand-new motorcycle sector, the 600 Super Sport.

In 1984, Kawasaki scored with the GPZ900R and, the following year, did it again with the smaller GPZ600R. In the process, it stole a march on the opposition by creating a whole new class, the liquid-cooled Super Sport 600. As such, the GPZ600R is a land-mark motorcycle in modern biking history. Without it, there would probably never have been the hyper-performance 600s of today, such as the Honda CBR, Yamaha R6, Suzuki GSX-R, and Kawasaki's own ZX-6.

The 600R shared numerous features with its older, bigger brother, such as being an across-the-frame, four-cylinder four-stroke with dual cams

The 1985 Kawasaki GPZ600R is an historic machine, as it was the very first of the modern Super Sport 600s to go on sale. The liquid-cooled 592cc across-the-frame engine produced 75bhp at 10,500rpm. Other features included anti-dive forks and Uni-Trak rear suspension. In this picture the bike is being put through its paces by John Robinson, technical editor of *Performance Bikes* magazine.

# PUSH-BUTTON STARTING

The taken-for-granted luxury of electric (push-button) starting really began its life as a common feature thanks to the Japanese manufacturers. Before this, kickstarters, either on the nearside or offside of the machine, were the norm.

Honda led the way first with their twin-cylinder models followed by the CB750 four. Today, virtually every motorcycle and scooter has an electric button. It has played a vital role in bringing two wheels to the masses. In the bad old days, if you stalled your bike at the traffic lights, it was often a case of having to get off, put the bike on its centre stand, and kick it back into life. Now, a rider in the same position simply pulls in the clutch lever, fires the engine, and is instantly mobile again. Electric (push-button) starting is also a great bonus on the Super Sport 600s used for racing, as previously the bike had to be bump-started; now, it's simply a case of pressing the starter button. What could be easier?

and four valves per cylinder. However, it was far from being simply a scaled-down GPZ900R; it was, in fact, very much a motorcycle in its own right. The engine, while possessing many similarities to the 900R, was actually much more closely related to the then current air-cooled GPZ 550's engine, which had proved surprisingly successful in production-class racing events on both sides of the Atlantic – in the USA, it was particularly competitive in the popular 'box-stock' category. Another asset of the 550 power unit was its exceptional reputation for reliability, with many professional race tuners openly con-

firming the Kawasaki engine to be one of the toughest ever built.

The new liquid-cooled 592cc continued this bullet-proof reputation. It followed the 550's centre cam chain, chain primary drive with an intermediate shaft and crank-end mounted alternator. The 600's engine also had the added advantage of being more compact than the smaller air-cooled brother, being some 40mm (1.6in) narrower. The five-bearing bottom end was virtually the same as the 550's; however, the bore centres of cylinders two and three had been moved inwards 1mm (0.03in). The 600

## KAWASAKI GPZ600R (1985)

**Engine:** 4-stroke, across-the-frame four, dohc, 4-valves-per-cylinder, water-cooled
**Bore and stroke:** 60 x 52.4mm (2.4 x 2.1in)
**Displacement:** 592cc
**Compression ratio:** 11:1
**Carburation:** 4 x Keihin CVK 32
**Ignition:** Electronic
**Lubrication:** Wet sump
**Gearbox:** 6-speed
**Clutch:** Wet, multi-plate
**Frame:** Rectangular section steel tubing, with twin downtubes

**Suspension:**
*Front:* 38mm (1.49in) telescopic with automatic anti-dive
*Rear:* Single shock
**Brakes:**
*Front:* twin 280mm (11in) hydraulically operated discs
*Rear:* Single 270mm (10.6in) hydraulically operated disc
**Tyres:**
*Front:* 110/80 V16
*Rear:* 120/80 V16
**Dry weight:** 195kg (430lb)
**Power:** 75bhp at 10,500 rpm
**Top speed:** 217km/h (135mph)

## CBR600F (2001)

**Engine:** Water-cooled, across-the-frame, double overhead cam shaft, 4-cylinder, with 16-valves-per-cylinder
**Bore and stroke:** 67 x 42.5mm (2.6 x 1.7in)
**Displacement:** 599cc
**Compression ratio:** 12:1
**Carburation:** Fuel injection
**Ignition:** Electronic
**Starter:** Electric
**Gearbox:** 6-speed
**Frame:** Twin-spar aluminium main frame, square-section swinging arm
**Suspension:**
  *Front:* telescopic fork
  *Rear:* rising-rate single shock absorber
**Brakes:**
  *Front:* 2 x 296mm (11.7in) discs with 4-piston calipers
  *Rear:* single 220mm (8.7in) disc with 2-piston calliper
**Wheels:** Aluminium, 3-spoke
**Tyres:**
  *Front:* 120/70 ZR17
  *Rear:* 180/55 ZR17
**Dry weight:** 170kg (374.8lb)
**Power:** 109bhp at 12,500rpm
**Top speed:** 249km/h (155mph)

also featured wet cylinder liners. Coolant entered each water jacket through an inlet onto the back of the cylinders, flowed around the liners, passed through the head, and exited via two outlets at the top. The single radiator was aluminium and equipped with a thermostatically controlled electric fan. Except for its cam-chain location, the head and valve train were similar to the GPZ900R's, with valves actuated by cam followers carrying screw-type adjusters.

The GPZ600R sported a brand-new frame, manufactured primarily from

**Honda's CBR has dominated the Super Sport 600 class since it entered production in 1987. Rivals have, from time to time, been faster or lighter, but the CBR's all-round ability has seen it remain at the top of the sales charts year after year.**

rectangular-section steel. Twin downtubes were bolted to the main section near the steering head and swinging-arm pivot, while a trio of large cross-tubes in the main section ensured rigidity. An aluminium brace across the downtubes supported the radiator and oil cooler. The 406.4mm (16in) wheels ensured a user-friendly 770mm (30in) seat height. An all-up weight of 195kg (430lb) certainly went a long way towards making the new 600 controllable around town, while out on the open road a very respectable 75bhp (10bhp more than the air-cooled 550) at 10,500rpm ensured workmanlike performance.

During its first two years, Kawasaki's GPZ600R had the field to itself,

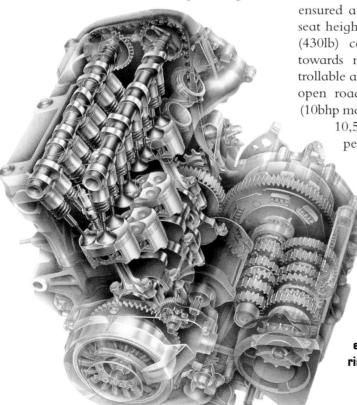

**Cutaway view of the Honda CBR600 engine, showing the double overhead camshafts, four-valves-per-cylinder, pistons, crankshaft, primary drive, clutch, and gearbox. The engine has proved extremely reliable both for road rider and racing competitor alike.**

with its Japanese rivals struggling to compete with older technology air-cooled engines. In fact, the 600R was just about the best-selling middle-weight motorcycle of its era all around the world. This very success, however, was to prove its undoing, as Honda, Suzuki, and Yamaha all pressed the panic buttons and came up with Super Sport machines of their own.

### THE OPPOSITION FIGHTS BACK

By late 1986, Yamaha was able to announce the new FZ600 (albeit an air-cooled design), Suzuki was working on their its 600 sportster, and Honda was about to put a massive spanner in the works by announcing its brand-new liquid-cooled 16-valve CBR600F, which subsequently went on sale in early 1987 to great press and public acclaim and has remained a top seller ever since. As the Honda has been the class leader for almost a decade and a half, we shall look at this bike first.

The CBR600F's huge success has been thanks to Honda's ability in keeping it competitive, with a series of updates over the years, to add to the original design's great all-round performance. Even for a company the size of Honda, the CBR's success has been phenomenal. Actually, the first CBR fours were the 400 and 250, which went on sale on the Japanese domestic market in 1986; by the summer of that year, rumours had reached Europe that 600 and 1000cc versions would soon follow.

The 250 four was the highest-revving road bike ever produced up to that time, with a red line that went up to an amazing 17,000rpm and a maximum power of 45bhp being produced at 14,500rpm. The 400 version of the motor punched out 59bhp at 12,500rpm and featured an engine raked forwards at an angle of 35 degrees and fed by a quartet of downdraught Keihin VG02 carburettors. A six-speed gearbox was mounted in a race-style (steel) box-section frame which supported the engine both fore and aft. A bodyshell similar to that of the Italian Ducati Paso (originally launched at the Milan Show in late 1985) was claimed to give the machine, as Honda sources described, the aerodynamic qualities of an arrow. Other details of the CBR400 included

three-spoke alloy wheels, triple disc brakes, a four-into-one exhaust, and a dry weight of 164kg (363lb).

With the launch of both the CBR600F and CB1000F for the 1987 model year, Honda had truly thrown down the gauntlet. At the time, these moves were controversial to say the least, as they came after Honda had, it seemed, committed its future to the V-configuration and turned its back on the design which had made its name, the across-the-frame four. At the beginning of the 1980s, Honda had introduced the VF750 V-four and subsequently followed this up with the VF1000, VF500, and VF400, plus the VT250 V-twin. The switch back to the use of the traditional across-the-frame four layout came as a result of Honda's

## CBR600F EVOLUTION

**1986** CBR600F launched late summer. Across-the-frame four-cylinder engine configuration, liquid-cooled, 16 valves, dohc, six-speed, steel frame, 431mm (17in) tyres, three-spoke alloy wheels, fully enclosed bodywork.

**1987** First production version, the FH goes on sale.

**1989** First update. Power increased from 85bhp to 93bhp, as a result of a host of engine modifications, including higher 11.1:1 compression ratio.

**1991** Major revision. Engine fitted with 15 per cent larger cylinder head ports, bigger 34mm (1.3in) carburettors and airbox, larger and lighter valves with narrower included angle, strengthened (and lighter) crankshaft, lighter pistons, compression ratio increased from 11.1:1 to 11.3:1. Clutch reduced in diameter from 138mm (5.4in) to 125mm (4.9in), number of plates increased from six to nine. Relocation of gearbox mainshaft meant new, more compact crankcases fitted. New exhaust system. Power output increased to 98.6bhp. New cycle parts including six-spoke wheels, modified frame (still steel), and swinging arm, revised suspension, and braking. Restyled bodywork and graphics.

**1995** Mechanical revision including higher compression (now 12:1) larger carburettors (36mm/1.4in) and introduction of ram-air system; power boosted to 100bhp.

**1997** Major update including 105bhp at 12,000rpm, torque increased 6.7kg (14.8lb) at 10,500rpm, new wheels and brakes, revised suspension, revised bodywork. Smaller detail changes including ignition, exhaust, and air-induction system.

**1999** Virtually a new bike. Almost every component was changed, including the engine – now 67 x 42mm (2.6 x 1.7in), compared to 65 x 45.2mm (2.6 x 1.8in). Maximum rpm increased to 14,600rpm. Cooling efficiency improved by 17 per cent, as a result of increased radiator area and revised coolant channels in the cylinder block. Cylinders have aluminium liners coated in graphite and ceramics for improved heat transfer and reduced friction, while other internal losses are minimised by changes to valves, pistons, and bearings. Carburettor size increased to 36.5mm (1.4in). New ignition system. All-new, twin-spar aluminium frame and new bodywork. Stainless steel exhaust, with aluminium/stainless muffler.

**2001** Fuel injection replaces carburettors. Revised bodywork, including fairing. Larger air-inlet ports for the airbox. New instrument console; modified electronic control unit (ECU). Cylinder head and cam cover redesign to accommodate cam-shaft pulsar and coolant temperature sensor needed for fuel injection system. 109bhp at 12,500rpm. In addition to the CBR600F, a new 'F' Sport model also available.

# CAST ALLOY WHEELS

Motorcycles began to be fitted with cast alloy wheels in the middle of the 1970s. While a few racing machines had cast alloy wheels in the early 1970s, in series production bikes, the first to be equipped with these as part of the original specification were: BMW (1977 R100RS), Ducati (1977 Darmah), Moto Guzzi (1976 Le Mans), Laverda (1976 Jota), Honda (1978 CBX), and Kawasaki (1978 Z1-R).

At first, some wheels were magnesium (on some Ducatis) or composite (Honda Comstar type), rather than simply aluminium. These early types were not without their problems – even BMW had a faulty batch on its 1980 models. Whatever their construction, however, the term 'alloy' or simply 'cast' has been a universal description. These replaced the long-running wire (with usually either 36 or 40 wire spokes) connecting the hub to the rim. The rims were of either steel or aluminium construction, sometimes flanged. The latter type, although marginally stronger (hence their use on pure-bred racers), had the disadvantage of the flanged 'well' retaining water. As for the cast wheel, to save weight, it has now become common practice to make these hollow. Another consideration

Cast alloys wheels began to be fitted as standard equipment during the mid- to late 1970s. Today, the spokes are often hollow to save weight. The three-spoke wheel shown here is from a Ducati 916 Senna. Note single-sided swinging arm for easy wheel removal.

is that, since the mid-1980s, tubeless tyres have become a standard fitment on all performance-related motorcycles, whether for road or circuit use, so the rim also has to act as a sealing device.

main rivals Kawasaki, Suzuki, and Yamaha continuing to enjoy success with the formula. The final straw for Honda came with the big sales success that Kawasaki enjoyed with the launch of its GPZ600R in 1985. The Honda philosophy seemed to be: 'If you can't beat them, join them – only do it better.'

The first CBR600F, the FH went on sale in early 1987 and, in addition to the aerodynamic bodywork, was notable for its use of 431mm (17in) wheels, which were at the time seen as a fashion whim, yet today are the acknowledged as the correct course to take. The 598cc engine ran on an 11:1 compression ratio and had a six-speed

gearbox, an electric start, transistorised ignition with electronic advance, four 32mm (1.3in) carbs, three-spoke aluminium wheels, air-assisted 37mm (1.5in) front forks with TRAC anti-dive, and Pro-link rear suspension. Dry weight was 182kg (400lb). There was also a lightweight, aluminium oil cooler and radiator, while the power output was a very respectable 85bhp, which meant a maximum speed of around 225km/h (140mph). One feature of the machine that was soon quietly dumped was the TRAC anti-dive, followed soon after by the front fork air-pressure adjustment.

The first update came in 1989, with the power bumped up to 93bhp as a result of a substantial list of engine modifications. Even more power came

**For the 1999 model year Honda introduced an aluminium frame for the first time on its best selling CBR600. The engine also gained a new shorter-stroke 67 x 42mm bore and stroke dimension, improved cooling, new cylinders, together with a revised ignition system.**

in 1991 (98.6bhp). More importantly, the rest of the bike received its first major redesign, with many new cycle parts, including wheels, frame, swinging arm, suspension, and braking. At the same time, the bodywork was completely restyled. In 1995, a mechanical revision included larger carbs and the introduction of a ram air system. Power was now up to 100bhp. Another major update occurred in 1997, including a power boost to 105bhp, new wheels, brakes, revised suspension, and smaller detail changes including ignition, exhaust, and air-induction system.

In 1999, Honda introduced what amounted to a virtually new bike. The engine featured shorter bore and stroke dimensions – 67 x 42mm (2.6 x 1.7in). There was improved cooling, new cylinders, lighter moving parts, larger carbs (now 36.5mm/1.4in), and a new ignition system. The biggest development was the adoption, for the first time, of an aluminium frame. The picture was completed by new bodywork and exhaust, the latter in stainless steel.

Finally, in 2001, fuel injection replaced carburettors, power output was increased to 109bhp, and there was a new fairing with larger air-inlet ducts, a modified ECU (Electronic Control Unit), and redesigned cylinder head and cam cover. The CBR was also made available in two guises: the standard 'F' and a new 'F' Sport model.

So what has been the reason for its success? One word: rideability. Other manufacturers might, for a short period, have had faster, better handling, sharper braking, and better styling. Honda's CBR600, however, has consistently been the best overall package in the hotly contested Super Sport arena and a classic in its own lifetime.

## SUZUKI AND YAMAHA
Suzuki and Yamaha were not normally known for lagging behind Honda and Kawasaki, but, in the Super Sport 600 battle, that is exactly what happened. While the two latter marques forged ahead with up-to-the-minute liquid-cooled bikes which really deserved the

Super Sport name, Suzuki and Yamaha dragged their feet. Yamaha seemed to think that simply slotting an ageing air-cooled four into its racer-replica styled FZ 600 would be enough. Suzuki was even slower, with it being the last to introduce a 600 in the shape of the 1988 GSX600F (which had an air-oil cooled engine) and then leaving it in production for far too long, before finally replacing it with the GSX-R600 in late 1996 – almost a decade later!

Yamaha's FZR600 replaced the air-cooled FZ600 for 1989. The middle-weight FZR followed the Genesis concept of Yamaha's inclined four-cylinder engine and Deltabox frame which had made the bigger FZRs such a success. But it did not boast the five-

**For the 2001 model year, Honda engineers fully updated the CBR600, with fuel injection replacing carburettors. There was revised bodywork, larger air-inlet ports for the airbox, and a modified ECU. Power went up to 109bhp at 12,500rpm. A new 'F' Sport model (shown) was also introduced.**

valves-per-cylinder technology of the 750 and 1000cc models; instead, it shared the four-valves-per-cylinder configuration of the smaller FZR400 instead. Displacing 599cc, this double overhead camshaft engine delivered a shade over 90bhp, at 10,500rpm. The motor was kept on the boil thanks to a six-speed box in which fifth and sixth gears employed reverse-tapered dogs (back-cut) for positive engagement and improved reliability. Much of the 600's technology was identical to the larger FZR's, but with the components coming in smaller sizes: 38mm (1.5in) fork stanchions, dual 298mm (11.7in) front discs, and a single 245mm (9.6in) rear disc, together with 110/70 V17 (front) and 130/70 V18 (rear) tyres.

The FZR600 at last gave Yamaha a viable Super Sport bike, a model not just for the showroom, but one that, at least in its early years, was a serious contender for the by now keenly contested 600 production-based racing class.

As for Suzuki, their 599cc GSX600F model, although a reasonable performer, could not touch the other three Japanese makes in terms of either sales or performance. It soon was downrated to the status of an also-ran and was thereafter seen as a budget buy for those who could not afford a CBR, FZR, or GPX/ZZ-R. ( Kawasaki had replaced its trend-setting GPZ with two models. The first, the GPX, arrived for the 1988 season, while the ZZ-R arrived in the autumn of 1989.)

## KAWASAKI'S SECOND-GENERATION 600S

Kawasaki's GPX, which went on sale in 1988, was the first 'second generation' model in the middleweight Super Sport 600 sales war. The arrival of Honda's CBR600F for the 1987 model year had effectively killed off sales of Kawasaki's GPZ. 'Big K' responded by producing this second-generation liquid-cooled 600, arming it with features from the company's new GPX750R.

This resulted in the 600's engine being reduced in weight by 1.5kg (3.3lb), while at the same time power output was increased by some 13 per cent. The latter was achieved by improved design

**Arriving at the end of the 1980s, Yamaha's FZR600 followed the 'Genesis concept' of inclined engine and Deltabox frame pioneered on the FZ750/FZR1000. It did not, however, boast the five-valves-per-cylinder layout, instead sharing the four-valve arrangement of the smaller FZR400.**

to the inlet porting and creating new inlet valves, lighter pistons, chrome-molybdenum connecting rods, and a larger airbox. To match the increase in horsepower (85bhp at 11,000rpm), the radiator's cooling capacity was up by 23 per cent. These changes gave a top speed of 230km/h (143mph) and allowed the GPX to sprint the standing 400m (0.25 mile) in 11.6 seconds.

The GPX600R's frame was similar to the lightweight double-cradle structure of the GPX750. This meant that there were two major frame sections: a high-tensile steel main frame and a short, bolt-on box-section aluminium rear section. The 600's frame design differed on the size and placement of gussets, brackets, and engine mounts. Other new components included the fairing, while the 38mm (1.5in) front forks shared the same electronic suspension system introduced on the GPX750. Called ESCS (Electronic Suspension Control System), it combined the functions of automatic damping and anti-dive in one lightweight unit. ESCS valves opened and closed automatically according to the inner pressure of the fork to adjust compression damping in response to speed and distance of fork travel. For an instantaneous anti-dive effect, valves were electrically activated whenever the front brake was applied. There were also new brakes – with BAC (Balanced Activation Calliper) – and these were a feature not only of the larger GPX750, but of the newly introduced ZX10 Super Bike, too.

Although 406.4mm (16in) wheels were still fitted, the weight of various components (including hubs, brakes etc.) had been pruned by 3.5kg (7.7lb). The Dunlop Tyre Company had created special V-rated rubber for the GPX 600. The low aspect ratio of this rubber (80 per cent front and 60 per cent rear) helped to lower seat height and also improve handling.

Although it never displaced Honda's CBR as number-one seller, the GPX did have considerable success on the track during its launch year, when, in 1988, it won many Super Sport 600 races in Britain and the rest of Europe. Yet, strangely, for a period of months the 'old' GPZ was also offered. Was this a case of giving customers an option or Kawasaki having a surplus of old stock? Perhaps it was the former, as, when the company introduced the new ZZ-R600, the GPX continued to be available until as late as 1996.

In October 1989, Kawasaki launched both the ZZ-R1100 and its smaller brother, the ZZ-R600. The latter bike was the first Super Sport 600 class machine to be equipped with an aluminium frame (even the class-leading Honda CBR600 did not receive this treatment until almost a decade later). Nevertheless, the ZZ-R was in many ways a strange offering. At the time of its launch, it was not only the first to sport an alloy frame, but it was also the most comfortable bike in its class and the most powerful. It was a physically larger motorcycle

than both the GPZ and GPX, and also the opposition's offerings.

The 599cc engine was not, as one would expect, a development of the GPZ/GPX, but actually brand-new, even though it was an across-the-frame, dohc, 16-valve four. The cylinder head featured straight-shot inlet ports, with 26mm (1.02in) inlet and 22mm (0.9in) exhaust valves set at a compact 30-degree included angle. Added to this was an 11.5:1 compression ratio, 36mm (1.4in) Keihin carburettors, digital ignition and a four-into-two exhaust system. Like the engine, the frame was also new, with double box-section aluminium extrusions mated to a cast-alloy steering head, swinging arm pivot, and downtube/side brace junction. At the time, Kawasaki claimed that the ZZ-R600 featured the stiffest frame ever fitted to one of

**In October 1989, Kawasaki launched both the ZZ-R600 and its bigger brother, the 1100. The 600's 599cc engine was a new dohc unit with 16 valves, 36mm (1.41in) Keihin carbs, digital ignition, and, for the first time on a 600-class bike, an aluminium frame.**

# HYDRAULIC STEERING DAMPERS

For many years, the old-fashioned 'tank slapper' was controlled by the fitment by many motorcycle manufacturers of some sort of friction steering damper. This usually comprised an adjusting knob above the steering column, with upper and lower plates underneath the bottom yoke with a couple of fibre washers. It was basic and it worked – up to a point. Then, in the late 1950s, it was realised that, by fitting a version of a shock absorber without the spring, and by fitting it between one of the front fork legs and the frame, a more effective form of damping could be achieved. In those early days, very few manufacturers (BMW was an exception) fitted a hydraulic damper as standard equipment. Instead, made by the likes of the British Girling concern, hydraulic steering dampers were sold as an aftermarket accessory.

By the mid-1970s, with machines such as the Kawasaki Z1, performance levels had reached a point where hydraulic steering dampers began to be specified as standard equipment (combined with the fact that most Japanese big bikes of the era were not blessed with the best of handling!). In fact, Kawasaki was one of the first motorcycle marques to equip its dampers with a method of adjustment. Before this, it was very much a case of either putting up with what was too stiff an action for normal road use, or disconnecting the device from the bike! Adjustable dampers meant that the rider could set the level of damping to his or her particular requirement and so became far more practical for use by the average road rider, rather than simply being for the racer.

Today, the adjustable steering damper is not only almost always a standard fitment, but also almost a science. Adjustable steering dampers from the likes of racing suspension specialists Öhlins can cost several hundreds of pounds. In addition, the famous designer Massimo Tamburini has repositioned the damper across the steering head, between the instruments and tank, on bikes such as the Ducati 916 and MV Agusta F4, to begin a new trend.

the middleweight designs. At the rear, a high-tensile steel sub-frame, bolted on, supported the rider and provided mounting points for the battery, wiring, and other detail components.

With its aluminium frame, almost 100bhp, and looks which aped its bigger brother, the ZZ-R1100, the new Kawasaki 600 outsold every other model in its class during 1990. This feat was not repeated until the present day by anything other than Honda's super-successful CBR600 in all its various versions. The smaller ZZ-R's Achilles heel was its weight – 195kg (430lb) – the heaviest of the time in its category. Even so, the ZZ-R was good enough for John Reynolds to clinch the British Super Sport 600 championship in 1990. Reynolds's task was made easier by several worthwhile improvements over

the GPX, including a switch to 431mm (17in) tyres, beefy 41mm (1.6in) front forks (the same size as ZX-10 Super Bike), and uprated braking (new four-piston calipers with larger 300mm (11.8in) floating discs up front and a single 230mm (9in) disc at the rear). It was in the area of rider comfort, however, where the ZZ-R really scored, for both the pilot and passenger benefited from an expansive dual seat, plush suspension, and a large fairing.

The definitive ZZ-R600 arrived for 1993. Coded E1 (the original was D1), this not only had a more powerful engine (*Motor Cycle News* tested a new ZZ-R at over 257km/h (160mph) that year), but also possessed a stronger frame and stiffer swinging arm, a larger diameter rear disc (240mm/9.4in), a more efficient fairing, a shorter wheel base, and other smaller changes.

### SPORTING INTENT

By the mid-1990s, the Super Sport 600 class had become the most important – sales wise – in the motorcycle industry, certainly in Europe. Honda, Kawasaki,

**It was the huge success of its R1 model that convinced Yamaha to go for a smaller-engined version for the important Super Sport 600 category. The result was the R6, which arrived in time for the 1999 season.**

**The R6's combination of a short wheelbase, aluminium chassis, extra long swinging arm, low weight, and a free revving 599cc four-cylinder engine has put Yamaha back at the top for both performance-minded riders and serious circuit racers alike.**

Suzuki, and Yamaha were all intent on updating or bringing out totally new models. Honda led the class, with its CBR600 winning both in the showroom and on the race circuit. As a result, the remaining three decided to act.

Yamaha had continuously updated its FZR entry, but even so never quite managed to catch Honda. So, amid a fanfare of trumpets, Yamaha launched the YZF600R Thundercat (599cc) in 1996. At first it was hailed as a CBR-beater – and in many ways it was, too. Unfortunately for Yamaha, not enough of the public agreed. The result was that, after the first year, the press was labelling the Thundercat as a 'second rank' 600. This was actually grossly unfair because it more than matched the Honda as an all-rounder and was comfortable, fast, and had some of the best brakes of any road bike on the planet. In fact, the Thundercat's brakes were truly outstanding and were the same, in fact, as those fitted to its bigger brother, the YZR1000R Thunderace (and also, later, the R1).

The Thundercat's engine was an updated version of the old FZR600R (the final version of the FZR series). Producing a healthy 98.6bhp, it offered lots of top-end power, but lacked mid-range torque. The Yamaha's Deltabox chassis was extremely stiff and, connected to well-damped forks and rear suspension, the ride was well controlled for road use (solo or with a pillion), but

**Launched in 1996, the Yamaha YZF600R Thundercat (above) was, and still is, an excellent all-rounder. The engine is based on the old FZR, rather than the new R6, and thus lacks torque.**

too soft for track action. In fact, in many ways the Thundercat was a more modern version of Kawasaki's ZZ-R600: fast, comfortable (even two up), and with brilliant brakes.

It was the huge success of its R1 that convinced Yamaha to go for a more sports-orientated entry in the shape of the R6, which arrived for the 1999 model year. The R6 did not replace the Thundercat, which remained in production, but gave Yamaha a bike which could match, and in some areas clearly beat, Honda's CBR. The R6's 599cc engine was much sharper than previous 600 Yamahas. This was not simply because it had a bigger bore and shorter stroke. Like its bigger brother, it was engineered with performance as its priority. Compared to the Thundercat's 98.6bhp at 11,500rpm, the R6 put out a whopping 119.9bhp at 13,000rpm. At 169kg (372.6lb) against the Thundercat's 187kg (412.2lb), the R6 was a rocketship. In fact, Super Bike magazine called it the 'Bad boy, bad boy'.

The R6's combination of short wheelbase, aluminium chassis, extra-long swing-arm, low weight, and a free-revving powerful engine managed to place the new Yamaha at the top for both performance-minded riders and serious circuit racers alike. In its first year, it managed a string of World Super Sport 600 race victories to back up its performance credentials.

Also, like the R1, the R6 did not have much wrong with it on its launch. This meant that all that was changed for the 2000 model year update were new pistons and a slicker-shifting transmission; for 2001, the biggest change was yet more power to keep it on the pace.

## GSX-R600

For years, it had been a mystery as to why Suzuki had not followed up its hugely successful GSX-R750 with a smaller 600 version. Instead, it had clung grimly to the low-tech GSX600F and later the RF600, neither of which made much impression. Finally, for the 1997 model year, Suzuki succumbed to both inside and outside pressures and launched a smaller GSX-R. Although this new 600 shared much of its frame, bodywork, and engine components with its bigger brother, the newcomer had a character all its own. You really had to work the engine hard to get the best out of it, while the suspension was more basic than the 750 (for example, the bigger bike had inverted forks, the 600 conventional telescoping forks).

Even so, the steering response was just as sharp, with plenty of feel. Braking, although not in the Yamaha class, was more than adequate. The alloy frame was identical to the 750, although the swinging arm lacked the bigger bike's bracing, and the 600 ran a slightly narrower rear wheel and a 180/55 ZR17 tyre (the 750 and 190).

However, of all the latest generation of Super Sport 600s, the Suzuki is, as What Bike? commented: 'for committed hooligans and track day blasters only'. This statement still stands, even though from the 1998 model year the engine was modified to deliver more mid-range torque and top-end power, with new cam timing for greater valve lift, improved engine airflow, and a larger exhaust collector box.

Finally, for 2001 the GSX-R600 was re-engineered. Compared to the 'old' engine, the new 2001 unit has shorter stroke dimensions of 67 x 42.5mm

**For years, one of motorcycling's mysteries was why Suzuki did not produce a 600 version of its highly successful GSX-R. Finally, for 1997, just such a machine arrived. Overnight, the GSX-R600 was acclaimed for its single-minded racer-like appeal, including razor-sharp handling.**

The latest incarnation of the GSX-R600 has seen a major update for 2001, with shorter stroke, new crankshaft, bearings, con-rods, pistons, clutch, and gears. Dry weight is a low 163kg (359lb), while maximum speed approaches 257km/h (160mph).

new. Original features include the frame, swinging arm, front forks, rear shock, wheels, brake calipers, and final drive chain. The bodywork also has improved aerodynamics and a new, smaller dual-beam headlamp. Dry weight is 163kg (359lb), while maximum speed is nearly 260km/h (160mph).

### KAWASAKI'S ZX-6R

As the company which had invented the class, Kawasaki has always made serious efforts with its Super Sport 600 offering. First came the GPZ, then the GPX, followed by the ZZ-R and, finally, for 1995, the ZX-6R. In reality, the ZX-6R was Kawasaki's most serious sales prospect, as the GPZ had the field to itself before the arrival of the other Japanese makers. Here was a bike which at last could challenge the Honda CBR and in some areas actually beat it.

Starting with the engine, the design team virtually threw away its old blueprints and set out to create a brand-new, lighter, more compact power plant. To achieve this, the engine was given a cam-chain relocation from the centre to the offside end of the crankshaft; this meant a crank 30mm

(2.6 x 1.7in) – as against 65.5 x 44.5mm (2.6 x 1.8in) – to reduce mechanical losses at high rpm. In this latest incarnation of the GSX-R600, the valves are set at a narrower included angle (28 instead of 30 degrees), making the combustion chamber more compact and increasing the compression ratio from 12:1 to 12.2:1. The inlet valves are positioned 13 degrees and the exhaust valves positioned 15 degrees from the cylinder centreline, versus the previous bike's 14 degrees and 16 degrees, respectively. The downdraught angle of the inlet ports is steeper, 44 degrees from the horizontal instead of 41.5 degrees. The inlet valves are of a larger 27.2mm (1.07in) diameter compared to 26.5mm (1.04in), while the stem diameter of the exhaust valves has been decreased from 4.5mm (0.17in) to

4mm (0.15in). The remainder of the valve gear has also been modified. The cylinder-head casting is also changed and weighs less. The crankshaft, bearings, connecting rods, gudgeon pins, pistons, clutch assembly, and most of the individual transmission gears are new. Furthermore, it is not only the engine of the 2001 GSX-R600 that is

Kawasaki had always made a serious effort in the Super Sport 600 class. First came the GPZ, then the GPX, followed by the ZZ-R and finally, in 1995, the ZX-6R. With this last bike, the company could at last offer a serious rival to Honda's class-leading CBR.

(1.18in) narrower than before. This also had the advantage of reducing width, while maintaining crankshaft strength and still needing only five main journals to support the crank (one less than on the ZZ-R), thus reducing weight and friction. There were new bore and stroke measurements of 66 x 43.8mm (2.6 x 1.7in) – 64 x 46.6mm (2.5 x 1.8in) for the ZZ-R – giving 599cc. The shorter stroke meant shorter connecting rods, while a pentroof combustion chamber design and an 11.8:1 compression (12:1 on ZZ-R) offered higher combustion efficiency from the larger bore size.

Reducing the included valve angle from 30 to 25 degrees allowed the use of larger valves – inlet 26mm (1.02in) to 27mm (1.06in), exhaust 22mm (0.87in) to 22.6mm (0.88in) – for improved breathing. The cylinder block was canted forwards 28 degrees (13 degrees more than the ZZ-R) for reduced engine height. Two additional benefits from this were: a more downdraught position of the carbs for the mixture into the inlet ports and a lower centre

of gravity. To cope with the extra power output, new coolant passages around the exhaust area of the cylinder head were put in to help maintain consistent operating temperatures.

The ZX-6R's main frame, subframe, and swinging arm were all manufactured in aluminium. There was also attention paid to the suspension, brakes, wheels, and tyres, the latter being three-spoke, cast-aluminium 431mm (17in) wheels with 120/60 ZR (front) and 160/60ZR (rear) tyres.

In a comparison test by the US magazine *Motorcyclist* in December 1994, the then soon-to-be-released ZX-6R achieved a top speed of 251km/h (156mph); Honda's CBR600, the same speed; Yamaha's FZR 600, 227km/h (141mph); and Suzuki's RF 600 230km/h (143mph). This also shows what a lead Honda and Kawasaki had over the other two Japanese manufacturers at the time.

For 1998, Kawasaki engineers carried out an update of the ZX-6R, centring on a new short-wheelbase aluminium frame with revised steering

**By the 2000 ZX-6R (shown) Kawasaki engineers had given the bike new carburettors plus a new short-wheelbase frame with revised steering geometry, offering improved handling.**

geometry, offering improved handling. The engine also received attention, gaining new carburettors with K-TRIC (Kawasaki Throttle Control), which smoothed out the power characteristics. There were several smaller changes to the engine, suspension, brakes, tyres, and bodywork. Finally, for 2000, came the ZX-6RJ1. This was lighter and more powerful, and had R1-type headlights, new front brake calipers, and very few other changes. To sum up, the current ZX-6R is not as sharp or aggressive as an R6, not as soft as the all-round CBR, and more user-friendly than the GSX-R.

### THE BRITISH OPTION

At the time of its 2000 year model launch, the long-awaited British entry into the Super Sport 600 class was the TT600. The reborn Triumph marque

## WHEEL SIZES

During vintage and veteran days, 533mm (21in) or even 584mm (23in) wheel sizes were common. In the 1920s and 1930s, these sizes had decreased to 508mm (20in). In the aftermath of World War II, they dropped to 482mm (19in), spurred on by racing motorcycles such as the Featherbed Manx Norton and AJS 7R. Wheel sizes of 482mm (19in) were also widely used on the new high-performance singles and twins of the postwar era, including the BSA Gold Flash, Triumph Speed Twin, and BSA Gold Star.

At the beginning of the 1970s came a new trend of fitting 482mm (19in) front and 457mm (18in) rear tyres, before generally settling on 457mm (18in) front and rear. Again, after another decade, the 1980s saw a switch to 406mm (16in) at the front, with either a 406mm (16in) or 457mm (18in) rear. All motorcycles with 406mm (16in) rubber at the front tended to sit up in a corner if the brakes were applied. In the latter half of the 1980s, with a new breed of motorcycle such as the Honda CBR600 and CBR1000, came the adoption of 432mm (17in) on both wheels. At last, the right size had been found and a trend had begun which endures to this day, both for high-performance roadsters and racing motorcycles alike.

The gap between race and road tyres has never been narrower than it is today, as is the level of performance available to the road rider in comparison to his track brother.

could claim the distinction of offering the shortest stroke engine in its class. Otherwise, the Segem fuel injection apart, the liquid-cooled four employed tried and tested engineering, rather than start with its own new technology – in fact, the first ever 100 per cent European four-cylinder Super Sport 600 followed in the well-marked tyre tracks of the Japanese big four in overall design concept terms. The TT600 owed nothing to any of Triumph's previous models, not even the one-litre (0.22-gallon) and 1200cc fours which kicked off their comeback

in 1991. As tester Alan Cathcart summed up the TT600 in the June 2000 issue of *Motorcycle Sport & Leisure*: 'It's light, fast but not radical – that's what Super Sport buyers want'.

Triumph claimed 108bhp at 12,750rpm from the 599cc liquid-cooled 16-valve dohc four. Other specification details included a six-speed gearbox; 12.5:1 compression ratio; aluminium frame and swinging arm, 43mm (1.7in) forks; 2 x 310mm (0.07 x 12.2in), four-piston calipers at the front and a single 220mm (8.7in) two-piston caliper at the rear; 431mm

(17in) tyres; and a dry weight of 170kg (374lb). Overall, the TT600 seems to have got it just about right first time around. It can match the best machines Japan has to offer in power output, handling, braking, comfort, and level of finish.

### STREAMLINED SUCCESS STORIES
All the bikes described above have, in no short measure, been built around the incredible developments in aero-dynamic streamlining that have occurred over the past few decades. At first, streamlining was employed in

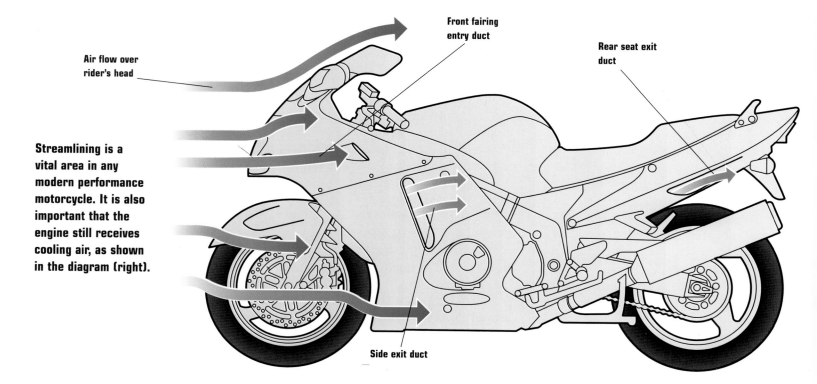

Air flow over rider's head

Front fairing entry duct

Rear seat exit duct

Side exit duct

Streamlining is a vital area in any modern performance motorcycle. It is also important that the engine still receives cooling air, as shown in the diagram (right).

speed-record attempts, then racing, and finally on production roadsters. Although several motorcycles had some form of enclosure, even in pre–World War II days, actual streamlining did not really catch on until the 1950s.

It was in Grand Prix racing that it snowballed from the simple flyscreen at the beginning of the decade to full dustbin enclosure by the mid-1950s. It all got out of hand, however, resulting in the sports governing body, the FIM, banning full streamlining from the end of the 1957 season in all forms of road racing.

In its place, from the beginning of 1958 came the dolphin fairing, a much less cumbersome device than that of the fully streamlined dustbin shell of the previous year. Even today, the dolphin still rules in racing; it is also essentially what is used on series production bikes described in this book. Dolphin fairing is far from perfect, but it does not suffer from the problems in high side winds that caused the 'dustbin' to be banned.

Aerodynamics are now an important area in designing a machine's fairing. The first fairings to be fitted to road bikes came thanks to the British industry, certainly as part of the original specification. In 1955, Vincent produced the fully faired version of its 998cc V-twin, the Black Knight. As the 1960s dawned, then came the Royal Enfield Airflow and the Ariel Leader as two other important examples. In the mid-1970s, it was the likes of BMW (the R100RS) and Ducati (with the SS and Mike Hailwood Replica) models that appeared on the scene. For once, these caught the Japanese off their guard as, even by the early 1980s, most machines from Japan were still naked. However, with the advent of the racer replica (such as the Suzuki GSX-R750) and tourer (Kawasaki GTR), the Japanese soon had the majority of their bikes 'covered'. Today, the only bikes which do not have a fairing of any sort tend to be 'Retros'.

Most road riders today would be lost without the comfort and wind-cheating abilities of their bike's

**From 2000, enthusiasts had the chance to buy a British Super Sport model, in the shape of the brand-new Triumph TT600. This had the distinction of offering not only the shortest stroke engine in the class, but also Segem's advanced fuel injection.**

fairing. Streamlining also improves fuel consumption figures, so it is not just a matter of comfort or aesthetics.

With incredible streamlining and other equally significant advances, the bike consumer has no fewer than five manufacturers all offering serious Super Sport 600 machinery. It is probably the hottest battle for showroom sales and track success in motorcycling. The would-be purchaser has never had it so good because they are excellent value. Any of these 'middleweights' has the performance which would have done any Superbike proud only a few short years ago, but for far less money and a much easier ownership experience thanks to their race-track bred handling and lower running costs for the likes of insurance, fuel economy, and purchase price.

# RACER REPLICA BIKES

Racer Replicas first emerged in the mid-1980s when the Japanese Suzuki company introduced its race developed GSX-R750. Clearly based around an endurance race bike, the GSX-R's introduction made all other 750s seem pedestrian by comparison. Since then the Race Replica has been the chosen mount for those riders who want to own a big four-stroke, but also want one as near a circuit racer as possible. And the bike that started it all, the GSX-R750, still lives on today.

One company, Suzuki, and one model, the GSX-R750, changed the face of motorcycling, through the invention of the 'Racer Replica', a bike that was as near to being a full racing machine as any street motorcycle had a right to be. While there had been roadgoing motorcycles which aped their track brothers for years, there was never one anywhere as close to this ideal as the GSX-R. Furthermore, the Suzuki's success ensured that a new breed not only had been created, but was also here to stay. Even to the present day, the GSX-R750 endures, although other larger (1100 and 1000) and smaller (400 and 600) variants on the theme have been subsequently built. Not only this, but Honda, Kawasaki, Yamaha, Ducati, and Laverda have all joined in.

Yamaha's superb R7 is the Japanese factory's World Superbike entry. And it shows with a mouth-watering specification which includes Öhlins inverted front forks, Nissin 6-pot front calipers, fully floating discs, and a tuned 20-valve engine.

## RACER BEFORE ROADSTER

From the beginning, the GSX-R was built as a racer first, street bike second. The man who stamped his identity on the project, Tansunobu Fujji, saw to this. Originally, what amounted to a working prototype was campaigned in endurance racing events during the early 1980s. One feature which was adopted – and which was to set the GSX-R apart – was its use of oil cooling. Although, in terms of motorcycling, this was new, it had been used to help control the temperature of aeronautical engines since the early 1920s. Nonetheless, it is still important to record the reasoning behind the introduction of this legendary performance motorcycle because of the effect it had on future design practices within the motorcycling industry.

When it was released in 1985, the GSX-R was a truly revolutionary design. Rather than being a street bike that could be adapted for racing, the GSX-R owed its development to the race circuit. With its air- and oil-cooled engine and state-of-the-art square-section aluminium tubular full cradle frame, it not only looked purposeful, but had class-leading performance, too, laying the foundations for a whole new era of sportsters. The machine's distinctive alloy twin cradle frame was a development of the design used on the factory's GS1000R XR41 racer which competed in World Endurance and AMA (American Motorcycle Association) Super Bike championships during the early 1980s. Together with Suzuki's Advanced Cooling System (where the engine lubricant took heat away from 'hot spots' such as the cylinder head and the undersides of the pistons), it created a motorcycle which in a single stroke achieved the then highly impressive combination of 241km/h (150mph) and 100bhp. Add the fact that, at 176.4kg (388lb), it was the lightest production 750 and Suzuki had come up with a true performance machine of the highest order. The GSX-R750 has continued, by way of evolution, to remain at the very forefront of performance and technical development into the 21st century.

**The Suzuki GSX-R750 was released in early 1985 and right from the start was more racer than roadster. Designer Tansunobu Fijji adopted oil/air cooling, which had been proven on a working prototype in endurance events during the early 1980s.**

Suzuki first successfully experimented with the concept of oil cooling to cure overheating problems encountered during development of the XN85 Turbo. Oil jets directed at the underside of the pistons prevented the turbocharged engine from dropping a molten cocktail into the crankcase. The same idea was also employed on the earlier GSX750EF (1983) motor to prevent the pistons in the two central cylinders from running hotter than their outside brothers. While it would be accurate to describe the GSX motor as air-cooled with oil assistance, the emphasis was switched the other way around in the 'R' engine.

Oil cooling came into its own in the new system, which employed a second oil pump to concentrate on flushing away engine heat. A sister unit, mounted on the same shaft and sharing a common housing, handled the lubrication. A large oil cooler was mounted on the front frame tubes. But why did not Suzuki use a water-cooled engine? The designer Fujji said at the time that it was 'because the oil/air cooled engine is both narrower and lighter'. In fact, a prototype liquid-cooled engine was constructed, but found to be appreciably wider and some 5kg (11lb) heavier than the oil-/air-cooled unit, which weighed in at just 75kg (165lb). This attention to weight – which was to form a key priority in the future design of Racer Replica 750s (and other sport bikes which were to follow) – was a vital part of the structure. The 'lowest weight' concept also led Tansunobu Fujji and his development team to create an aluminium chassis, where both the frame and swinging arm were constructed in aluminium. At the time, Suzuki claimed their alloy frame as a motorcycle first. In fact, however, the German Airdie firm had got there half a century earlier, when it built and sold a series of roadsters with aluminium frames during the early 1930s.

The exhaust was yet another area where weight saving dictated terms, the GSX-R using a four-into-one system, rather than the heavier four-into-two or four separate pipes and silencers on earlier fours. Inside the engine, yet more pruning took place by reducing the weight of the piston and connecting-rod assemblies, which in turn allowed the crankshaft journals to be reduced to 34mm (1.3in), 2mm (0.07in) less than the GSX750EF. In total, the crankshaft, pistons, and connecting rods weighed in at some 2kg (4.2lb) less than their counterparts in the earlier 750 Suzuki power unit. New materials were also used for components such as the crank-shaft bearings to reduce frictional losses in the transfer of power through the hydraulic clutch and six-speed gearbox.

Racer Replica were apt words to describe the GSX-R's power delivery,

## GSX-R750 EVOLUTION

### 1985 (750F)
Introduced with oil-/air-cooled, 16-valve, dohc, four-cylinder engine; 100bhp; aluminium frame.

### 1986 (750G)
Small increase in power, 25mm (0.98in) longer swinging arm, radial tyres, modified wheels.

### 1987 (750H)
Stronger front forks, with electronic anti-dive.

### 1988 (750J)
First major update, with 60 per cent stiffer frame, new short-stroke engine dimension of 73 x 44.7mm (2.87 x 1.75in). Maximum engine revolutions increased to 13,000 rpm; new, semi-flat slide carburettors; maximum power increased to 108bhp. Modified suspension, wheel size decreased to 431mm (17in).

### 1989 (750K)
Detail changes only.

### 1990 (750L)
Engine reverted to original longer stroke format. Four-into-one exhaust replacing earlier Four-into-two type. Carb size increased from 36mm (1.41in) to 38mm (1.49in). Inverted (upside-down) front forks. Power increase up to 110bhp, but also weight up to 198kg (436.5lb).

### 1991 (750M)
Cylinder head modifications, including the adoption of a single rocker-arm per valve in place of the original forked single rocker for each valve pair, thus reducing internal inertia. This helped raise power to 116bhp.

### 1992 (750WN)
A major change came with the adoption of water-cooling to supplement the existing oil-cooling system. Power increased to 118bhp and a new frame (24 per cent stiffer than before) was adopted. Suspension and braking also updated. Dry weight now 208kg (458lb).

### 1993 (750WP)
Only detail changes.

### 1994 (750WR)
The WR model had an extra 2bhp, while weight decreased to 199kg (438.7lb). There were also six-piston calipers and an increase in fork-tube diameter from 41mm (1.61in) to 43mm (1.69in). Other changes were made to the swinging arm and tyre sizes.

### 1995 (750WS)
Cosmetic changes only.

### 1996 (750T)
Major redesign saw not only brand-new styling (the same as the new GSX-R600), but also a rash of technical changes. The twin-cradle frame was ditched in favour of a twin-spar chassis (still of aluminium) based on that of the RGV-Gamma 500GP racer. There was also a new engine, making the 750T the most compact and lightest machine in its category. Forced air induction was also introduced. With 128bhp and 179kg (394lb), the GSX-R shot back to lead its class once more.

### 1997 (750V)
No changes.

### 1998 (750W)
Developments included fuel injection, a 50 per cent larger airbox, small engine modifications – giving 135bhp – and a closer ratio gearbox.

### 1999 (750X)
Minor changes only.

### 2000 (750Y)
Given the factory code Project 701, the 2000 model featured a brand-new engine (which was more compact and 5kg/11lb lighter) and a new frame. Overall dry weight was 166kg (366lb). Gearbox used staggered input and output shafts (reducing engine length) and the fuel injection was given twin butterflies to improve emissions and throttle response.

which testers and buyers soon discovered was very much like that of a genuine racer. It had little on offer in the sub-7000rpm zone and whirlwind-type performance above it, hardly surprising when you realise that the original 1985 model year GSX-R750's maximum torque was produced at 10,000rpm. The bike's ideal environment was certainly not around town, but take it on the open road – or, even better, a race circuit – and nothing then available on two wheels could match the Series One GSX-R for pure riding fun. An uncompromising machine, that first GSX-R was a true racer. As such, it was born to win races, which it did so by taking victory in the 1985 British Super Stocks series (Mick Grant).

During the mid-1980s, many manufacturers plumped for 406mm (16in) front wheels or 406mm (16in) for both wheels. Interestingly, Suzuki opted to give its new Racer Replica 457mm (18in) at either end, even though at the time most other Japanese sports bikes had adopted 406mm (16in) in the interests of ultra-quick steering. Monoshock rear suspension was yet another of the Suzuki's features. Taken for granted at the beginning of the 21st century, in the early-mid 1980s, it was in its infancy, certainly in the more effective vertically mounted shock, rising-rate variety given to the GSX-R. Then there was the riding position, which again closely reflected that of a purebred racer, with its 'tucked-away' style provided by the clip-on handlebars, sculptured tank, single racing saddle, rear set foot controls and closely fitting fairing. The GSX-R750 even needed a racing paddock stand to enable maintenance such as tyre changes to be carried out. On the fuel tank were the words 'R Hyper Sports' – a new name, but simply code, of course, for Racer Replica. That first series of the GSX-R not only firmly established it as a top showroom success, but also this very success ensured that others would now enter into competition.

Before moving on to developments among other Japanese manufacturers, it is an interesting aside to reflect on a particular technological feature that

## GSX-R750 F (1985)

**Engine:** 4-stroke, across-the-frame four, dohc, 4-valves-per-cylinder, oil-air cooling
**Bore and stroke:** 70 x 48.7mm (2.75 x 1.91in)
**Displacement:** 749cc
**Compression ratio:** 9.8:1
**Carburation:** 4 x Mikuni VM29SS
**Ignition:** Transistorised
**Lubrication:** Wet sump
**Gearbox:** 6-speed
**Clutch:** Wet, multi-plate
**Frame:** Aluminium, deltabox
**Suspension:**
  *Front:* 41mm (1.61in) telescopic, 4-way adjustable
  *Rear:* single shock, swinging arm
**Brakes:**
  *Front:* twin 300mm (11.81in), hydraulically operated discs
  *Rear:* single 220mm (8.66in), hydraulically operated discs
**Tyres:**
  *Front:* 110/80V-18
  *Rear:* 140/70V-18
**Dry weight:** 176.4 kg (388lb)
**Power:** 104.5 bhp at 10,500 rpm
**Top speed:** 249km/h (155 mph)

visited the GSX-R750 during the 1980s: anti-dive forks. Although 'Anti-dive front forks' was one of the biggest catchphrases among the 1980's much-publicised hi-tech innovations, together with the turbocharger, 406mm (16in) front wheels, and front fork braces, it was a phenomena of that decade only and was eventually quietly consigned to the rubbish bin of history. Many of the new wave liquid-cooled four-cylinder rocketships of the mid-1980s came with anti-dive, including, notably, the Kawasaki GPZ900R and the Suzuki GSX-R750.

Take the Kawasaki fitment (also found on other models such as the GPZ600R and GPZ750R), known as ADVS (Automatic Variable Damping System). In fact, you could say that

Ever since it went on sale at the beginning of 1985, Suzuki's GSX-R750 has been at the very forefront of Racer Replica development. The original bike was closely based on the Suzuki factory's successful endurance racer of the early 1980s.

# ALUMINIUM FRAME CONSTRUCTION

When the Japanese company Suzuki launched its stunning GSX-R750 Racer Replica to huge public acclaim at the German Cologne Show in September 1984, it was claimed to be the world's first aluminium-framed production motorcycle. This claim was inaccurate, as some 50 years earlier a German company, Ardie, had done just that. The Suzuki chassis was obviously far more advanced, but, even so, it was not the first.

The reason for using aluminium instead of steel is primarily about weight, or lack of it. Anyone who has attempted to lift a conventional steel-tube motorcycle frame will quickly realise that it is incredibly heavy! Manufacturing the main-frame in aluminium could save at least half the weight of a steel assembly. It was also found that, with computer-aided design processes, it was possible to pinpoint potential weak areas – such as the steering head – and so the GSX-R750 had a much improved steering-head design than on previous steel-framed Suzukis.

The original GSX-R's specifications also went a stage further, with the entire mainframe, integral sub-frame, and swinging arm fashioned from extruded aluminium. The actual frame was constructed in box-section with a full cradle, in which the bottom frame rails were detachable to ease engine removal. Suzuki described it as MR-ALBOX (Multi-Rib Aluminium Alloy Box Section) and the frame weighed only 17.8lb (8.1kg). The success of the GSX-R750 (it was the top-selling sports bike of 1985) ensured not only the further development of the model range at Suzuki, but also the taking up of the aluminium frame concept by rival manufacturers.

Again, as with many important technical innovations, aluminium frames are now very much a part of the performance motorcycle design, and they have played a big role in the much lower weight of modern bikes.

**Modern bikes often have aluminium frames, primarily to cut down weight. By using aluminium, it is theoretically possible to gain a saving of half the weight compared to steel. Aluminium frames can be purely of delta-box, all-aluminium layout or, as seen here, of combined steel/alloy construction.**

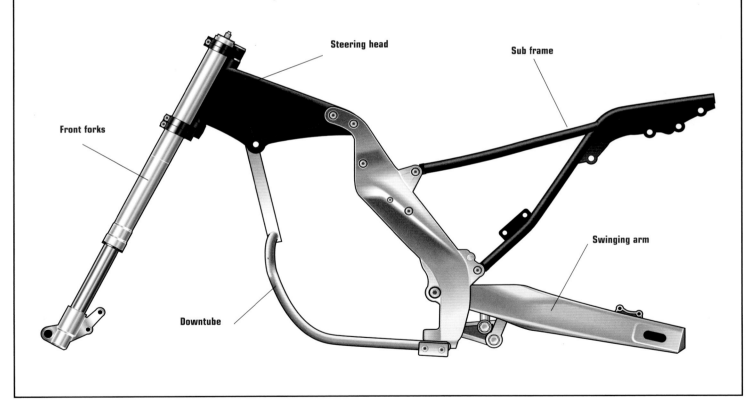

Steering head

Sub frame

Front forks

Swinging arm

Downtube

Kawasaki got there first, as in the company's publicity blurb it claimed a 'first on any Super Bike' for the system. The 'official' description of how it worked reads as follows: 'It provides truly progressive front suspension in two stages. First, as the speed/distance of the front suspension travel increases, the main fork spring pushes down on the AVDS valve assembly to restrict hydraulic fluid transfer, and effectively increase compression damping. Then, as the compression force continues to increase, the valve is progressively forced open as the secondary AVDS spring compresses, assuring optimum performance under a wide variety of conditions. AVDS begins working after, on average, 50mm of suspension travel. Total travel is 140mm.' Honda also tried its own version of the anti–dive theme on the original CBR600 and CBR1000 model, but it, like Kawasaki and Suzuki, quietly dropped the idea.

So what had happened to the rest of the Japanese industry? The truthful answer was that the GSX-R750 had caught them on the hop – to be kind. At worst, it had made them all look very, very stupid.

## YAMAHA AND CO

Yamaha, at least, had already thought of a similar machine. Kawasaki, meanwhile, was too busy with its own best sellers at that time, the GPZ900R and GPZ600R models. As for Honda, it was in the process of sorting out its V-four range after a disastrous beginning. This would lead to the much-improved VFR750 and eventually the truly great, limited production and very expensive RC30, followed by the RC45.

Yamaha's Racer Replica 750 arrived a year too late. Had it debuted in 1984 instead of 1985, the story might well have been very different. The FZ would have provided a more than stiff challenge to the GSX-R 750's dominance of the class, yet its launch date meant that the Yamaha was always destined to live in the Suzuki's shadow. And, although the Suzuki invented the Racer Replica class, it was the Yamaha which was by far the most sophisticated of the two machines. The other strange thing is that the FZ project actually began several years before the Suzuki one, back in 1977.

What Yamaha's engineers were looking for was a four-stroke which could equal the power of a two-stroke. Not unnaturally, this entailed some fairly drastic thinking in the company's research and development division. If you consider the subsequent five-valve technology a little excessive, you will be even more amazed to learn that this was only one option considered. It was actually discovered that seven was the optimum number of valves for ensuring the highest volume of inlet mixture into a combustion chamber up to a rev ceiling of 20,000rpm. The engineering team even went to the trouble of building both single- and twin-cylinder prototype engines to evaluate its ideas, but ultimately came to the conclusion that there were simply too many technical problems, particularly when it came to putting the idea into production. Also, as it transpired, putting seven valves into a single combustion chamber was not best suited to the comparatively small displacement engine used in motorcycles.

Six valves were also extensively tested, but these suffered from major shortcomings caused by hot-spots

**The GSX-R750 has always been closely connected with the race circuit. Examples have taken part in various disciplines of the sport, including endurance, Super Stock, and open class short-circuit events, with considerable success in all these forms.**

between the trio of exhaust valves. Eventually, by elimination, Yamaha's development squad got down to five valves. It was soon discovered that by having two exhaust valves there was enough room to eliminate the troublesome hot-spots, while the three inlets still allowed the advantage of the six-valve layout of high intake volume.

As is always the case in practical engineering, combining the right set of design features is the key to a successful outcome. Utilising the five-valves-per-cylinder layout meant that enough gas flowed into the (theoretically superior) lens-shaped combustion chamber to provide the potential for a relatively higher output than conventional two- or four-valve heads. Using a single spark plug – as opposed to the twin-spark layout on the seven-valve prototype head – the biconvex chamber gave excellent flame propagation. In other words, all the fuel that flows into the chamber is burnt quickly and efficiently. This has the added advantage of allowing high compression ratios with a slightly dish-topped piston. Yamaha engineers claimed that this set-up provided a 10 per cent power advantage

over a four-valve head using the traditional pentroof chamber.

By 1982, the Yamaha engineering team decided that it was on the right track and began a variety of projects, all using the five-valve head, lens-shaped combustion chamber allied to a displacement of 750cc to comply with the forthcoming FIM regulations for F1 and endurance racing. Many varied configurations were tested along with additional technical features, including hydraulic valve lifters. As an additional spur, Yamaha kept its various project team leaders apart, each being unaware of what his counterparts were up to. When the time came to make a choice, it was jointly decided to go for the ever popular across-the-frame four layout.

## BUILDING A BETTER DESIGN

Apart from the five-valves-per-cylinder technology, the other radical feature of the final, joint-agreed design was the 45-degree slant of the cylinders, which lowered the centre of gravity. This was a decision influenced by studying the very latest trends in the layout of automobile racing engines. The down-draught carburettors were borrowed

**A Suzuki tester with the throttle pinned on the latest version of the GSX-R. In the 750cc class, it is still the nearest one can get to owning a racing bike to take on the street. The GSX-R name continues to excite genuine enthusiasts.**

from Yamaha's ill-fated XZ550 V-twin. The result was the FZ750, launched in time to go on sale in the spring of 1985 and destined to be the first in a family of similar engines which led to the present day and the awe-inspiring R1.

A feature of all these engines was an old Yamaha obsession with narrowness. Unlike Suzuki and its GSX-R, Yamaha did not resort to oil/air lubrication to achieve this; instead, it placed the generator on top of the gearbox behind the cylinders and drove it via a chain from the crankshaft. Not content with that, the electronic-ignition trigger was to be found on the nearside crankshaft web and the sensors mounted on the crankcase halves. As a result, the FZ's crankcases were 9mm (0.35in) narrower than the XJ400 air-cooled four – in fact, as narrow as a V-four would have been! The width across the barrels had been kept to a minimum by a hybrid wet/dry liner system which directly water-cooled the top section of the cylinder liners only.

On the FZ750, the carbs and airbox lived inside a dummy tank and the paths from the 100mm (3.9in) bell-mouths which protruded into the airbox were routed past the flat, plastic sides down the inlet tracts to the valves in straight and equal lengths. Similarly, the exhaust ports and header pipes were straighter than would have been possible with an upright engine or, as Yamaha was keen to point out, with a V4. Another advantage of this arrangement was that the airbox was in still, cool air.

The only truly conservative engineering feature of the liquid-cooled dohc 749cc engine concerned the centrally located cam-chain, which makes things awkward when a replacement is required. To justify this, Yamaha engineers explained that the torque loadings caused by a cam-chain on one side of the power unit would have been unacceptable when the engine was race kitted. The valve train design saw a cam lobe for every valve –

direct operation without rockers – and hollow chrome molybdenum camshafts. Valve-lash adjustment consisted of shims under the bucket seats. Yamaha claimed that, after the running-in period, the valves were virtually maintenance-free (a fact borne out in service), helped by the entire circumference of the cam lobes being carburised, not just the lifting surfaces. The bucket-and-shim arrangement meant that load-bearing areas were larger than with conventional tappets; also, the bucket tops were manufactured from sintered material for improved wear resistance. On the hot side (exhaust), the valve seats were also manufactured from sintered metal (as one might have found in an air-cooled engine running at much higher temperatures than the liquid-cooled FZ), thereby minimising heat-inducing wear. The valves themselves were each equipped with a single, oil-tempered, silicon-chrome spring, and had to cope with less severe lift than on a four-valver due to superior gas flow.

This all added up to a very durable valve train. Automobile designers, after

all, have managed to do away with the sort of regular adjusting that the bike industry had grown accustomed to, so there was no reason why Yamaha should not have followed this route. Today, over 15 years later, the bike industry has largely caught up with the car world in longer mileages between servicing; Yamaha played an important role in this. Even so, the actual mileage distances between services are still smaller than cars. This is largely because most motorcycle engines far exceed the power output per litre figure of their four-wheel cousins.

The balance of the 1985 Yamaha FZ750 engine looked quite conventional when compared to the top end. There was a six-speed gearbox and a hydraulic clutch, but otherwise the FZ

**To make a renewed attack on the World Super Bike scene, Yamaha introduced the improved YZF750 during the mid 1990s. Effectively this gave the 20-valve machine improvement in key areas – more power, better handling, superior brakes and a lighter weight.**

mostly followed standard 'UJM' (Universal Japanese Motorcycle) practice, although there were some nice touches such as the positive oil feed to the gearbox, pressure equalising holes inside the crankcases to cut down on pumping losses, and baffles in the sump to reduce the lubricants tendency to create crankshaft drag. In contrast to its hi-tech engine, the FZ's chassis almost looked ordinary. It was a box-section affair, but, unlike the Suzuki GSX-R, manufactured from steel not alloy and derived from the YZR500 Grand Prix racer of the early Kenny Roberts era (late 1970s). The front downtubes were detachable for easier engine removal, while the toptubes splayed dramatically for better access to the top end. The box-section swinging arm was aluminium alloy, pivoting on needle roller bearings and controlled by the rising-rate Mono Cross suspension system. Up front, the 39mm (1.53in) fork stanchions were manufactured from tubing with a robust 3mm (0.11in) wall

thickness. A trio of opposed piston calipers with semi-metallic pads took care of the braking. The six-spoke cast alloy wheels were 406mm (16in) up front and 457mm (18in) to the rear.

The 1985 FZ750 broke the 100bhp barrier, putting out 106bhp at 10,500rpm. Yet the most impressive feature (as in the later five-valve Yamaha fours) was the torque. The almost flat torque curve saw 8kg/m (63ft/lb) at 8000rpm, which were excellent figures indeed. *Bike* magazine achieved an electronically timed 228.5km/h (142mph), while the standing 0.4km (0.25 mile) was despatched in 11.76 seconds, a terminal speed of 200km/h (124.2mph).

In retrospect, the FZ had an absolutely superb engine, which was to lay an ultra-firm foundation for the type, using the same basic technology which was to follow. These included the FZR750R (OWO1), FZR1000 Genesis, Thunderace, and finally today's R1. The balance of the FZ was not so

good, with weak brakes, that 406mm (16in) front wheel, and a rock-hard seat (best described as a plank!). From 1989 until production ceased in 1991, the FZ was to receive more powerful brakes and a 431mm (17in) front wheel. That hard seat, however, was to remain to the end.

### OWO1 – A REAL RACER

The FZR750R (OWO1) arrived for the 1989 model year and employed a new version of the FZ, five-valves-per-cylinder, slanted block, dohc, four. The new engine had ultra short-stroke 72 x 46mm (2.8 x 1.8in) bore and stroke dimensions and was derived from the 1988 Yamaha YZF750 works

**The Yamaha FZR750R (OWO1) arrived for the 1989 model year and used a shorter stroke version of the preceding FZ power plant. The OWO1 was equally effective as either a fast street bike or a competitive racing bike. Rob McElnea puts one through its paces at Donington Park, 1990.**

# INVERTED FRONT FORKS

Although the theory goes that there must be a more effective type of front suspension than the long-serving oil-damped telescopic front fork, to date no major bike manufacturer has managed to replace its use. ELF, Bimota, and even mighty Yamaha have tried, but with very little success. Part of this is due to motorcyclists being extremely conservative – they do not appreciate radical change. The only major difference in telescopic front fork design has come through, in effect, mounting the legs upside-down! Known as the inverted fork, this was pioneered, like so many other two-wheel developments, on the race circuit.

The trend began during the late 1980s on Grand Prix racers. It was already known that, by reversing the rear shock absorbers on a conventional twin-shock chassis, damping characteristics could actually be improved – and the same has been found true with front fork design. This means that, instead of the slider (the outside tube which holds the stanchion) being at the bottom of the fork, it is transferred to the top. The result is that a smaller outer tube is required at the bottom so that the wheel spindle can pass through in the conventional manner. Apart from the fork being inverted, the same basic technology to achieve damping is there, together with, on the latest bikes, a varied range of adjustments enabling the riders to set their motorcycles up with a finesse that would have been impossible even for a GP bike a few short years ago.

Today, the inverted front fork has almost taken over from the conventional telescopic type on high-performance sports bikes, although this is far less the case with more touring-orientated machinery.

---

endurance racer. The redesign was actually so intensive that it was virtually a different engine, compared to the proceeding FZ power plant.

During 1987 and 1988, Yamaha had won the prestigious Suzuka Eight Hours race, one of the most gruelling events in the world for four-stroke racing machines. Riders around the globe were now to have the opportunity to buy a replica of the victorious YZF750 factory racer. The new bike – known officially as the FZR750R, but more commonly called the OWO1 – was a costly, limited-production 'replica'. Although fully street legal, it was really a homologation special and produced in just enough quantities to allow Yamaha to take part in both the F1M Superbike and F1 world championships.

With its shorter stroke, the OWO1 effectively had the advantage (for racing) of reduced piston speed, so the engine had the ability of revving higher without the limiting factor of piston failure. The corresponding increase in bore meant a larger diameter combustion chamber, with space for larger valves. Besides the bigger valves, there were very light, immensely strong titanium-alloy connecting rods, plus lightweight pistons with only two rings (one compression, one oil control). Other notable features included flat slide carbs, digitally controlled electronic ignition, a 15mm (0.59in) lower cylinder block due to the shorter stroke (in turn allowing an alteration in the engine inclination from 45 to 40 degrees), and a 20mm (0.78in) shorter wheelbase, to quicken the steering.

Racing also demanded a close-ratio six-speed transmission (there was also an even closer ultra-expensive £2000-plus Works C box), a special wet clutch, and the removal of the radiator cooling fan. In addition, the OWO1 was upgraded with alterations to the aluminium FZR1000–derived Deltabox frame, an Öhlins racing rear shock, 431mm (17in) hollow-spoke wheels, and race-type Michelin radial tyres of wider and lower profile. There was also an extensive (and expensive) factory race kit. This included forged pistons, an exhaust to be used with the existing EXUP system, an inlet camshaft, and carburettor-tuning components to enable adjustment of the air/fuel mix required for the increased power output. It should be noted that Yamaha experienced a series of con-rod breakages, which, although eventually cured by a stronger less break-prone type, all the same destroyed many engines. The result was that, in Britain at least, many OWO1s now exist with transplanted FZR1000 power units.

To emphasise the racer aspect, the OWO1 was equipped solely for the rider, there being no pillion seat. This was more than a mere Racer Replica – it was the real thing! There is no doubt that, in its day, the OWO1 was probably the fastest and finest 750 available to the general public and certainly the best across-the-frame-four.

## 'BIG K' ARRIVES ON THE SCENE

Unlike Suzuki and Yamaha, 'Big K', Mr Kawasaki, took longer getting off the mark with a sporting 750, and even longer, as events were to prove, in producing one which could make an effective challenge. Kawasaki's first stab, the GPX750R, was launched in September 1986 and was the first four-cylinder model from the factory designed exclusively as a 750. Based on existing technology derived in previous liquid-cooled Kawasaki engines, the GPX power plant was clearly influenced by the smaller GPZ600R, but even more so by the twin-cylinder GPZ250R. For example, its valve-train was virtually stolen from the smaller bike. This meant a minimum mass of component parts throughout, including the likes of pistons weighing just 0.165kg (0.36lb) each, a compact new primary drive and gearbox design, and a belt-driven alternator behind the cylinders. The result was a 750 which put out 106bhp at 10,500rpm and 7.8kg/m (5.2lb/ft) of torque at 8500rpm.

Powered by a liquid-cooled, 16-valve, dohc motor, the GPX750 displaced 748cc and ran a compression ratio of 11.2:1 with maintenance-free, electronic ignition and a quartet of Keihin CVK 34mm (1.3in) carbs. With a dry weight of 195kg (430lb), it was the second lightest machine in its category when launched. The GPX750 was also the first Kawasaki to employ the BAC (Balanced Actuation Calliper) system. These were dual-piston brake calipers with a difference: the leading piston had a smaller diameter than the trailing ones.

However, even though it was a fast motorcycle – 243km/h (151mph) and only 1.6km/h (1mph) slower than the bike which ultimately replaced it in Kawasaki's line-up, the ZXR750) – the GPX has to be adjudged a failure. To begin with, its styling was bland. Also, it did not have the racing pedigree of the GSX-R750, FZ/FZR750, or Honda V-four RC30. In addition, it suffered a number of problems, including carb icing (not the only Kawasaki to be so afflicted), annoying hesitation between 3000 and 4000rpm, the 406mm (16in) front/457mm (18in) rear wheel sizes, a fairing which did not do the pillion any favours, and a woefully weak horn. It was also seen as an all-rounder, rather than a sexy Racer Replica.

### ENTER THE ZXR750

When Kawasaki realised that the GPX was never going to make the grade as a Racer Replica 750, the company resorted to a more focused bike. The result came at the end of 1989, when it launched its first ZXR750, the H1 model. Although in some respects clearly a development of the GPX, it also benefited from the company's participation in F1 and endurance racing with a series of prototype bikes. Axing the GPX's conventional steel-tube frame, there was instead an all-aluminium perimeter component, although manufactured from box-section extrusions rather than sheet, welded to aluminium castings at the steering head and swinging-arm pivot. Race-track practice was clearly evident in the distinctively braced, box-section aluminium swinging arm with a bolt-on bracket at the rear to speed chain replacement, plus features such as built-in provisions for fitting a race-stand and hydraulic steering damper.

As in the factory's F1 racer, conventional wide-diameter, cartridge-style

**The view Kawasaki hoped most riders would see of its ZX-7R. To help achieve this, there was a heavily revised 748.3cc engine, with improved combustion efficiency, a stronger cylinder block, increased carb downdraught, and a larger ram-air system. Top speed was 269kph (167mph).**

fork stanchions were employed, while the brakes featured semi-floating discs with four-piston calipers – a first for Kawasaki. Yet more track influence was revealed by use of bottom-link Uni-Trak rear suspension, which now featured an eccentric cam in its linkage to alter the ride-height settings. The 431mm (17in) wheels were ready to take racing tyres, too, featuring extra wide rims and massive hollow hubs and spokes to minimise unsprung weight. Visually, the ZXR looked every inch a race bike, which in this class was, of course, all-important. It was distinguished by the dramatic twin

'Hoover' tubes which ran from the front of the fairing to the fuel tank, although in reality they were merely ducting extra-cool air onto the cylinder head. The engine itself was extensively up-rated from the GPX750, with an all-new top end giving superior breathing, a higher compression ratio, larger (36mm/1.4in) carbs, revised ignition, and a four-two-one exhaust system.

For those interested in racing in either F1 or the then fledgling WSB (World Super Bike), an engine race kit was offered, while the factory limited its activities to the specially built ZXR-7, which finished runner-up at Le Mans 24 Hours that year. For 1990, the production ZXR incorporated many of the engine components from the

previous season's race kit. At the same time, a new cylinder head with larger ports was fitted, together with bigger carbs, a larger capacity (curved) radiator, and new four-into-one exhaust. Useful weight – 5kg (11lb) – was taken from the chassis, while the braced swinging arm was ditched in favour of a stiffer, neater item based on the factory's latest F1 racer. More track influence was seen in the front suspension which gained both spring preload and damping adjustment, and the rear-wheel rim grew still wider. For the first time, the ZXR750 began to attract

# MONOSHOCK REAR SUSPENSION

As far as modern motorcycles go, the pioneers in the field of mono- (single-) shock rear suspension were Kawasaki and Yamaha. The latter's system was first found on Yamaha's works racers during the mid-1970s, but its near horizontal shock absorber and cantilever swinging arm were crude when compared to the monoshock set-up of Kawasaki.

Kawasaki's patented Uni-Trak was developed over a relatively long period; indeed, Kawasaki was the first manufacturer to produce a progressive rising-rate, single-shock rear suspension system. Uni-Trak was first utilised on a prototype KR250 in-line twin racer of 1976 – two years before Kork Ballington captured both the 250 and 350cc world titles on machines equipped with Uni-Trak. Kawasaki also used Uni-Trak on its 500cc motocross GP bike, ridden to runner-up in the 1979 championships by the American Brad Lackey. Clearly the system worked: it had been proven in the white-hot competition of world championships sport on both the tarmac and dirt.

The following year, customers could buy production motocross and enduro mounts fitted with the system. The first production Uni-Trak roadster was the GP550 of 1982. The system was developed and fitted to Kawasaki's street bikes, benefiting from the extensive competition developments, but specially adapted for the particular needs of the road rider. Priority was given to a progressive action which permitted very light and rapid suspension movements in

response to minor road unevenness, while providing increasingly firm response to large road shocks.

Kawasaki's engineers wanted, and got, first-class road holding allied to greater rider comfort than the conventional twin-shock system could give. The top of the shock absorber was attached to the lower part of the frame, the bottom being linked by a compound lever action to the swinging arm; being thus located close to the machine's centre of gravity increased handling stability. A leverage ratio of approximately 2:1 in the linkage meant that the speed of the shock absorber's movement was about half that of the swinging arm's, causing very little heat build-up in the shock absorber, and providing consistent damping. While both spring pre-load and damping characteristics of the shock absorber could be varied (the method of adjustment varying between different models), the highly progressive control that the Uni-Trak system provided meant frequent readjustment of suspension settings became a thing of the past.

By 1985, no fewer than 14 of Kawasaki's production roadsters were kitted out with Uni-Trak. More crucially, the rest of the industry had realised the breakthrough it was. Today, the rising-rate, mono-shock system is almost universally favoured for high-performance bikes.

**Modern single-shock suspension systems provide both handling and comfort far superior to the older twin-shock variety. The shock is operated via a series of linkages as shown in the drawing.**

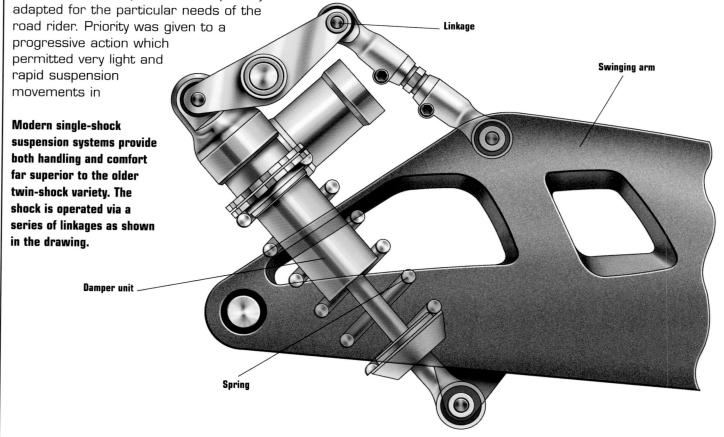

Linkage

Swinging arm

Damper unit

Spring

attention, especially when the Australian Rob Phillis put in a number of excellent rides during the 1990s WSB series.

By now, Superbike racing had really begun to take off, capturing the hearts and minds of sponsors, spectators, and the media – and the manufacturers, including Kawasaki. The result was two new ZXR750s for 1991: the 'J', which was aimed squarely at the road rider, and the 'K' version which, although street-legal, had a track-biased specification with a comprehensive race kit available. By using this twin-bike approach, Kawasaki was able to at last offer both the road enthusiast and the racer viable machinery and at competitive prices.

Although both the 'J' and 'K' models were in different states of tune, they shared the same basic engine update which saw the original bore and stroke changed to 71 x 47.3mm (2.8 x 1.9in), allowing higher revs; the wider bore also brought benefits of increased combustion and breathing efficiency. Both models also shared an all-new cylinder head, valve train, pistons, crank, and oil system. The camshaft drive redesign incorporated a lightweight individual rocker train. All this allowed Kawasaki's design team to opt for an amazingly compact 20-degree included valve angle. Other changes included larger 320mm (12.59in) – previously 310mm (12.2in) – semi-floating discs at the front, and wider rims and tyres, plus F1 works pattern bodywork: the 'J' roadster had a dual-stepped seat, the 'K' (also known as the 'R') a solo-only type. The latter model also featured revised cam profiles, flat-slide carbs, close-ratio gearbox, uprated suspension, and an aluminium fuel tank.

In 1991, Rob Phillis was the highest placed non-Ducati finisher in the WSB rankings, while Scott Russell won the American AMA 750cc Super Sport title, with a perfect score of nine wins in nine races. For the 1992 model year, the ZXR750 was little changed except for graphics and an improved race kit. John Reynolds became double British champion that year, winning both national and Supercup titles.

At the end of September 1992, Kawasaki launched the ZXR750L and 'M' series. This simply built on continuing success, which grew in 1993 when the American Scott Russell became the first non-Ducati or Honda rider to become World Super Bike Champion on a factory-entered ZXR. He then went on to finish runner-up in the series the following year. From then on, however, the ZXR's fortunes waned, resulting in a brand-new model for 1996, the ZX-7R. Despite this, the ZXR-750 still remains an important milestone in the evolution of the class.

## ZX-7R

The ZX-7R arrived in time for the 1996 season and came after Kawasaki had launched the ZX-9R in 1994 and the ZX-6R in 1995. Of the three, the 7R had probably the most difficult task. For a start, it had to take over from the successful and much-loved ZX-R750 and, at the same time, offer a serious challenge in WSB racing. Unfortunately, it has largely failed on

**Honda's RC30 V-four was not a Racer Replica like the GSX-R, but instead a pukka race bike, one that could also be ridden on the street. The letters 'RC' stood for Racing Corporation and this was proved when the RC30 won the first two WSB championships in 1988 and 1989.**

both fronts. In racing, Ducati and Honda have dominated since Kawasaki's glory days of 1993 and 1994, while in the showroom it never made a significant impact, always being outsold by its smaller and larger ZX brothers and by its direct competitors. As with the earlier GPX750, the ZX-7R has struggled to attract buyers, even though in many ways it is a significant improvement over the machine it replaced.

At the ZX-7R's heart is a heavily revised engine displacing 748.3cc, while there is improved combustion efficiency, a stronger cylinder block, new direct actuation valve train (shim and bucket), and a more downdraught angle (50 degrees) for the carbs. These changes, combined with a larger volume, twin ram-air intake system, have resulted in superior engine response and more mid-range power compared with the ZX-R. Carburettor size of the R (coded P) street bike is 38mm (1.49in), while the RR (coded N) racer employs 41mm (1.61in) Keihin flat-slide instruments featuring a smooth bore to maximise air flow. The RR's carbs feature an accelerator pump and fuel enricher.

The lubrication system was also updated and improved, consequently giving increased reliability, particularly under racing conditions, over the ZXR. There were also improvements

(shared with the ZX-6R) to the transmission, resulting in more positive gear changing. A curved radiator reduced the frontal area of the bike, while the four-two-one exhaust features a balancer pipe between numbers one and four header pipes to assist engine torque.

Improvements to the engine also brought the need for a fresh look at the chassis. So the ZX-7R has a new, stronger alloy frame (on the RR version, the rake and trail are adjustable), and the suspension was given new inverted 43mm (1.69in) cartridge front forks and a nitrogen gas-charged rear shock; both the front and rear suspensions feature a multitude of adjustment. Although brake disc sizes remained as before, there the ZX-7R has the advantage of more powerful six-piston calipers up front, rather than the old four-piston assemblies.

Adding to the Racer Replica image are the bike's hollow three-spoke, cast alloy wheels, with a new 152mm (6in) rear rim being able to take the very latest in racing tyres. As before, the RR version has a number of race circuit

# FORCED AIR INDUCTION

Like other developments, forced air induction was first used and proven on the race circuit, notably in Formula 1 racing cars. The primary reason for using it is to increase volumetric efficiency. In the beginning, Formula 1 race-car type technology was introduced, at least into the ranks of the series production motorcycle, with the launch of the Kawasaki ZZ-R1100 towards the end of 1989. Forced air induction functions by drawing incoming air via an inlet duct or ducts at the front of the motorcycle's fairing. On the ZZR-1100, a single duct was located, letterbox-like, below the headlamp, and thus cool fresh air was fed via a sealed duct straight to the airbox. The fact that it was sealed (unlike any production motorcycle at the time) meant that there was no chance for the induction air to be heated by the radiator or engine. On the Kawasaki, this air duct had also been so shaped that any rainwater would lie at the bottom and not be drawn into the carburettors.

Forced air induction works at its best at higher speed, there being a ramming effect which actually pressurises the airbox and thus improves carburation. The effects of this in racing can be as much as 66 per cent more power output – the difference between winning or not winning a race. For the normal motorcyclist, the effect is to improve the performance of his or her machine in comparison to those with an unsealed airbox. In effect, forced air induction is a power booster, relying on cool air as its medium.

By the time of the launch of its updated 1993 D1 model, Kawasaki included twin instead of single ram-air intake ducting, refinement of the engine to capitalise on the advantages of the pressurised intake system and increased overall breathing efficiency. Today, several manufacturers have adopted the basic principle, each with its own particular layout, but all with the same concept, that of improving performance.

**Forced air induction began on F1 race cars. The Kawasaki ZZ-R1100 was the first production bike to use it. The system works by drawing incoming air via an inlet duct/s at the front of the bike's fairing. This photograph shows ducts from a GSX-R Suzuki.**

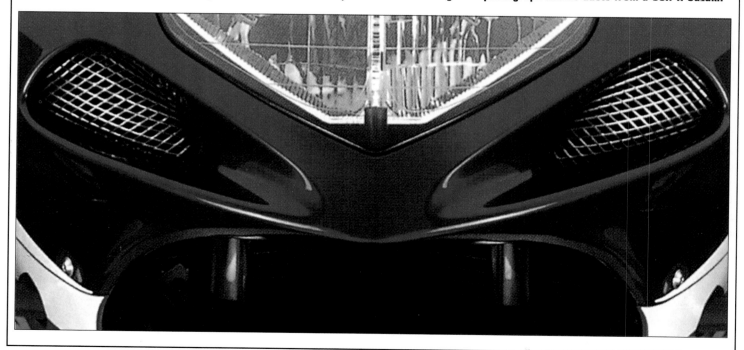

features such as a special clutch and close-ratio gears.

In a 1997 test, *Ride* magazine compared the standard ZX-7R with the latest Suzuki GSX-R750W ('W' stood for 'water') and, even though the Kawasaki was 25kg (55lb) heavier, it was marginally faster at 269km/h (167mph), the GSX-R achieving 262km/h (163mph). The following was *Ride*'s verdict: 'Ride a GSX-R750 in the sunshine on smooth, empty roads and you'll want one. My heart says buy one, but after two breakdowns my head says get the ZX-7R instead because it's just as good but in a different way. Not quite as raw and exciting, but not as scary or flimsy-feeling either. The Kawasaki is faster, better built, handles just as well on the road and looks the business too!'

The ZX-7R is still built today, but has not seen the myriad changes of the 6R or 9R. This is because it came out later and was in many ways more suited to its task thanks to its WSB racing background. Unfortunately,

because the 750cc class is not as important as it was a few years ago, it has not achieved the success its capability deserves.

## HONDA V-FOURS

It has to be said, the V-four Honda did not get off to the best of starts. It was 1982 when the company gave the world the first mass-produced V4 production bike and, as one commentator rightly said: 'the 750S was met with all the enthusiasm one accords cold porridge'. Unfortunately, the revolutionary engine was compromised by appalling styling, an appalling riding position, and very bad handling. A year later, Honda introduced the VF750F, a super-sports version of the original, which outsold every other 750 that year. The F was plagued by mechanical reliability gremlins (including cams and cam chains!) and, by the time Honda had extended its V4 range to include a 400, 500, a 1000, and a 1000 Racer Replica, the public had lost faith in the concept.

**The RC45 replaced Honda's much-loved and very successful RC30. It was essentially a technically updated version of the same basic formula. By the time it was launched in 1994, however, Ducati was top dog in WSB racing. Even so, the American John Kocinski won the title on an RC45 in 1997.**

Unused to being at the end of a humiliation such as this, Honda licked its wounds and retreated to its design shop. In 1985, it launched the VFR750 and, in so doing, reinvented the V4 configuration and produced an all-time great. But the VFR was an all-rounder, not a Racer Replica. For this, the company went a stage further and created the RC range. 'RC' stood for 'Racing Corporation' and has subsequently produced four WSB championship winning machines – three V-fours and finally, in 2000, a V-twin – and in the process has given Ducati its biggest challenges.

The RC30 was not a Racer Replica like the GSX-R or ZXR; instead, it was a proper race bike that could be

ridden on the road. It also had the distinction of winning the first two World Super Bike championships (in 1988 and 1989). Built from 1988 through to 1992, the RC30 was a WSB homologation special. Even so, it was not only fast and surefooted, but also, despite its competition bias, a thoroughly refined and surprisingly comfortable road bike. The problem is that, as so few were built in comparison to more mainstream models from other manufacturers, finding a good one today is likely to be difficult, if not impossible. The best ones are in museums or private

**The RC45 and RC30 shared not only the liquid-cooled dohc V-four engine layout, but also a twin headlamp fairing. Major differences between the two bikes included inverted front forks and programmed fuel injection for the RC45.**

collections, with the remainder having been raced to destruction. A good RC30 is still a match for virtually anything else on the road, except for outright power. Official Honda figures reveal 103bhp at 11,500rpm and 246km/h (153mph), from the liquid-cooled 749.2cc 90 degree V-four.

After the RC30 came the RC45. Much of the RC45, which ran from 1994 through to 1998, aped the RC30, including the engine size, aluminium frame, and single-sided swinging arm. Yet it was very much a case of attempting to improve on an existing successful design. Attention was given to comprehensive updating and weight reduction, the latter saving 4kg (8.7lb) – total weight 189kg (416.6lb) against 193kg (425.4lb) for the RC30.

A feature carried over from the RC30, the lightweight titanium connecting rods on the RC45 were now attached to low-friction slipper pistons with three-rings replacing the RC30's two, which operated in new powder-metal composite cylinder liners. Some 1.5kg (3.3lb) were saved through this exercise alone (the RC30s being made of steel). Another major change was that of programmed fuel injection, a first on a series production Honda motorcycle. This was borrowed from the company's hi-tech oval piston NR750. There were also improvements to both the six-speed gearbox and NR-derived hydraulic clutch, the cooling system (now with two, instead of one radiator), and a revised four-two-one exhaust.

Also new were the inverted front forks (the RC30 featured a conventional telescopic fork assembly), while the massive, cast aluminium single-sided swinging arm was modified. The RC45s had been redesigned to hold a larger 190 section rear tyre than the same type found on the RC30. The redesigned fairing's upper cowling incorporated a pair of slit-shaped ducts to flow a maximum volume of cool,

dense air into the fuel injections giant 7-litre (1.5-gallon) airbox.

For the customer, Honda attributed 120bhp at 12,000rpm to the RC45. On paper, this was a considerable improvement over the bike it replaced. In truth, however, the RC45 did not actually work significantly better than the RC30 and, at £17,780 in 1994, was double the price of the lighter and faster Fire Blade. Neither could it match its older brother's WSB record, as even the signing of Carl Fogarty could not bring a world title. Eventually, the GP star John Kocinski was drafted into the team for 1997 and won the RC45's only world championship. From then on, Ducati dominated WSB, resulting in the RC45 being ditched in favour of the SP-1 1000cc V-twin for 2000, which, it is worth noting, promptly beat Ducati at its own game.

## THE HONDA FIRE BLADE

Before we turn to Ducati, it is worth noting that, in the Performance Premier League, two motorcycles dominated the 1990s: the fabulous

Ducati 916 and Honda's equally ground-breaking CBR900RR Fire Blade. Coming first, the Japanese bike rewrote the rules, putting all its Japanese four-cylinder rivals at a distinct disadvantage with its combination of extreme lightness and stunning power. Honda's engineering team led by Tadeo Baba came up with an 893cc liquid-cooled 16-valve dohc across-the-frame four, which in its original 1992 'N' model form developed 122bhp at 10,500rpm, giving a maximum speed of 266 km/h (165mph). This, combined with its low 186.5kg (411.15lb) weight, saw the new Fire Blade lavished with praise, repeatedly earning 'bike of the year' awards from magazines throughout the world. Only its sub-900cc engine size was questioned, but even this in later

**The amazing Honda NR750 used oval piston, V4, 32-valve technology. Racing prototypes appeared in 1987, before going into limited production during the early 1990s. Few were sold because it cost a cool £35,000!**

years was rectified with increases first to 918cc and eventually 929cc.

Its technical specification, however, was truly impressive for a series production street bike and also helps to explain why the power-to-weight ratio is so good. Tadeo Baba and the rest of the Honda engineers involved in the design and development of the Fire Blade had set out to create a performance motorcycle with no compromise in the quest for minimum weight. Flat-topped, ultra-lightweight slipper pistons allowed high rigidity and equally lightweight connecting rods and crankshaft, thus minimising inertia and providing extremely crisp engine response and smooth control. Another weight-saving device was the fitment of a magnesium instead of aluminium cylinder head (from 1994 onwards).

The Fire Blade's 16 valves are operated directly by twin camshafts, resulting in a compact, low-friction valve train that requires adjustment only every 25,700km (16,000 miles). Originally, a bank of four 38mm (1.49in) diameter flat-slide carburettors, assisted by a single-port induction system, provided the engine with its diet of fuel. However, later an electronically controlled PGM-F1 fuel injection took over, providing even more precise throttle response. The ignition system is computer-controlled and digitally transistorised, with electronic advance. A cartridge-type liquid-cooled oil cooler ensures lubricant temperatures are kept strictly under control for stable output and maximum engine life.

The Fire Blade's chassis has also

## FIRE BLADE EVOLUTION

**1992** Launched with 893cc 16-valve liquid-cooled dohc across-the-frame four-cylinder engine. Aluminium frame, with 24-degree steering head angle, six-speed gearbox, four-into-one exhaust, 122bhp at 10,500rpm. Top speed 266km/h (165mph).

**1994** New fairing, new 'fox-eye' headlamps, modified suspension, including revalved, fully adjustable front forks. Engine given magnesium cylinder head in place of aluminium original. Electronic speedometer, redesigned warning lights.

**1996** Major changes undertaken.

*Engine:* cylinder bore size increased to give 918.5cc; compression ratio raised from 11 to 11.1:1; the big-end bearings, crankshaft, and clutch all strengthened; new slimmer alternator reduces engine width by 9.5mm (0.37in); modified gear change with three new ratios; 3-D ignition mapping; curved alloy radiator; silencer capacity increased from five to six litres (1.09 to 1.31 gallons).

*Chassis:* Thinner wall frame rails, with three instead of four internal boxes; stronger cross-bracing to swinging arm and pivot plate made of reinforced open casting; lighter final drive chain. Rear suspension given increased damping control and lighter internals. Forks have lighter internals and wide range of adjustment. Bodywork given more aerodynamic lower fairing; top section remains unchanged. Front mudguard redesigned to provide down-force at speed. Riding position modified to give more upright and relaxed stance.

**1998** Engine size, bore and stroke dimensions left unchanged, but some 80 per cent of internal components modified; crankshaft, connecting rods, and camshafts left unchanged. Power output increased to 128bhp; combustion chambers and intake and exhaust ports reprofiled to reduce air flow resistance. 38mm (1.49in) carburettors retained, but vacuum piston size changed to produce sharper throttle response. Clutch plates reduced from 10 to eight; top-gear ratio increased for higher maximum speed. Radiator capacity increased by seven per cent; silencer larger, but lighter. Small changes made to frame to increase strength and reduce weight. Combined with engine changes, weight dropped 3kg (7lb). Steering head modified to provide more responsive steering, with fork offset reduced from 35mm (1.37in) to 30mm (1.18in), and a 5mm (0.19in) increase in trail. All-new, braced swinging arm; modified front suspension, also fork legs moved apart by 10mm (0.39in) to increase torsional rigidity. Front brakes: new opposed, four-piston calipers and floating discs increased in diameter from 296mm (11.65in) to 310mm (12.2in). Wider and higher fairing, with new headlamp shape. New 28mm (1.1in) thick, one-piece, electronic instrument panel, with centralised tachometer; more powerful headlamp.

**2000** Radical changes made. New bore and stroke dimensions of 74 x 54mm (2.91 x 2.12in), giving 929cc. Computer-controlled fuel injection (PGM-Fi); Honda Variable Intake Exhaust Control (H-VIX), higher compression ratio 11.3:1; larger diameter valves (operating at narrower angle), forged instead of cast piston material; new, hollow (20 per cent lighter) camshafts. Semi-pivotless frame with new longer swinging arm. Inverted 43mm (1.69in) cartridge-type front forks. Larger 330mm (12.99in) front brake discs; front wheel diameter increased from 406mm (16in) to 431mm (17in). Smaller battery, but with 10 per cent increase in output.

played a vital role in the machine's success as, during its life, the frame, together with the rest of the Fire Blade, has seen a steady evolutionary process which has kept Honda at the very forefront of motorcycle technology. Right from the start, the concept was to provide the Fire Blade with a light yet sophisticated chassis. For example, the 1997 V model frame was based on twin main spars of extruded aluminium, weighing in at a mere 10.5kg (23lb). Featuring a semi-floating rubber engine mount to combat engine vibrations, it supported a high-rigidity aluminium swinging arm designed using in-depth computer analysis and rigorous track testing. Up to the introduction of the 2000 model year 'Blade', which

became Honda's first big-bore Sports Bike to come equipped as standard with inverted front forks (43mm/1.69in diameter), the front suspension consisted of a special version of the conventional telescopic front form, with massive 45mm (1.77in) stanchions. At the rear

**Honda's CBR900RR Fire Blade arrived in 1992 (a line-up of the models stretching from 1992 through to a 2000 Fire Blade, nearest camera, is shown above). At first, the CBR900RR Fire Blade used a 893cc engine. This was enlarged to 918.5cc for the 1996 model year.**

**The 2000 model of the Fire Blade saw radical changes, including an increase in engine size to 929cc, computer-controlled fuel ignition, increased power output (larger valves, forged pistons etc), modified frame, and an increase in front wheel size from 406mm (16in) to 432mm (17in).**

**The Honda engineering team which was responsible for designing the Fire Blade was led by Tadeo Baba. Their primary requirement was to create a motorcycle in which no compromise was made in the search for the best possible power-to-weight ratio.**

was a refined version of Honda's Pro Link system, with a remote-reservoir single shock absorber.

Honda was the first manufacturer to use the combination of 406mm (16in) front wheel and 431mm (17in) rear wheel on a production roadster, ensuring razor-sharp response and sure-footed handling in a single package. From the 2000 model year, however, Honda switched to 431mm (17in) rubber for both wheels, a move it made, according to Honda, because of difficulty in obtaining supplies of high-performance 406mm (16in) tyres.

Braking has been another area where the Fire Blade has seen changes during its life. At first, there were twin 296mm

## FIRE BLADE (2000)

**Engine:** Water-cooled, dohc, 16-valve-per-cylinder, across-the-frame 4-stroke, four cylinder

**Bore and stroke:** 74 x 54mm (2.91 x 2.12in)

**Displacement:** 929cc

**Compression ratio:** 11.3:1

**Ignition:** Computer-controlled digital transistorised, with electronic advance

**Fuel system:** Electronic fuel injection

**Gearbox:** 6-speeds

**Frame:** Aluminium construction with triple-box spars and multi-point diamond configuration; aluminium alloy swinging arm

**Suspension:**
*Front:* inverted front forks
*Rear:* Honda Pro Link monoshock

**Wheels:** 431mm (17in) hollow-section triple-spoke cast aluminium

**Tyres:**
*Front:* 120/70 ZR 17
*Rear:* 190/50 ZR 17

**Dry weight:** 170kg (374.7lb)

**Power:** 152bhp at 11,000rpm

**Top speed:** 273.5km/h (170mph)

The Fire Blade has had considerable track success, having not only won the British Production Powerbike championship, but also several Isle of Man TTs. By the end of 1998, Honda had sold more than 14,000 Fire Blades in the UK alone. This success was largely thanks to its unique combination of being as light as a 600, but with the power of an 1100.

At the time of its launch in 1992, machines such as the Suzuki GSX-R1100 and Yamaha's 1000 EXUP reigned supreme. Both these examples were brilliant bikes in their day, hugely powerful and extremely rapid. With one fell swoop, the Fire Blade destroyed them both. After riding the Honda, the GSX-R and EXUP felt somewhat like dinosaurs – heavy and cumbersome.

(11.65in) discs up front, but, over the years, size has increased to 310mm (12.2in) and finally 330mm (12.99in). It is worth noting that these are all of the floating variety and feature four-piston calipers. At the rear, a single solid 220mm

(8.66in) disc with two-piston calliper has remained standard fitment. In any case, even early Fire Blades possessed brakes which were capable of hauling the bike down from three-figure speeds with the minimum of rider effort.

### DUCATI 748

The huge success of Ducati's 916 led to the launch of the smaller displacement 748cc, which first went on sale in the spring of 1995. Although, except for engine size and narrower tyres, the 748 is virtually the same as the 916 (or, for that matter, the 916's replacement, the 996), on the road the 748 is very much its own motorcycle, not simply a smaller engined, cheaper 916/996. In fact, the 748 has its own character – revvier and with a smoother power delivery – while retaining its bigger brother's handling, braking, and looks. In fact, for many, the 748 is a better choice than the 916 or 996.

At first, there were two versions of the 748, the Biposto (dual seat) and SP (Sport Production). The latter differed from the Biposto in having increased power, carbon-fibre fairing and silencers, an Öhlins rear shock, cast-iron fully floating front brake discs, metal-braided front brake lines, adjustable brake and clutch levers, and, of course, a single seat. When first deliveries of the 748SP arrived, they soon found their way onto the race circuit. The Super Sports racing category began to be run at the same meetings as the World Super Bikes from 1996 and it was a move which benefited Ducati, as the F1M allowed 750cc V-twins to compete alongside 600 fours. The first ever World Super Sport champion was Fabrizio Pirovano, on, you guessed it, a 748!

**Although it looks like a 916 or 996, Ducati's 748 is actually very much its own bike, with an individual character thanks to its revvier, smoother power delivery. Like its bigger brothers, the 748 has made its mark in racing at the highest level.**

This success, but with Paolo Casoli riding, was repeated in 1997. Like its bigger 916 and 996 brothers, the 748 can boast an enviable racing pedigree.

### THE OTHER ITALIAN – LAVERDA

In the world of the Racer Replica, there is another Italian worthy of inclusion here: Laverda.

In the 1970s, Laverda built some genuine Superbikes, such as the SFC750 twin and Jota 1000 triple. During the 1980s, however, the company ran into a financial storm, ending up on the rocks. In 1992, it was rescued by local businessman Francesco Tognon and Laverda rose from the ashes. Its first model, which went on sale during 1994, was the very pretty little Racer Replica-styled 650 Sport. This used a 668cc dohc, 180 degree, parallel-twin engine, with four valves per cylinder, chain-driven cams, and air-oil cooling. Equipped with six speeds and the excellent Weber-Marelli electronic fuel injection (as fitted to Ducatis), the 650 Sport was acclaimed for its superb handling and brakes, but largely criticised for the engine. This was because it was related to the less-than-successful 500 Alpino of the 1970s. Not

only was it old technology (even with some modern updates), but also the Alpino was not known for its smoothness or flexibility.

To progress further, Laverda realised it needed a new bike, but funds were limited, so the company brought out an interim 750. Arriving in mid-1997, the 747cc was eventually built in several versions, ranging from 72 to 90bhp; however, although re-engineered, it still used the basic engine configuration of both the 650 Sport and Alpino. The biggest difference between the 650 and the 750 was the amount of engine torque generated below 5000rpm. On the smaller model, there was very little; on the new 750, it felt and performed like any other modern 750 twin, in other words plenty of low-down power. The base model was the 750S, which in its 1999 guise generated 82bhp at 8250rpm. This equated to a maximum speed of 220km/h (137mph), compared to 216km/h (134mph) for the 650. The real 748 challenger, however, was the 750 Formula which went on sale in spring 1998.

For 1999, the engine underwent several improvements, particularly as regards lubrication and cooling. This came in response to problems encountered with the first batches of 750s. At last, Laverda's twin was almost, but not quite, up to matching the stunning Ducati 748. However, Laverda had cost on its side, as in Britain the comparable 748 sold at a between 20 and 25 per cent higher price. The Formula, with its distinctive black-and-orange paintwork, looked professional, while, like the 650 Sport and 750S, the small size and excellent tucked-in riding stance made the rider feel instantly at home.

Further financial trouble eventually resulted in Laverda being rescued by rivals Aprilia in late 2000. While it is well known that Laverda had been developing a new triple, this is likely to be a 1-litre (0.21-gallon) Superbike, rather than a 750 class machine.

There you have it, the Racer Replica class – just about the nearest you are likely to get in a four-stroke when it comes to owning a racing bike which can be ridden on the street. Well, that is

# TYRE TECHNOLOGY

Tyres are the most vitally important piece of equipment on any motorcycle. After all, they are your sole link with the tarmac. Just as wheel sizes have changed over the years, so has tyre technology. Until the early 1980s, most tyres were ribbed at the front, with a block tread at the rear. However, companies such as Dunlop (with the TT100 series), Avon (Roadrunner), and Pirelli (Phantom) had begun to offer a more sporting type by the mid-1970s.

Yet the real change has come since the mid-1980s. With a new breed of high-performance bike such as the Suzuki GSX-R, Yamaha FZR, and Kawasaki GPZ series, speeds had in effect outstripped tyre suitability. Developments from then on have been thick and fast; metric instead of imperial sizes, tubeless rims and tyres, radial tyres (launched by Michelin in 1986), lower profile tyres, and ever wider sections (some rears are now a massive 190 section). And that's just the start. Compounds also play an important role. Today, you can have anything between a virtually full race tyre which on the rear of some bikes will only do 482–643km (300–400 miles), right through to tyres which, on a touring bike, will do many thousands of kilometres service, but with less outright grip. Usually, the softer compound, the more sticky the rubber. Like a race tyre, rubber found on a sports bike will usually get up to working temperature, as the priority for both is maximum adhesion.

In racing, there are slick (bald tread) tyres for maximum performance in dry conditions, intermediate (treaded) for damp or colder conditions, and full wets (a much chunkier tread profile). The latter can only be used in wet conditions, otherwise they will soon overheat and their adhesion qualities will be lost. Another facet of modern-day racing is the tyre warmer. This is wrapped around the wheel covering the complete tyre. Usually run in conjunction with a generator, tyre warmers allow the tyre to be preheated. Preheating allows the rider to go at full pace from the drop of the flag. However, at the beginning of the racing season (March) and at its end (October), even tyre warmers struggle to get the tyre hot enough, so that by the time the rider leaves the start grid the tyre is still not at the optimum temperature.

**The 748 stripped of its bodywork to show the 90-degree vee of its cylinders, under-seat exhaust, rising rate (vertical) rear shock, steel trellis frame, curved radiator, and side-mounted battery. The latter, together with the engine-located swinging arm, was needed due to engine length.**

the theory at least. The more likely fact is that, in the face of the ultra-low weight and vast power of Yamaha's new R1, the 750 class, so long at the top, could well be consigned to history in a few short years. Suzuki's announcement of its new GSX–R1000 for 2001 could well have been seen as an admission of this fact from the company which had created the Racer Replica category in the mid–1980s.

# MINIATURE SUPERBIKES

Packing the most into the least size is what Miniature Superbikes are all about. Today it's possible to own a 250 two-stroke or 400 four-stroke which is capable of phenomenal performance levels. The first such series of bikes was the famous LC (Liquid-Cooled) Yamaha twins of the early 1980s and the series has culminated, most recently, with Aprilia's stunning RS250. But if you don't fancy a two-stroke then try one of the various 400cc four-cylinder four-strokes such as the Yamaha FZR and Kawasaki ZXR.

In years gone by, the word 'Superbike' meant not only a super specification, great performance, but also a big engine displacement. However, in the past few years, an entire group of smaller bikes has made its debut that casts aside this perception – and, judged on sophistication and speed, these bikes are worthy of inclusion in this book. These are the Miniature Superbikes.

### YAMAHA MINIATURES

Miniature Superbikes are generally split into distinct groups: 250cc two-strokes, 400cc across-the-frame fours, or 400cc V-twins/fours, or, for the Japanese market, jewel-like 250cc fours. The first small-capacity modern machine with a performance to worry bigger bikes was Yamaha's trend-

Using a modified Japanese Suzuki RGV250 90-degree two-stroke V-twin engine, the Aprilia RS250 is the nearest thing to a Grand Prix racer on the street.

setting LC (Liquid-Cooled) 250/350cc two-stroke twins.

The world had its first glimpse of the new RD350LC in the autumn of 1979, at the Paris Show. In launching its LC series, Yamaha took several major technological steps, including introducing cantilever rear suspension and liquid cooling, to bring ordinary riders a new dimension in two-stroke performance. The 250 and 350LC models were primarily aimed at the European market and started to arrive in the spring of 1980. Compared to earlier Yamaha two-strokes, they contained all manner of new developments. The most obvious was liquid cooling. Yamaha used a mixture of 50 per cent distilled water and 50 per cent ethylene glycol (antifreeze), forced around the aluminium cylinders by a crankshaft-driven pump. Another common factor of the LC series was reed-valve

induction (pioneered by Yamaha on its earlier air-cooled RD series models). This system comprised reed-valve blocks and petals mounted in the cylinder/carb inlet tracts. Reed-valve induction was largely responsible for the LC's easy starting and lusty low-mid range power. It was so efficient, in fact, that rivals such as Honda, Suzuki, and Kawasaki had little choice but to follow, largely ditching in the process the previously used piston-port or disc-valve methods. Components such as the six-speed transmission and crankshaft were derived from the outgoing air-cooled RD models.

The new cantilever suspension found on the 250/350LC models was a development of that pioneered on the company's YZ motocross bikes. It offered increased rigidity and much longer rear-wheel movement compared with the previous pivoting fork/twin shock

**The world's first miniature superbike was launched at the Paris Show in October 1979, in the shape of the new Yamaha RD350LC. In launching the bike, the Japanese company had taken several technological steps, including cantilever rear suspension and liquid cooling.**

set-up of the RD. A single De Carbon-type rear suspension unit was tucked away under the frame and the unit received little in the way of cooling air – what it did get had already been warmed by the engine and radiator. Not surprisingly, under arduous conditions, the LC twins tended to suffer from damper failure.

Another major development on the LC range was the anti-vibration engine mounting system. Again simple, but effective, the motor was pivoted at the rear and retained by high-deflection rubber bushes at the front.

The engine simply 'bounced' up and down; so noticeable was it that you could literally see the engine moving independently of the frame!

The LCs, both the 350 and 250, had the same engine and bore/stroke sizes as the air-cooled RD models they replaced. The bigger motor displaced 347cc, while its smaller brother came out at 247cc. As for power outputs, the RD350LC put out 47bhp at 8500rpm, the RD250LC 35.5bhp at 8500rpm. In terms of performance, the 350 could reach 177km/h (110mph), while the 250 topped 161km/h (100mph).

More than 20,000 LCs were sold in 1980 alone. In racing, the LCs won nearly everything in sight, from club championships to major international production events. 'Legal' modification of LC engines for production racing made it possible to extract some 46bhp at 9000rpm from the 250 and 54bhp at 9500rpm from the 350.

In 1980, Yamaha introduced its power-valve TZ250H racer. The only question then was how long it would

# EXHAUST - ITS EFFECT UPON PERFORMANCE

The exhaust has always played a vital role in the evolution of the motorcycle – and its ultimate performance. Of course, in racing, where noise is far less of a priority than on a bike which has to be ridden on public roads, a designer has much more freedom. Even so, it is still possible to affect the performance of an engine by getting the exhaust right.

As a journalist once wrote: 'When a musician blows into a wind instrument, the sound which comes out at the other end depends upon what happens to the air inside the instrument.' This statement was never truer than when explaining a motor-vehicle exhaust system. Ideally, the exhaust gases should be allowed to escape as smoothly, completely, and quickly as possible, but these gases come in pulses as the sequence of exhaust strokes takes place and poor tubes and silencer design can result in too much back pressure building up, having a strangling effect. Taken to an extreme, such as if the exhaust was blocked, the engine would not run at all.

It is quite common practice on multi-cylinder engines for the exhaust header section (the part bolting directly to the cylinder head) to be siamezed; this means that you then have two-into-one, three-into-one, four-into-one, or even six-into-one. This obviously also plays a role in the power-to-weight ratio. For example,

when Benelli built its first six-cylinder model, the 750 Sei in 1972, the Italian company used six separate pipes and silencers! However, when it launched the 750s replacement, the 900 Sei, a few years later, it employed a six-into-two system.

The black art of two-stroke tuning sees the exhaust taking on as an important a role as that of engine preparation, whether the machine is to be used for fast road work or racing. Up to the early 1950s, two-strokes lagged behind four-strokes in GP racing. Once the technology of expansion-chamber exhausts was understood, however, a giant leap forwards was made. The Germans, in particular, led the way, thanks to the efforts of engineers such as Walter Kaaden (MZ) and Helmut Georg (DKW).

Increasingly, exhaust systems are being manufactured in stainless steel. This is because, for years, owners were faced with having to purchase new components (particularly silencers), often only a few months after the motorcycle was purchased new.

**The exhaust system plays a vital role in the performance of every motorcycle. It can often have as much effect as, or even more than, camshaft profile and compression ratios combined. The 'four-into-one' system shown below has the advantage of providing substantial weight saving.**

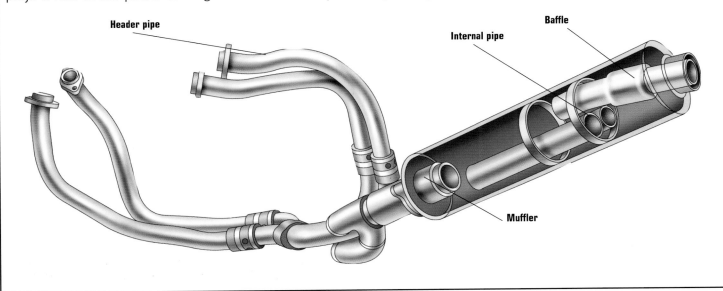

Header pipe

Baffle

Internal pipe

Muffler

Cutaway view of the RD350LC YPVS, which debuted at the 1982 Cologne Show. The biggest change when compared to the original 350LC was the YPVS (Yamaha Power Valve System). This race-developed valve operated in the exhaust port window, giving greater engine flexibility.

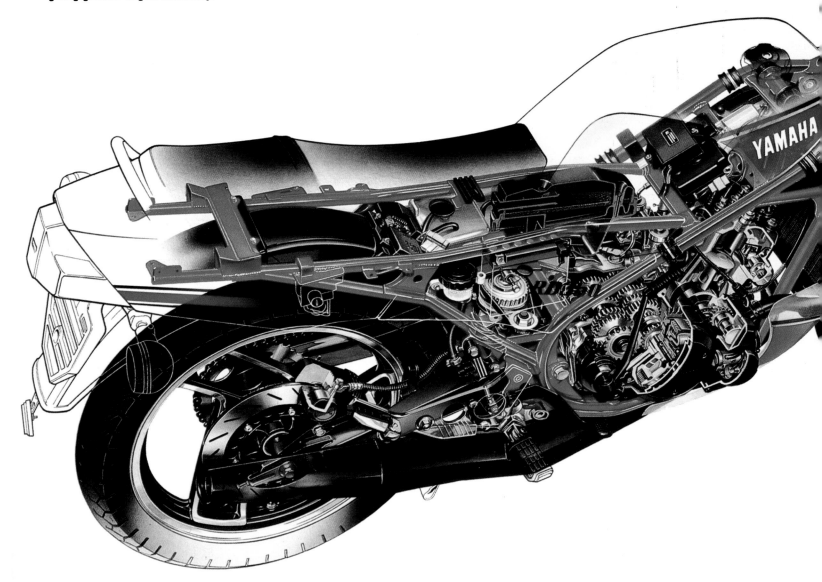

take for the company to transfer this device to a series production street bike. Sure enough, at the 1982 Cologne Show, Yamaha unveiled the all-new RD350LC YPVS.

## YAMAHA RD350LC YPVS

At first, many observers thought that the new bike was simply a restyled and tuned 350LC. How wrong they were. In fact, it was considerably different, with the YPVS producing 59.1bhp at 9000rpm, 12bhp more than the bike it replaced. Its chassis had a specification

that a few years earlier would have put any 350 circuit racer to shame.

One of the most vital changes over the original 350LC was the YPVS (Yamaha Power Valve System). Very simply, this was a valve that operated in the exhaust port window. The timing on a 9000rpm, high-output engine would exceed 200 degrees to obtain the necessary port area to handle the exhaust gas within the time available. This would produce, on a conventional engine, a power delivery far worse than on the RD400; as well as poor response

at low rpm, the power would arrive like a kick from a horse. The answer was obviously to change the exhaust port height while the engine was running, increasing the port height and area as the speed increased. The Yamaha Power Valve System afforded high gas-trapping capability at low speeds and provided the necessary port area for peak power at high rpm. Producing a mild-mannered street racer was not the only effect the YPVS system had: at low and medium rpm, it also restricted the amount of unburnt fuel that

## YAMAHA RD350LC YPVS (1983)

**Engine:** 2-stroke, with reed-valve induction and YPVS, twin cylinder, water-cooled
**Bore and stroke:** 64 x 54mm (2.5 x 2.1in)
**Displacement:** 347cc
**Compression ratio:** 6:1
**Carburation:** 2 x Mikuni VM26
**Ignition:** CDI
**Lubrication:** Autolube
**Gearbox:** 6-speed
**Clutch:** Wet, multi-plate
**Frame:** Steel tube, full cradle
**Suspension:**

*Front:* Telescopic forks
*Rear:* Yamaha monocross, cantilever swinging arm
**Brakes:**
  *Front:* 170mm (6.7in) hydraulically operated discs
  *Rear:* Single 260mm (10.2in) hydraulically operated disc
**Tyres:**
  *Front:* 90/90-18 51H
  *Rear:* 110/80-18 58H
**Dry weight:** 145kg (320lb)
**Power:** 59bhp at 9000 rpm
**Top speed:** 193km/h (120mph)

converter, the battery driving the 0–12 volt motor, which in turn rotates the power valve: 0–5000rpm equals 0 volts (valve closed); 9000rpm equals 12 volts (valve fully open). Since Yamaha introduced the technology, the power-valve theme has been taken up by several other manufacturers, who have all produced their own variations, including Suzuki, Honda, Cagiva, Gilera, and Aprilia.

The heritage of the 350 YPVS's frame can be seen by viewing photographs of the company's TZ racers of the late 1970s and early 1980s. Even so, the YPVS's frame was totally new, with a wide-tubed chassis employing a rising-rate rear suspension system to control

disappeared down the exhaust, hence promoting more efficient running and therefore improved fuel economy.

The valve control system of the 350YPVS was electronic, but, during development on the TZ racer, a mechanical centrifugal type (similar to a contact breaker advance) was tried, as was a hydraulic system employing the engine's water pump. The electrically driven system emerged a clear winner, consuming less power and having more accurate control over the valve than its rivals. It works on the following basis. The engine speed is first detected from the ignition through a simple frequency to a voltage

**The year 1984 saw the arrival of the magnificent four-cylinder Yamaha RD500LC. This model featured not one but two crankshafts. Like the later 350LC, the RD500LC featured YPVS; it produced just over 70bhp and had a maximum speed of 238km/h (148mph).**

wheel movement and a generously proportioned box-section swinging arm to resist rear-end flexing. Air-assisted front forks added a final touch to what was then the best Yamaha sports bike to reach mass production. Except for adding a full fairing for the 1985 season, the same 350YPVS remained in production for many years. After production ceased in Japan, the bike still continued to be built in Brazil.

### LEADING THE PACK

When studying Yamaha, it is also necessary to include the RD500LC. Its 499cc liquid-cooled 50-degree V-four motor caused both Honda and Suzuki to rush back to their drawing boards to produce similar machines (the Suzuki 500 Gamma four and the Honda NS400 triple). Also, technically, the RD500LC (introduced in 1985) was perhaps the most glamorous miniature Superbike ever built.

The RD500LC's engine featured not one but two crankshafts; at the same time, Yamaha was clever enough to incorporate components first seen on the 250/350LC twins. Although its two cranks had a 50mm (1.96in) stroke,

**Over the years, the technology developed on the race circuit through Yamaha's range of TZ250 racers. Research has been ploughed back into the development of improved two-stroke street bikes.**

they were nevertheless copies of the unit fitted to the twins. The reed-valve induction differed from earlier Yamaha practice by having two distinct arrangements on the same engine. The front two cylinders were fed from reed blocks mounted directly onto the crankcases and those at the rear were fed by the more conventional cylinder fitted components. This configuration allowed all four carburettors to be grouped inboard between the vee of the cylinders, producing a very narrow, compact engine. The crankshafts, both rotating in the same direction, drove a massive 14-plate clutch which in turn operated an engine-speed double-weighted balancer shaft. The gearbox, deviating from the normal splash-fed variety seen on the LC twins, featured a trochoid pump that delivered lubricant to shafts, primary gears, and sundry smaller items. Equipped with a single electrically powered servomotor,

all four YPVS valves were mechanically linked. As well as a desirable reduction in production costs, the system also eliminated out-of-balance effects and ensured that all valves operated in unison.

The magnificent RD500LC was a genuine roadgoing V-four two-stroke and not – as some believed – a 'Kenny Roberts Replica'. The power plant was not adapted from a Grand Prix engine, many of its components coming instead from the existing LC series, thereby maximising reliability. However, the cycle parts, unlike the engine bits, had been specifically created for the V-four. The frame was a wide, rectangular steel-tube affair with a single rising-rate gas/oil shock mounted horizontally beneath the engine. Everything spoke of performance, the bike having anti-dive forks and triple-ventilated disc brakes as standard. The YPVS system is now recognised as one of the classic innovations in two-stroke technology and a credit to the technical wizardry of the Yamaha Motor Co. It also placed Yamaha at the very front of two-stroke development. Its rivals have had to work long and hard to catch up.

# ELECTRONIC IGNITION

In the early days of the internal combustion engine, the fuel/air mixture was ignited by a platinum tube which passed through the cylinder wall and was heated on the outside by a petrol-burning flame. Virtually extinct by 1900 it was superseded by the magneto, which served from the early 1920s right through to the 1950s. After this came coil ignition, in which there was a battery to supply electricity and a coil to transform the low-voltage supply to a much higher electrical pressure with the assistance of a contact breaker, which triggered it to a very high pulse. There was also a condenser, wired to the contact breaker to prevent excessive arcing or sparking across the points.

During the 1970s came the first of the now almost universally used electronic ignition systems, but before examining this it is worth noting a vital difference between coil and magneto ignition. Coil ignition gave its healthiest spark at low revs and grew progressively weaker as the spark rate increased; the magneto, by contrast, gave a stronger spark as the engine revolutions and thus spark rate increased. The problem was that you could not have both. This is where electronic ignition comes in.

The most advanced electronic ignition systems now function with notable accuracy and consistency over a doubly wide range of operating speeds. Increasingly stringent emission laws have forced manufacturers to use electronic ignition, in place of either magneto or coil types, not just because of superior performance, but also because of environmental considerations. A vital breakthrough for electronic ignition has also been economies of scale in the electronics industry, making microprocessors affordable for both bikes and cars.

Even in the early 1970s, electronic control of the ignition advance had proved its worth in a few racing cars and motorcycles; by the end of that decade, the great feat had been achieved of programming a miniature computer to attend to the generation, timing, and prolongation of each successive spark according to the demands made by the rider, and the vicissitudes of engine load, speed, temperature, and even fuel supply. No longer did an arbitrary or approximated ignition advance curve, simple enough to be mechanically determined, have to suffice in all these exigencies; at last every spark was correctly timed so that the engine could operate much closer to the limits of pre-ignition than before, meaning it could operate more efficiently and economically.

Finally, the combination of fuel injection in place of the carburettor has led to an integrated electronic fuel injection and ignition system, such as that pioneered by the Italian Weber-Marelli and German Bosch concerns. Ignition and injection systems are able to make use of the same sensors, the same transducers, and, to some extent, the same circuitry, making full electronic engine management a reality.

In 1987, Yamaha again stole a march on the opposition, when it launched its new TZR250. This was an entirely new motorcycle, even though it still used reed-valve induction and an updated form of YPVS. Its 249cc parallel-twin engine set a new class record for a production roadster 250, with 50bhp at 10,000rpm. Other details of its specification included a six-speed gearbox, monoshock rear suspension, 431mm (17in) wheels, and a dry weight of 128kg (282lb). It, like the LC models, was hugely successful in sports-machine class racing events, winning just about everything in sight. That

**In 1987, Yamaha again stole a march on the opposition, when it launched its new TZR250. This was an entirely new bike, even though it still employed reed-valve induction and an updated form of YPVS. It produced 50bhp at 10,000rpm.**

was, until the opposition, in the shape of Suzuki (RGV), Kawasaki (KR1), and Honda (NSR), suddenly caught up at the end of the 1980s. Together, and later joined by Aprilia, they have produced a series of fabulous, super-fast 250s, with the performance and technical features of the GP circuit. As for the TZR, this has been updated over the years, but has never given Yamaha the stranglehold it once had on the 0.25-litre (0.05-gallon) division.

## SUZUKI'S RGV

In the 1960s, Suzuki had its T20 Super Six, then, in the 1970s, the GT250 and X7. During the mid-1980s, it introduced its first liquid-cooled 250 twin-cylinder two-stroke, the RG250 Gamma (49bhp) of 1984. The really big news arrived at the beginning of 1987, however, with the trendsetting RGV250 V-twin. The first version to be exported was the 1989 'K' model, followed in 1990 by the 'L', which was virtually identical.

Both the K and L models shared the same 90-degree V-twin two-stroke engine, which displaced 249cc and featured dual slingshot carburettors, a new air-induction system, a radial-flow radiator, and AETC (Automatic Exhaust Timing Control). The latter was a variation of the Yamaha-conceived variable exhaust valve and it gave the RGV a reasonably wide spread of power for a highly strung two-stroke. This resulted in a power output of 57bhp at 11,000rpm and a top speed of 209km/h (130mph).

The earlier RG250 Gamma parallel-twin had been the first Suzuki 250 street bike to feature an aluminium frame. However, this effort was eclipsed by the high quality and substantial DC-ALBOX frame made from cast aluminium to reduce weight while still maintaining maximum strength. There was an updated version of the link-type Suzuki 'Full Floater' rear suspension, while at the front was a pair of sturdy 41mm (1.61in) diameter

**The first Suzuki RGV250 arrived in 1987, with the first examples of the machine being exported in 1989. The much-improved M version went on sale in 1991. The power output of 59bhp remained unchanged, but there were many improvements to both the engine and chassis.**

stanchion telescopic forks. Braking was taken care of by twin 290mm (11.41in) front discs and a single 210mm (8.26in) disc at the rear. This system incorporated four pistons for each calliper for both front discs, reduced to two pistons at the rear. Wheels were of the racing three-spoke variety: 431mm (17in) at the front, 457mm (18in) at the rear. With a dry weight of 128kg (282lb), these early model RGVs suffered from borderline reliability: problem areas were broken/seized exhaust valves and piston/cylinder seizures.

For 1991, the Suzuki engineering team redesigned the RGV to such an extent that it owed virtually nothing to the original, except for the basic concept and 90-degree cylinder configuration. It was also to be a much-improved motorcycle, both in terms of performance and reliability. The engine was updated, including completely new exhaust valves – now referred to as 'power valves'. The original had been derived from the Suzuki motocross type, whereas the 1991 type was purpose-built for the job.

Another major departure concerned the swinging-arm design. On the original RGV, this had been straight, but the new model (coded M) featured a Grand Prix–derived crescent-shaped, aluminium-alloy device. This modified design also had the advantage of allowing both expansion chamber exhausts to exit on the offside and provide an incredible 58-degree banking angle. Other notable developments over the earlier RGVs included a coaxially mounted gearshift lever, a needle roller

**Kawasaki's KR1, launched in 1988, was the closest thing to a race bike that the giant engineering concern had ever put onto the street at that time. At its heart was an all-new 249cc liquid-cooled parallel twin two-stroke, with crankcase reed-valve induction.**

bearing on the shaft for greater strength, and revised gear ratios to improve acceleration. The main-frame was also substantially improved and the sub-frame modified for easier maintenance. Front forks were now inverted and of an entirely new design, while there was a marginally steeper steering-head angle. Both wheels were now 431mm (17in), with wider section rims. The brakes, too, had been uprated; front discs were enlarged to 300mm (11.8in).

Although the quoted power out of 59bhp remained unchanged, the engine-management system had been reprogrammed to provide more usable power characteristics. This displayed itself not only during normal road use, but also on the race circuit, benefiting both types of rider. These changes converted the RGV250M into a class winner during 1991, both for show-room sales and as a race winner in the by now hotly contested Super Sport 400 racing category. This success continued into 1992 with the 'N' model and subsequently the 1993 'P' version. Both were still able to compete with the growing tide of 400cc four-stroke models, such as the NC30 Honda,

ZXR Kawasaki, and FZR Yamaha. As an example of the RGV's race-track prowess, in the first three seasons of the British Super Teen Championship (then for either 250cc two-strokes or 400cc four-strokes), an RGV won the title in 1991, 1992, and 1993.

### KAWASAKI KR1

In the mid-1980s, Kawasaki built an inline twin Super-Sports model loosely modelled on its multi world championship winning liquid-cooled inline twin-cylinder two-stroke racers. Coded KR250, the 249.1cc tandem twin was based around the bikes raced so successfully by world champions Kork Ballington and Anton Mang. Included in the KR250's specification were triple discs, cast-alloy wheels, Uni-Trak rear suspension, hi-level exhaust, and a three-quarter fairing; however, the KR was a Japanese-market–only model.

Later that same decade, the high-performance 250 class became the most important on the Japanese domestic market. This was to result in a rash of superb little bikes such as the Yamaha TZR, Honda NSR, Suzuki RGV, and the Kawasaki entry, the

Rider's eye view of Kawasaki's ZXR400, showing the minimal instrumentation of a racer, with a centrally mounted tachometer. The speedometer is to the left. Other details visible are the front brake master cylinder and air-box induction hoses.

KR1. The first KR1, the B1, arrived in 1988. At its heart was an all-new 249cc liquid-cooled parallel-twin engine with crankcase reed-valve induction. It ran a compression ratio of 7.4:1 and produced 55bhp.

The KR1 was the closest thing to a race bike that 'Big K' had ever put on the street at that time. Technical features included power valves, a cassette-type gearbox, a box-section aluminium frame and swinging arm, adjustable 41mm (1.61in) front fork, semi-floating 247mm (9.72in) front discs and dual piston calipers, fully floating rear calliper, hollow-spoke wheels, and low-profile 431m (17in) tyres. There were twin 28mm (1.1in) Crescent-slide carbs and, to keep the engine's low-end and mid-range as wide as possible, there was the newly introduced KIPS (Kawasaki Integrated Power-Valve System). Controlled by a tiny computer and servomotors, KIPS operated with maximum precision to knock out power right through to 11,500rpm; however, it is true to say that, like other high-performance 250s, the best power is generated at the top end of the scale.

The factory claimed 210km/h (131mph) at the standing start 0.2km (0.12 mile) in 12.5 seconds. Road testers raved and customers flocked to their local Kawasaki dealer, cheque books at the ready. The KR1 was an immediate success, both on the street and in production-class racing. The first KR1 to be exported in serious numbers was the B2 of 1989. This had a number of changes from the B1: new frame gave increased rigidity of the steering head and swinging arm pivot; the size of the box-sectioned aluminium beams, front cross beam, and seat rails was increased for extra strength; gussets had been added to strengthen the swinging arm; and bosses for a steering damper (hydraulic) and centre stand had been added. Performance and power output remained unchanged.

### IMPROVING ON A CLASS ACT

By the end of 1989, the KR1 was firmly established around the world and it was a KR1 that was ridden by Ian McConnachie when he won the British Super Sport 400 race series. If all this seemed a hard act to follow, Kawasaki brought out an even more potent piece of kit for the 1990 model year, the KR1S. The KR1 had never been short on horsepower, but the KR1S had an extra 5bhp, gained

**Brilliant as the hi-tech GP derived two-strokes were, upcoming emission controls saw a general move to smaller versions of the four-cylinder four-strokes, including Kawasaki's ZXR400. These 'pocket rockets' are extremely popular in Japan. Their biggest fault is lack of engine torque.**

without altering engine revolutions. This boost had been achieved through revised cylinder porting and a new exhaust system which included different expansion chambers and aluminium-bodied (rather than steel) silencers, together with new, stronger pistons. Another bonus was that the silencers and exhaust pipes were no longer one unit; in the event of damage, the new silencers could be replaced separately. The KIPS was retained, but with modified porting to help boost top-end torque without sacrificing middle or bottom-end output. The micro-computer controlling ignition was also modified to provide a faster throttle response throughout the rpm band.

While the wall thickness of the twin-spar aluminium frame was unchanged,

## RS250 (2001)

**Engine:** Water-cooled, two-stroke, 90-degree V-twin with reed valve induction and sequential 2-stage exhaust valve
**Bore and stroke:** 56 x 50.6mm (2.2 x 1.99in)
**Displacement:** 249cc
**Compression ratio:** 13.2:1
**Fuel system:** 2 x Mikuni TM34SS flat-slide carbs
**Ignition:** CDI digital, with advance mapping programme
**Gearbox:** 6-speed
**Frame:** Double-beam in alloy and magnesium, with thin wall structure
**Suspension:**
  *Front:* inverted Showa fork, with 41mm (1.61in) stanchions
  *Rear:* aluminium swinging arm with single shock absorber
**Brakes:**
  *Front:* 2 x 298mm (0.07 x 11.73in) floating discs with 4-piston calipers
  *Rear:* single 220mm (8.66in) disc with 2-piston calliper
**Wheels:** 431mm (17in), 5-spoke aluminium.
**Tyres:**
  *Front:* 120/60 ZR17
  *Rear:* 150/60 ZR17
**Dry weight:** 140kg (308lb)
**Power:** 68bhp at 10,000rpm
**Top speed:** 220km/h (137mph)

included new style chain adjusters, shortened front forks, a nitrogen charged alloy-bodied rear shock with remote reservoir, and revised spring rates, and larger (300mm/11.81in) and thicker front discs. The rear brake was given a revised calliper and there were five-spoke (instead of three-spoke) alloy wheels, wider and lower profile tyres, and revised cosmetics.

Throughout 1990, the KR1S was the bike to beat in Super Sport 400 racing, until, in 1991, Suzuki brought out its revised RGV V-twin and the Kawasaki's days of glory and maximum showroom sales were over. Kawasaki, like Suzuki and Yamaha, was from then on to develop a new range of miniature across-the-frame four-cylinder four-strokes to take over from the two-stroke. As events were to prove, however, it was not to prove that simple.

### THE FOUR-STROKE CHALLENGE

Brilliant as the hi-tech GP-derived two-strokes were, upcoming emission regulations, particularly in the USA, were stacked against them. This led the Japanese to downsize their bigger models to create a miniature four-cylinder four-stroke category.

The motorcycles this move spawned all follow the technology of their particular company's bigger brothers. So, you have the Yamaha FZR400, Honda CBR400 or NC30, Suzuki GSX-R400, and Kawasaki ZXR400;

**When it went on sale in 1994, Aprilia's RS250 shot to the top of the high-performance 250cc two-stroke league. It used a bought-in Japanese Suzuki 249cc RGV V-twin engine in a race-derived aluminium chassis to offer class-leading speed and handling.**

even the Italian marque Ducati got in on the action by building its 400SS V-twin. This latter bike was especially big in Japan, even though the Japanese had plenty of four-stroke 400 multis of their own. So which of this four-stroke line-up is best? This is a difficult question, as all would meet most people's needs, providing you enjoy riding solo. This is because none of the 400s (this also of course applies to the 250 two-strokes) is blessed with the low-down torque, let alone the outright power, of a bigger bike such as a 600 or 750.

The true home of these Miniature Superbikes (or Pocket Rockets, as I once named them) is really Japan. There they sell by their thousands, but sales are less strong in other countries. However, even in Europe, they do have their admirers, who appreciate their lack of bulk, their single-minded sporting character, and their often beautiful looks. Others question the need for the complication of four cylinders (this obviously does not apply to Ducati) in an engine of only 400cc. Furthermore, some riders are aghast at the way these tiny four-stroke multis

the cross-section had been modified to provide increased rigidity, the smoother finish being another feature of the KR1S compared to its older brother. The front cross brace was increased in size and the cross-section of the swinging arm changed to increase torsional rigidity and welded gussets added to provide extra strength. The length of the swinging arm was increased by 10mm (0.39in) to allow fitment of a larger 140-section rear tyre and the outer diameter of the pivot spindle enlarged from 17mm (0.66in) to 20mm (0.78in). Other changes need to be revved to the heavens to make the most of their somewhat restricted power figures.

It is generally accepted, certainly if track results are consulted, that the FZR400 Yamaha is top in this class. It was also the first production Yamaha to feature EXUP and, at the same time, (spring 1987) was 'Japan only'. Like its 600 brother, the FZR has only four valves per cylinder, as against five for the 750 or 1000cc class models. There is also very little power below 7000rpm and it is only above 10,000rpm that the FZR really sings. The ZXR400 Kawasaki is not quite in the same class as the Yamaha, certainly not as a track tool. That is not to say it has not got its virtues, including the look and feel of a 'bigger bike' than the Yamaha. Honda's NC30 is the engineering jewel amongst these 'Pocket Rocket' 400

fours. Virtually a scaled-down RC30, this smaller machine retains the 90-degree V-four engine layout.

Motorcycles such as the CBR400 and GSX-R400 were never officially imported into Britain. However, many subsequently arrived as 'grey' imports, a thriving trade in itself. Actually, the grey import industry was initially brought about by enthusiasts buying Japanese-market models, which were predominantly these 400 fours.

Another popular grey import over the years has been Honda's NSR250V-twin two-stroke. Perhaps this bike more than any other in this chapter represents the ultimate in maximum performance on minimum engine size. The latest version is a true work of engineering genius and is very closely related to Honda's RS250 over-the-counter racing machine. In addition, the

advanced technology utilised on this model extends to a card-type security system for the ignition, thus preventing would-be thieves making off with your pride and joy!

## APRILIA RS250

The most talked about – and probably the best – of the current crop of Miniature Superbikes is the Italian Aprilia RS250. This bike was planned over a long period of time, uses a Japanese rival's engine, and has proved a major reason for the rapid growth in Aprilia's fortunes worldwide.

**From 1996, the Aprilia RS250 came with revised CDI ignition and carburation. This combination resulted in a power increase from 65 to 68bhp and a more flexible spread of power. Top speed is 220km/h (137mph). This is a year 2000 model.**

When the company first mooted the idea of a high performance 250 V-twin two-stroke back in the late 1980s, the stumbling block was related to a suitable power plant. The solution came from a most unexpected source, Suzuki. Its RGV250, which together with Kawasaki's KR1, Yamaha's TZR, and the Honda's NSR, had created a whole new generation of high-performance GP technology two-strokes at the end of the 1980s and the beginning of the 1990s. Aprilia reasoned, correctly, that as fellow Italian bike constructors Bimota had been able to purchase and use engines from all the big four Japanese manufacturers, why couldn't it? To begin with, the RGV seemed the best engine for Aprilia's needs and Suzuki were ready to play ball.

**With the advent of the 160km/h (100mph) 125, such as the 916-styled Cagiva Mito Evo, the term 'performance motorcycle' has spread to even smaller-engined bikes. Speed, race-bred handling, and light weight combine to offer great fun for less money.**

Although the RS250 did not materialise until 1994, it was an open secret for months – if not years. In an interview for the UK trade magazine *Motor Cycle Dealer* in October 1991, Steve Reynolds of newly appointed British importers Aprilia Moto UK said: 'Suzuki have sold 800 RGVs this year, and if, when the 250 comes out we did half that number I'd be ecstatic.'

In the 250's first full sales year in the UK in 1995, Reynolds' company actually sold 550 examples, 350 more than its original allocation. In fact, the Aprilia V-twin was so good that, in Britain at least, its arrival signalled the demise of the RGV itself! Not only was the 249cc 90-degree V-twin Suzuki-built engine better than the one that powered the Japanese maker's own machine, but also the rest of the RS250 simply made the RGV obsolete overnight. It was lighter, blessed with superior handling and more powerful (Brembo) brakes, and had a much more modern styling job. Motorcycle journalists simply loved the newcomer and penned headlines such as: 'One of

the best-handling machines on the road'; 'Big leans, high corner speeds, high grins'; 'Want a bike that can stuff R1s in corners on track days? Well look no further than Aprilia's RS250'; and 'The RS is just about the closest you can get to a GP bike on the road.'

## AN UNUSUAL ADVANTAGE

The real mystery has been why Suzuki agreed to supply (and have continued to supply) engines at all, when the Aprilia was so much better than Suzuki's own bike. Did Suzuki consider it had developed its own bike as far as it could or had it simply lost interest in the class? Whatever the reason, there is no doubt that the combination of the Italian chassis and Japanese engine has proved an outstanding success. The Suzuki-constructed engine is built to Aprilia's own specification. Most informed observers agree that the engine found in the Aprilia is not only more flexible than when fitted in the Suzuki, but faster, too, and has become

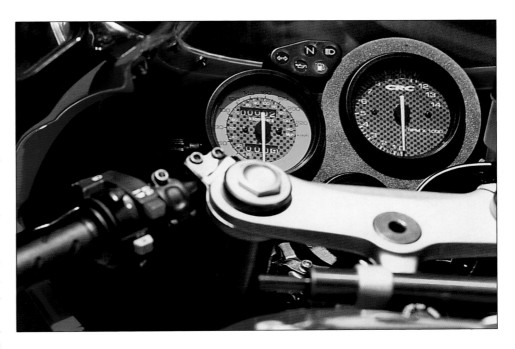

Cagiva Mito instrumentation, switch gear, warning lights, top yoke (triple clamp in USA), and across-the-frame mounted hydraulic steering damper. The Mito Evo was designed by Massimo Tamburini, creator of the Ducati 916 and MV Agusta F4.

even more so following changes introduced for the 1996 model year and onwards This update saw not only a new CDI ignition module, but also re-setting of the twin Mikuni 34mm (1.33in) flat-slide carburettors, resulting in a power increase from 65 to 68bhp. The post-1996 bike is also easier to ride, with speed being maintained with less cog swapping than in the six-speed Suzuki gearbox.

One other area where the Aprilia wins over the Suzuki original is in the instrumentation. On the Japanese model, there was no calibrated temperature gauge, whereas the Italian bike has a proper LCD temperature gauge, which cleverly doubles up as a lap timer and clock. Once the engine reaches 45 degrees centigrade, it is ready for real action – and the fun really starts. It pulls crisply from 6000rpm, hits the power at 8000, and really starts to move at 9000rpm. This frantic urge continues to build until the 12,000rpm redline, when power simply dies. As the exhaust note rises, it changes from a civilised burble to a deep, racer rasp,

## LIQUID-COOLING

Since the waste heat generated by a motorcycle has ultimately to be shed into the atmosphere, all bikes are, in the final analysis, air-cooled. Yet air is not the most effective medium for removing heat from some critical regions deep within an engine, so water or oil are now common intermediaries. The amount of heat to be removed is considerable; of all the calorific value of the fuel consumed by the engine, only around a third is converted into useful work, the remainder being lost, in roughly equal proportions, through the exhaust and cooling systems.

The choice of air- or liquid-cooling has always been controversial. Air is cheaper, lighter, and more readily obtainable than water, as the latter has to be carried and circulated. The earliest water-cooled engines had no radiators and no circulatory systems; they relied on the evaporation of the coolant. When a closed circuit utilising a radiator was evolved, natural convection currents were trusted to keep the water circulating. The introduction of an engine-driven water pump improved the efficiency of the water-cooled system considerably.

The effectiveness of a water-cooling system may be improved by raising the temperature of the coolant; the introduction of ethylene glycol was originally based on its boiling point being very much higher than that of water. Hence, in modern engines, glycol is retained as an anti-freeze agent, but more than 30 per cent is undesirable; water is a superior coolant over any other liquid at the same temperature, so complete is its heat transfer ability. Indeed, the higher the boiling point, the better water does compared with any other liquid coolant in this respect, so that adding even a small amount of water to glycol improves efficiency greatly. By the time the proportions reach 70 per cent water/30 per cent glycol, heat transfer is virtually as good as plain water.

The presence of the thermostat valve is explained by the need to bring the working temperature up as quickly as possible. The bulk of the cooling water is therefore isolated from the engine by this valve, allowing the relatively small amount in the engine water jackets to be heated quickly. When working temperature is reached, the valve opens and normal circulation begins. Originally, radiators were always made of copper, a material possessing exceptionally good thermal conductivity. Aluminium is now virtually standard practice throughout the motorcycle world, for, although its conductivity is slightly less, it is much lighter. Additionally, many motorcycles now use either two smaller radiators or in the case of, say, the Ducati 748, 916 and 996 series, a curved radiator.

which signals acceleration strong enough to hoist the front wheel well clear of the ground in first gear without needing to slip the clutch.

Aprilia's superb aluminium-beam frame provides road-holding and handling abilities that make larger sports bikes such as the Honda CBR600 or Kawasaki ZX-6 seem dull and overweight by comparison. The 40mm (1.57in) inverted front fork and rising-rate monoshock rear end blend suppleness with superb control and rider feedback. Only details such as

poorly positioned mirrors, unlacquered graphics and a small, fiddly fuel tap blemish the RS250's record. Testing a 1996 model, *Motor Cycle News* recorded 220km/h (137mph).

At the Milan Show in 1997, Aprilia displayed an updated RS250 for the 1998 model year. This was no mere cosmetic makeover, but a comprehensive re-engineering package. There was now completely adjustable suspension. In addition, the Showa inverted front fork had had its stanchion diameter increased from 41mm (1.61in) and

now featured adjustable rebound, as well as damping and spring load. The rear shock was now adjustable in extension, compression, spring preload, and length.

Attention had also been focused on the brake, wheel-rim width, and tyre type. The front calipers (still four-piston Brembos) had been rehashed for additional rigidity, in order to improve braking performance, while the floating-disc diameter had been reduced from 320mm (12.59in) to 298mm (11,73in), thus decreasing has always been its frame – perimeter beams of extruded aluminium and magnesium alloy with a torsional stiffness of 197kg/m/degree (132lb/ft/degree). The rear fork was also manufactured from aluminium to provide what Aprilia claims to be the highest degree of torsional stiffness to be found in a series production motorcycle: 162kg/m/degree (114lb/ft/degree). A Grand Prix–inspired fairing – and the entire redesigned bodywork – had been extensively tested in the wind tunnel. Aprilia claimed that it offered an increase of some eight per cent over the previous model. The hand shields were completely integrated in the fairing, helping to eliminate the majority of turbulence and fully enveloping the rider. There was also a more powerful headlamp and new mirrors, analogue and digital instrumentation, and, as already mentioned, original graphics on the bodywork. Finally, the fuel-tank capacity was increased from 16.5 litres (3.5 gallons) to 19.5 litres (4.25 gallons).

## OWNING AN RS250

Unlike with four-stroke Superbikes, Racer Replica 750s, and Super Sport 600s, owning a high-performance two-stroke is slightly different and there are a number of important things to watch out for when owning, or considering buying, a (used) RS250. Compared to other high-performance two-strokes, the Suzuki-sourced power unit is quite reliable, at least for normal road use. Racing use will require regular maintenance and feeding of components such as pistons, rings, small-ends, gaskets, and seals.

There are a number of potential trouble spots. The three-stage power valve – which opens and closes depending upon engine revolutions – is held together by pins. These can wear, causing, in extreme cases, the lip of the valve to touch the top front of the piston. The power-valve covers should be removed at regular intervals and the assembly sprayed with a suitable aerosol contact cleaner. Otherwise, a black mass of unburnt carbon deposits will clog up the valve.

Dealers report that the front-fork oil

seals blow on a regular basis, particularly if the machine is used under extreme conditions, such as track days or actual racing. Furthermore, with virtually no engine braking, the RS250 can eat up brake pads. Many owners prefer after-market components such as Carbone Lorraine, Dunlopad, EBC, or Ferodo. Pads, like tyres, are very much a matter of personal choice; every rider should test out a range of products to see which one suits best.

The RS250 has proved very popular for clubmans-type racing. It also has, in many European countries, a series at national level for only RS250 (one-model racing) machines. So it is very important for a road rider to check carefully that you are not being sold a clapped-out ex-track bike. Obvious (but not always reliable) signs are accident marks on the bodywork (notably the fairing) and in wired-up components such as the gearbox drain plug. Look for other evidence of crash damage such as scraped handlebar ends, control levers, and wheel spindles/nuts.

The cylinder bores are plated. This means that worn cylinders will need replacement or replating. For road use, it is recommended that the pistons/cylinders are examined for wear between 11,200 and 16,000km (7000 and 10,000 miles), depending upon use or riding style. In competition (racing) use, examination of the cylinders will be part of the maintenance programme.

Turning to tyres, choosing the best tyres for the RS250 is all a case of grip versus cost. For example, super-sticky rubber in the shape of Dunlop's track-based D207 GP will provide more grip than a set of Pirelli Dragons tyres, but this should be balanced against the fact that the latter last almost 50 per cent longer.

These comments are not intended to give the reader the idea that an RS250 is a liability. If maintained correctly, it is one of the most exhilarating performance bikes of any size on the road. Living with a high-performance two-stroke, however, is not the same as owning a large displacement four-stroke. Still, there are few bikes which can provide the same level of fun.

Bimota's revolutionary 500V Due went on limited sale in 1997 and was the first of a brand-new breed of high-performance two-strokes that aimed to ensure low pollution emissions and improved fuel consumption, failings of the conventional two-cycle engine.

unsprung weight. The width of the front rim had been increased from 76.2mm (3in) to 88.9mm (3.5in) and the front tyre from 110/70 to 120/60. The rear wheel and rear brake remained unchanged.

Yet the heart of the Aprilia RS250

# TOURING BIKES

For years touring bikes meant big heavy motorcycles with poor performance and road-holding abilities. But today the buzz word is Sports/Touring, and a vast array of superbly engineered bikes are available. BMW, Ducati and Honda, together with the reborn British Triumph marque lead the race to provide potential owners with these fun and freedom machines. The top touring models include the Honda ST1100 Pan European, BMW K1200, Ducati ST2/4 or Triumph's ST Sprint.

In the past, touring machines were built for comfort, long distances, carrying capacity, and even sidecar use. Outright performance came way down the list of priorities. There were exceptions to this rule, including Vincent's short-lived Black Knight of the mid-1950s and the BMW R69S of the 1960s, but not very many.

Then came the 1970s and the era of the modern Superbike, spurred on by the introduction of Honda's ground-breaking four-cylinder CB750 in 1969. The explosion of high-performance models which followed led to a demand for speed, but coupled to machines which could carry two people long distances in comfort. BMW's R100RS and Moto Guzzi's SP1000 (Spada in the UK) were some of the first of this new breed.

**Launched in 1998, Triumph's Sprint ST is a superb all-rounder; its 955cc liquid-cooled 3-cylinder engine providing smooth flexible power delivery for either touring or autobahn blasting.**

As leisure time has increased in the Western world, so the era of the sports tourer has arrived. For many motorcycle enthusiasts, there is nothing to beat touring on two wheels. Manufacturers have been only too ready to tap into this booming motorcycle sector: currently several companies offer purpose-built high-performance touring bikes, not just Honda, Suzuki, Yamaha, and Kawasaki, but also BMW, Ducati, Triumph, Moto Guzzi, and Aprilia. The American giant Harley-Davidson also offers a wide range of machines aimed at the tourist, although it lacks a real performance bike.

### THE JAPANESE

Market leaders Honda offers potential buyers the ST1100 Pan European. This is a tourer in the truly grand tradition, featuring a 1084cc dohc 16 valve V-four engine, which puts out 99bhp and can touch 217km/h (135mph). The more expensive 'A' version features ABS,

traction control, and linked brakes. *Bike* magazine refers to it in the following terms: 'Mile munching tourer is surprisingly agile and almost indestructible.'

The ST is a *tour de force* as an example of how to build the ultimate touring bike. Honda's engineering team began with a brief to build a fast, practical, and reliable touring machine. It accomplished this in superb fashion. The liquid-cooled V-four engine is modern engineering at its best, offering high-torque, usable power in a smooth and unstressed fashion. This, coupled with a slick-operating gearbox and largely maintenance-free shaft final drive, makes living with the ST an easy task.

A choice of screen heights helps tailor the ST to the individual rider's needs. In the A version, Honda's Traction Control System (TCS) gives the machine great safety by preventing the rear wheel spinning under power in slippery conditions; with this and ABS, the ST is one of the world's safest big-bore bikes.

For riders wanting less both in terms of size and performance – plus a lower purchase price – there is the NT650V Deauville. This uses a 647cc six-valve liquid-cooled V-twin engine. With a power output of 55bhp at 8000 rpm and 185km/h (115mph) top speed, you should not expect too many thrills, but it does work as a small tourer.

Alternatively, although not strictly a sports tourer, the latest 1832cc Gold Wing 1800 has the potential to provide more performance and handling capabilities than the 1500 version it displaced for the 2001 model year. Like the 1500, the 1800 has at its heart a flat-six engine. But the latest incarnation of Honda's long-running Gold Wing (the

**Honda's ST1100 Pan European is an example of how to build the ultimate touring bike with its 1084cc 16-valve V4 engine, supreme comfort over long distances, comprehensive weather protection and shaft final drive.**

# ANTI-LOCK BRAKING SYSTEM (ABS)

BMW was the first company to offer ABS (anti-lock braking system) for motorcycles. It appeared at first as an option only, on the K100 during the 1988 model year, after being unveiled to the public at the Cologne Show in 1986.

BMW's experiments with anti-lock braking systems had begun in 1978 when one of its flat-twins was fitted with an adaptation of the ABS developed for BMW cars. Yet this required extensive modifications to the motorcycle's brakes and was very cumbersome; it was soon abandoned as unsuitable. After experimenting with a British-made hydro-mechanical type, BMW chose the electronic/hydraulic anti-lock device developed by FAG Kugelfischer, as it proved both easy to connect to motorcycle brakes and effective in operation. This was based on impulse sensor gears, carried on the inside of the front and rear discs. An improved and much lighter system, ABS II, arrived during the early 1990s.

**The German BMW company pioneered ABS on motorcycles from the late 1980s. Its working mechanism is shown below.**

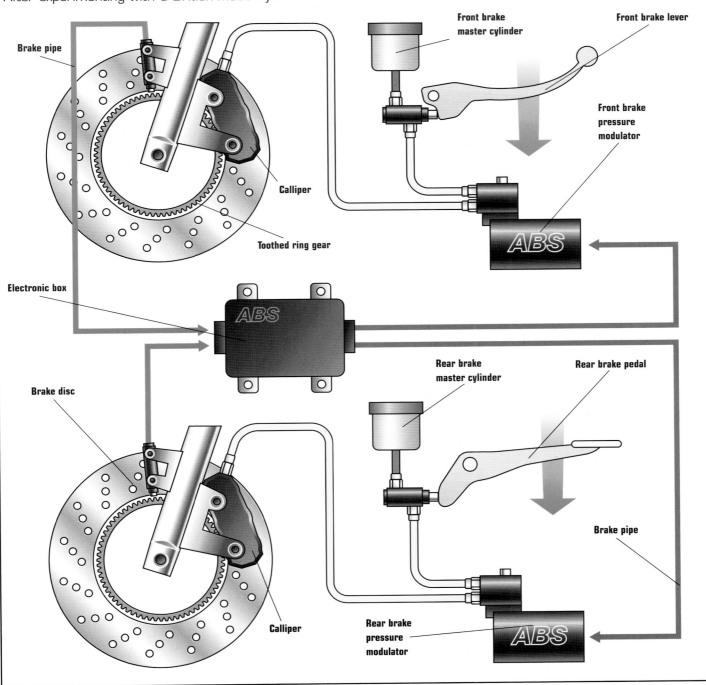

Brake pipe

Front brake master cylinder

Front brake lever

Calliper

Front brake pressure modulator

Toothed ring gear

Electronic box

Rear brake master cylinder

Rear brake pedal

Brake disc

Brake pipe

Calliper

Rear brake pressure modulator

**For riders who want to go touring, but do not want or need the ultimate in size or performance, there is Honda's excellent NT650V Deuaville, with its added benefit of a lower purchase cost. This bike uses a 647cc six-valve liquid-cooled V-twin engine and can top 185km/h (115mph).**

first naked GL1000 hit the streets in the mid-1970s) not only has a trendy single-sided swinging arm, but also a race technology twin-spar frame. As with the ST, the Gold Wing is available with ABS braking at extra cost.

For many years, Kawasaki offered the 1000GTR. Launched in the spring of 1986, it was one of the first of the new generation of touring machines for the rider who wanted to travel fast without sacrificing the comfort, convenience, and load-carrying capacity of something such as either a BMW or Moto Guzzi twin. Essentially, the GTR was a combination of a de-tuned 997cc 1000RX engine, with a new diamond frame, shaft final drive, and radial tyres. Compared to more

modern machines, however, it was showing its age by the early 1990s and was finally axed in 1997.

Kawasaki also offered the GPZ1100 (using a de-tuned ZZ-R1100 engine), but this only lasted from 1995 until 1998. Basically an excellent bike, it was killed by its unexciting style and, for a serious tourer, lack of shaft final drive. Kawaski's current sports tourer is the ZZ-R1100 (marketed in the USA as the ZX11). Launched in late 1989 and going on sale early the following year, the ZZ-R1100 was the world's fastest standard production model until it was ousted by, first, Honda's Blackbird and, later, the Suzuki Hayabusa. The 1074cc, 147bhp, 280km/h (174mph) cruise missile is now seen very much as a sports touring bike.

In 2001, Suzuki's sports touring range consisted of the GSX600F and GSX750F. Both were, as *Bike* was quick to point out: 'Capable, fully faired sports tourers. No frills, few thrills.' Of course, Suzuki also had the GSX1300R Hayabusa, but, with its 290km/h

(180mph) top speed, this should really be considered a Superbike.

In 1993, Yamaha launched its highly innovative GTS1000. Featuring hub centre steering, with a revised EXUP motor, the model suffered from an identity crisis. Although the company had created the GTS (Grand Touring Sport) with the accent on sport, as such, sales were abysmal. Yamaha then tried to refocus public attention towards simple touring, but things still did not work out. It was a decent, some would say excellent, motorcycle, which only proves that the motorcycle-buying public is very conservative. Yamaha should have looked at what happened to Bimota with the flop of its Tesi hub-steering project. Besides the GTS, Yamaha has also sold the FJ1100 and later FJ1200 air-cooled sports tourers with considerable success (the final FJ model was discontinued in 1995) and, more recently (and still in production), the XJ900 Diversion from 1994. This has a top speed of 204km/h (127mph), with the four-cylinder engine displacing

892cc; other specification details include eight valves, shaft final drive, and 89bhp at 8250rpm. There is also the smaller 598cc Division with chain drive, which can reach 185km/h (115mph). Finally, although they were originally listed as sports bikes, the YZF600R Thundercat and YZF1000R Thunderace are now regarded as sports tourers and very capable ones, too. The bigger engined bike has a 20-valve four-cylinder motor which puts out a highly impressive 130bhp and can reach 260km/h (162mph), while the Thundercat is virtually as quick, even though its 599cc 16-valve four 'only' produces a claimed 92bhp. The smaller bike is considerably lighter, but struggles against the larger model when laden with luggage two-up.

## BMW'S TOURING CHALLENGE

The German BMW company has always been one of the main challengers to the mighty Japanese industry when it comes to offering the best touring bikes. So it remains today, with both twin- and four-cylinder models being offered.

BMW's four-cylinder models are the K1200LT, which replaced the earlier K1100RT, and the still earlier K1000RT. The more sporting K1200RS can achieve 246km/h (153mph), against 196km/h (122mph) for the heavier more touring-orientated, gadget-ridden LT,

**Making its debut at the Munich Show in 1998, BMW's K1200LT is a giant among bikes, challenging the Honda Gold Wing with its 378kg (834lb) bulk. Its 1171cc engine features liquid-cooling, dohc 16-valves, Bosch electronic fuel injection, and a six-speed gearbox.**

the latter boasting the likes of a CD player, reverse gear, and even heated seats. Yet the 'Ks' employ the same 1171cc 16-valve inline four-cylinder engine with five-speed gearbox and shaft final drive. The fuel-injected engine is much smoother than the earlier K-series, while ABS is standard on both bikes.

The development of the K series was one of the seminal moments in BMW's developmental history. By the late 1970s, the motorcycle sales division of BMW was in deep trouble. Sales were holding up in Britain, but nowhere else. BMW had slumped to seventh spot in the domestic German market and, worse still, into eleventh place behind dirt-bike specialists Husqvarna in the USA. The importers had warehouses full of unsold bikes. Rudolf von der Schulenberg had resigned as chairman and the chief engineer and sales director had both gone. From the beginning of 1979, there were new men, who, luckily for BMW, had considerable motorcycle experience. Even so, BMW's senior management came very close to quitting two wheels altogether.

## WEATHER PROTECTION

Touring riders, even those who use large-capacity fast motorcycles, need to travel in as much comfort as possible. Unlike more sporting machines, which often travel only relatively short distances, a touring bike can notch up hundreds of kilometres in a day. To do this, the bike needs a powerful, smooth engine with plenty of torque, the riding position needs to be relatively upright with all the controls falling readily to hand, and, perhaps most of all, the motorcycle needs an efficient fairing, as it needs to provide weather protection for both rider and pillion passenger. Streamlining may help fuel consumption, but the most important requirement is that the rider/passenger is cocooned in a bubble of relatively still air. Turbulence is a sure-fire way of getting tired more quickly.

The most effective fairing currently fitted to sports/ touring bikes belong to Honda's Pan European and the various BMW twin- and four-cylinder models. There are also some excellent after-market touring-type fairings available. However, it is important to remember that Honda and BMW have spent a fortune developing their faired bikes as a complete package. After-market components will often be designed for more than one manufacturer, rather than a single dedicated model.

Besides the fairing itself, heated handlebar grips (an optional extra on many BMW models) can help make riding a real pleasure. These, together with a good fairing, can make a tremendous difference to the comfort of any serious touring rider.

**Capable of 246km/h (153mph), the BMW K1200RS is the highest performance motorcycle the German company has ever put onto the market. It is still classed as a touring machine, but one with sporting intent. Maximum power output from the inline four is 130bhp at 8750rpm.**

What many viewed as old-fashioned flat-twin engines were not what customers seemed to want anymore.

So it was decided that BMW needed a more sexy image. The engine would need to have more than two cylinders. Surprisingly, one of the company's staff, Josef Fritzenwenger, was already employed looking for a replacement for the long-running 'boxer' twins, a job he had been doing since 1975! Logically, the engine format for this planned newcomer would have been a liquid-cooled flat four. But Honda's introduction of just such a power plant for its newly released Gold Wing had stifled the idea at birth. BMW had no intention of fighting on a battleground chosen by the competition. BMW also needed the up-to-date successor for its

venerable twins to be in the same civilised tradition.

Furthermore, the new range would, if necessary, be based upon a model that would remain recognisably the same into the 1990s and beyond, thus reducing the huge cost of development which would have to include all

## K1200RS (2001)

**Engine:** Liquid-cooled, dohc, 16-valve, 4-stroke, inline flat four
**Bore and stroke:** 75 x 70.5mm (2.95 x 2.77in)
**Displacement:** 1171cc
**Compression ratio:** 11.5:1
**Fuel system:** Bosch electronic fuel injection
**Ignition:** Digital
**Gearbox:** 6-speed
**Final drive:** Shaft
**Frame:** Die-cast aluminium, monocoque
**Suspension:**
*Front:* telelever, inverted with
single shock absorber
*Rear:* paralever, aluminium single-sided swinging arm
**Brakes:**
*Front:* 2 x 305mm (12in) discs, 4-piston calipers
*Rear:* single 285mm (11.22in) disc, 2-piston calliper
**Wheels:** 431mm (17in) aluminium
**Tyres:**
*Front:* 120/70 ZR17
*Rear:* 170/60 ZR17
**Dry weight:** 279kg (615lb)
**Power:** 130bhp at 8750rpm
**Top speed:** 246km/h (153mph)

# CENTRE HUB STEERING

Although other manufacturers explored the separation of the steering and shock absorber functions as a way of maintaining a constant ride height at the front (with a conventional telescopic front fork the motorcycle dives under braking), the Italian Bimota company can take credit for first putting this revolutionary approach onto a series production motorcycle.

The Tesi ('thesis') project came from research carried out by two engineering students at Bologna, Pier Luigi Marconi and Roberto Ugolini. This research began in the early 1980s and, when the pair contacted Massimo Tamburini, then technical director at Bimota. Marconi was taken on by Bimota, at first under the supervision of Frederico Martini and later as technical director. The first Tesi prototype made its debut at the Milan Show towards the end of 1983. Powered by a VF400F Honda V-four engine, the steering was indirect with hydraulic control, while the frame was built up from a composite structure made of carbon fibres and a honeycomb of aluminium and kevlar, all of which was held together by special aeronautical adhesives.

Essentially, the steering had its hydraulic control housed within the front hub, while the pivot remained fixed. The pivot was connected to the hub via a second perpendicular pivot which constituted the steering axis and which, with its longitudinal inclination, determined the value of the train. This control mechanism was oil-damped, driven by a dual-pressure hydraulic pump, which sent pressurised oil to a second pump, set on the offside arm of the suspension fork. To prevent problems arising from variations in pressure, an air pump providing pressurised air was included, thus maintaining a constant pressure. The hydraulic circuit featured two small plungers. When the rider turned the handlebars to the right, the upper of the two plungers compressed the fluid, or alternatively, to the left, pulled on the fluid. The steering angle was 30 degrees, the train 120mm (4.72in) – adjustable – and the inclination of the steering-column tube 20 degrees.

By the fourth variation of the Tesi (now powered by a Yamaha FZ750), the steering operation had been converted to mechanical operation, rather than hydraulic. On the final Ducati-powered Tesi (1993), the front and rear swinging arms were different, being manufactured of Avoinal and machined, not cast. The shock absorber was an Öhlins unit. Total production of all Tesi models including prototypes was 346 examples.

The story ends with Yamaha, which, with its similar 1000GTS model, found that customers simply did not want to embrace centre hub technology. Instead, buyers chose to stick with the dated, but tried and tested, telescopic fork.

**The Italian Bimota company pioneered centre steering on production bikes. The first prototype made its debut at the 1983 Milan Show, but the public did not accept such a radical new look to the bike. Yamaha also used a similar system in its GTS1000 four manufactured in 1992.**

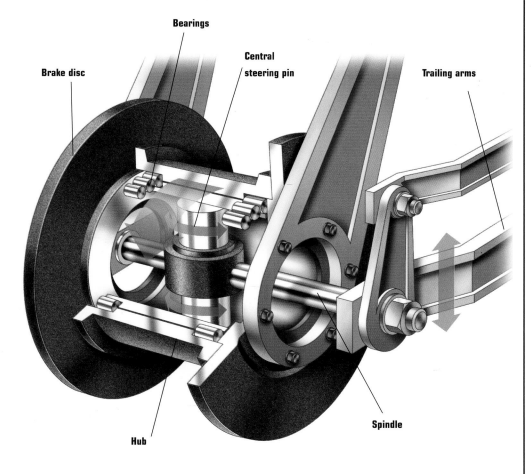

Bearings
Central steering pin
Brake disc
Trailing arms
Spindle
Hub

Rider's eye view of the BMW K1200LT cockpit. With just about every modern feature any touring rider could wish for, the options list is truly staggering. Standard features include adjustable windscreen, radio cassette with four speakers, electrically assisted reverse gear, and ABS.

current and foreseeable legislation over the next decade and more. The search was made even more difficult by the need to retain the firm's 'distinctive' image. This meant that vertical twins, V-twins of all kinds, square fours, transverse multis, two-strokes and chain final drive were all unthinkable, which narrowed choice to a fair degree.

It was to be experiments that Josef Fritzenwenger carried out with a water-cooled, four-cylinder engine from a Peugeot car (the 104) that led him to the concept of CDS (Compact Drive System), as BMW was soon to call it. Originally, this 1-litre (0.21-gallon) aluminium engine was intended for transverse and inclined installation in the 104, but it struck Fritzenwenger that, if he took this a stage further and laid the engine flat, but with its crankshaft in line with the frame, it could be what he and, more importantly, BMW were looking for. The configuration was entirely suitable for shaft final drive, had a low centre of gravity, mechanical accessibility, and no one had made a longitudinal

**The four-valves-per-cylinder BMW Type 259 engine, with high camshafts (chain-driven to short pushrods) and oil/air cooling, first appeared in 1993 on the R1100RS. Since then, it has been decreased in size for the R850 and enlarged for the R1200C.**

and horizontal inline four in the motorcycle world – ever. Various prototypes with either four or three cylinders were built ranging from 800 to 1300cc. But ultimately two engine sizes were chosen: the K100 in 997cc and the K75 in 740cc. As will be seen, both types shared the same slightly long stroke bore and stroke dimensions.

Work began on the two-tier range at Spandau, Berlin, in May 1979. The entire development team, now led by Stefan Pachernegg, initially concentrated on

the four (coded K589). Even at this early stage, however, some basic information was collected for the triple (coded K569). Although there were many years of hard work – and not a few problems – ahead, the first fruits of these exhaustive, costly, and long-rumoured labours were ultimately delivered to an eagerly waiting public in October 1983.

The original model to hit the streets was the unfaired K100, followed by the far more popular K100RS sports tourer and finally the K100RT. The fastest of the trio was the RS, with a maximum speed of 220km/h (137mph). A major feature of the K-series machines was the use of Bosch LE-Jetronic fuel injection, together with digital ignition. But it was not until the introduction of the K1 Super Sports (still more tourer than sports) in late 1988 that a K-series model sported four valves per cylinder.

As for the triple, the K75 was launched during September 1985 and employed much of the technology and most of the

K100's components. The second 750, the K75S (virtually a three-cylinder version of the K100RS), debuted in June 1986, with the range further strengthened at the Cologne Show later that year with the introduction of a budget K75 (the original K75 having a small handlebar-mounted device).

Technically, the only major differences between the three- and four-cylinder models were the K75 series lower axle ratio of 3.2:1, shorter inlet manifolds, new piston crown shapes, and the combustion chambers, which raised the compression ratio from 10.2:1 to 11:1, and a modified and better looking silencer – still in stainless steel – with three sides instead of four.

The K100 series frame was suitably modified to take the shorter three-cylinder engine. A feature of all the early 'K' series machines was the monolever rear suspension system with its single gas-damped strut. BMW not only produced a number of limited edition Motorsport K100RS machines, but also, in 1988, became the first bike manufacturer to offer ABS, on its K100 series machines, albeit as an option.

The 16-valve K1 Super Sport was launched at the Cologne Show in September 1988. Development had actually begun in 1983, the year in which the K100 was brought out. It retained the K100's 997cc engine displacement. The K1's biggest drawback was its none-too-popular futuristic styling, even though its 16 valves, new central computerised fuel injection, and improved ignition had pushed maximum power up to 100bhp. In addition, the latest braking package included larger discs and four instead of two piston calipers at the front (shared by the latest K100RS). Another feature of the K1 was the Paralever design of the rear swinging arm with two universal joints. A huge fairing and front mudguard set the style, together with unique, built-in small lockable side boxes (like miniature panniers).

For 1990, BMW gave the more conservatively styled K100RS the same technical specification as the K1. This resulted in sales of the K1 dropping away badly; it was finally dropped in 1993. Meanwhile, in 1991, the K1100LT (Luxury Tourer) was introduced. This

**At its launch in 1998, the new Triumph Sprint ST was almost universally hailed as the world's finest sports/tourer. Here at last was a bike which could beat Honda's long-running VFR. With 110bhp from its 955cc liquid-cooled three-cylinder engine, the Triumph offered versatile performance.**

1092cc engine had four valves per cylinder. Some versions were sold in a Special Edition guise with Connelly leather seat and top-box/panniers, crashbar fairing, rear carrier, and so on as standard equipment. For the 1993 model year, new 'Ferrari Testa Rossa'–style fairing lower panels gave the K1100RS a fresh appearance.

The final piece in the jigsaw of the K series family is the new K1200 series 1171cc, which began with the arrival of the K1200RS in October 1996 (the venue being the Cologne Show). This machine also carried a political message; it was the first BMW motorcycle offered for sale with a power output exceeding 100bhp (actually a very healthy 130bhp at 8750rpm. It was also the first production for BMW to feature a six-speed gearbox. In many

# HARD LUGGAGE

The question of luggage-carrying ability may seem at odds with that of the performance motorcycle. Unlike its four-wheel brother, the motorcycle is not normally blessed with much carrying capacity. However, the advent of serious touring as an important sector of the motorcycle industry has brought the need for luggage systems. These can either be soft or hard type. The former is usually either a pair of throw-over panniers or a tank-top bag. The latter is much more robust and has the advantage of being solid. Hard luggage usually consists of a pair of panniers, with

mounting frames and/or a large-capacity top box; this mounting frame doubles as a carrier. Most useful are top-boxes in which either one or two helmets can be stored. Also, panniers and top-boxes can usually be removed easily from the bike and thus act as suitcases. Several manufacturers, such as BMW, Ducati, and Honda, have factory-fitted hard luggage as optional extras. Models include the various twin-cylinder 'R' and four-cylinder 'K' series from the German manufacturer, the ST2 and ST4 from Ducati, and the VFR800 and Pan European from Honda.

---

ways, the K1200RS deserves to be classed as a Superbike. Even so, it is as a sports/tourer that it really excels. BMW claims a maximum speed of 245km/h (152mph).

Then there is the giant K1200LT. Debuting at the Munich Show in 1998, it went on sale early the following year. It is a mammoth among bikes, challenging Honda's Gold Wing with its 378kg (834lb) of what some would see as excess. There is no doubting its up-to-the-minute design and build qualities, but equally there is no disputing its sheer size. In American parlance, the K1200LT is a 'full-dresser'. With 70 litres (2.47 cubic feet) of storage in the pannier cases and 50 litres (1.76 cubic feet) in the top box (reduced to 15 litres (0.52 cubic feet) if

the six-disc CD changer is installed!), the LT can swallow two helmets and a considerable amount of luggage with room to spare. A cool box for the top case is considered essential by many stateside owners. Standard equipment includes an electrically adjustable windscreen, ABS brakes, a radio cassette with four loudspeakers, electrically assisted reverse gear, height-adjustable saddle, and length-adjustable passenger backrest. The options list is vast: onboard computer,

**New for 1999, the Triumph Sprint RS was a half-faired version of the 955i Daytona, the purpose of which was to allow owners to see the engine, instead of it being tucked away behind acres of plastic. The Sprint RS is seen as a sports/tourer.**

intercom system, heated handlebar grips, even a special chrome pack for US buyers. It is a fitting pinnacle to the prestigious K series bikes.

Turning our attention away from the K series, BMW tried to stop making its trademark flat twins during the 1980s but there was such an outcry from owners and potential owners that it was forced to do a rapid U-turn. In 1992, it introduced a new 1085cc four-valve engine. The first model was the R1100 RS, a sports tourer. Then came what many BMW enthusiasts see as the definitive tourer, the 1996 R1100 RT, which offered more weather protection, great luggage capacity, and a softer ride. BMW claims 204km/h (127mph) for the RT and 219km/h (136mph) for the RS. Even faster is the 227km/h (141mph) R1100 S, which, although BMW's sportiest bike ever, is still capable of touring. All feature shaft final drive.

## SHAFT FINAL DRIVE

This last feature is worth some consideration, for BMW was at the forefront of bringing this system into bike technology. The shaft final drive system for motorcycles was patented in 1897 by the German Alois Wolfmüller of Munich, after one of his employees Ludwig Rüb had invented it. Rüb, a former engineer at the Hildebrand & Wolfmüller motorcycle works, paved the way for subsequent designs with a longitudinally fitted driveshaft.

Rüb's designs, which never left the drawing board, were themselves based on the Belgian FN shaft-drive bicycles.

Indeed, at the beginning of the 20th century, FN became the first manufacturer successfully to apply the shaft-drive concept (which never quite made it with the pedal cycle) to motorcycles. In 1922, the shaft-drive returned to the city of Munich, thanks to BMW, when their chief, Franz Josef Popp, took the decision to begin motorcycle manufacture, resulting in the Max Friz–designed R23 flat twin with shaft final drive. The Friz concept featured a straight drive train, with the crankshaft, transmission shaft, and propeller shaft aligned in a row, facing towards the rear-wheel drive.

This early drive concept, with its shaft to the rear wheel, was referred to as the 'cardan drive'. Originally inspired by the Italian scholar Geronimo Cardano (1501–76), this form of power transmission had never before been considered in the context of a motorcycle. Cardano had invented the 'cardan suspension' for compasses and the same principle was subsequently

used for driveshaft joints. Early motorcycles, such as BMW's R32, did not require such joints because they had rigid frames without any rear-wheel suspension. A rubber disc was quite sufficient as a shock absorber.

Fourteen years after the debut of the R32, the flow of power to the rear wheel did require the use of a joint. At that time, BMW racers already featured a competition-only ohc engine with a supercharger, which had become so powerful that, to retain rider control, rear-wheel suspension was needed. So, in 1937, BMW's factory racers were equipped with a form of plunger rear suspension. The driveshaft thus required a universal joint (UJ). The following year, BMW introduced this technology into several of its production roadsters.

The first idea for further refining the BMW concept came in the 1950s, when, in 1954, Dipl. Ing. Alex von Falkenhausen (the designer of the first rear-wheel suspension in the mid-

**The first Moto Guzzi California was built in the early 1970s. In the summer of 1997, its concept was brought up to date with the introduction of the EV (Evolution). Boasting some 150 individual refinements, both large and small, it is a great touring bike.**

1930s) took up a proposal made by Helmut Werner Bönsch. He patented a pivoted rear-wheel drive housing with a driving-force support. Soon this gained its first working experience in the 1955 world championship, on a bike ridden by Walter Zeller.

The next update came thanks to BMW's involvement in off-road sport at the end of the 1970s. The problem with the shaft-drive system that was then in use was that the rear wheel would 'lift up'. This was solved in 1981, when, with the introduction of the new R80G/S, BMW again revolutionised the driveshaft concept by introducing the Monolever single swinging arm. The design team had been able to come up with a joint able to work efficiently

without play or distortion, even under the most arduous off-road conditions.

Developments made by BMW engineers René Hinsberg and Horst Brenner were reflected by a pattern registered in November 1983. The final design was a direct consequence of these developments: the Paralever double-joint swinging arm was made of cast aluminium and fitted to the four-cylinder K100 from 1983 onwards. A new refined version of the driveshaft debuted in 1987. Just as the R80G/S had been BMW's first model with the Monolever in 1980, the new enduro models R80GS and R100GS marked progress with the new Paralever. The K1 was the first K-series machine to feature this unique technology. Today, all BMW twins and fours use the device. Although other manufacturers have used, and still use, shaft final drive, it is BMW which has consistently pushed its development forwards.

## OTHER EUROPEAN OFFERINGS

Turning back to European touring bikes, British hopes are carried by the Hinckley-based Triumph concern. It currently lists four sports-touring models: the Trophy 900, Trophy 1200, Sprint ST, and Sprint RS. For many informed observers, the Sprint ST is the best sports tourer in the world, with its 955cc three-cylinder 12-valve engine putting out 110bhp at 9000rpm and capable of reaching 251km/h (156mph). The Sprint RS costs less and has 7bhp and 4mph less, but is just as capable as the ST. The two remaining Triumphs, the Trophies, have been around for some time and are beginning to show their age, a major failing being the fact that they tend to be top-heavy. In addition, with 212km/h (132mph) for the 1200 and 209km/h (130mph) for the 900, they are considerably slower.

Although many may view the Moto Guzzi California more as a custom

**At the end of 1996, the Italian Ducati marque shocked the biking world by launching its ST2 (Sport Touring two-valve) V-twin. Powered by a 944cc liquid-cooled Desmo 90 degree V-twin engine, it instantly made its mark and was soon joined by the 916-engined ST4.**

cruiser, this would be to do it a major disservice, as its real forte is serious touring. The 1064cc overhead-valve 90-degree V-twin, two-valves-per-cylinder engine can trace its ancestry back to the original 700cc V7 of the mid-1960s, but a major advantage of this long pedigree is virtually bullet-proof mechanical components and spare parts availability. All models now come with electronic fuel injection. This has cleaned up the big twin's low-down running and starting, so it is now able to perform with the best of them. The handling is good, too, with more ground clearance than one has a right to expect. There are currently two versions: the extensively fitted EV1100 with vast panniers, a usefully comprehensive screen, and masses of chrome and stainless steel, plus the stripped 'economy' version known as the Jackal. Costing almost a third less than the EV, it offers excellent value for money.

At the end of 1996, Ducati surprised motorcyclists everywhere when it introduced its own purpose-built touring model, the ST2 (Sport Touring 2 valve). Powered by a 944cc liquid-cooled 90-degree V-twin engine, the newcomer immediately made an impact on the sports touring sales sector, almost overnight challenging Honda's class-leading VFR for top spot. Supporting the engine was an updated Ducati trademark steel-trellis frame (pioneered on the Pantah 500SL back in 1979), inverted forks, triple Brembo Gold Line brakes, a comprehensive fairing and colour-coded matching panniers. Although only available with chain final drive, the Sport Touring Ducati did benefit from the excellent Weber-Marelli fuel injection, similar to that found on the 916 Superbike.

At the end of 1998, Ducati took its sports touring theme a stage further by

**The ST4 arrived at the end of 1998 and took Ducati's ST theme a quantum leap forward by slotting in the 4-valve-per-cylinder 916 engine into a lightly modified ST2 chassis. The result was sensational with the combination of superbike performance and touring practicality.**

introducing the ST4, a marriage of the ST2 chassis (suitably modified) with the four-valves-per-cylinder dohc fuel-injected engine from the 916. The result was a superb, if bland-looking, motorcycle, capable of hitting 257km/h (160mph), for touring two-up in comfort. For the 2001 model year, Ducati introduced an even more potent device, the ST4 S, using a de-tuned 996cc engine, which produced 117bhp and could reach 266km/h (165mph).

Italian pace-setter Aprilia has also joined the sport-touring scene, with the new SL1000 Falco, a 106bhp version of its RSV Mille Superbike, which is best described as more sports than tourer. However, this is likely to be followed, if successful, by a more focused version.

On the face of it, the performance-touring market is a straight fight between Japan and Europe. Who is the winner? This cannot be decided, as both parties offer their own blend of motorcycle. It also depends on priorities such as whether you demand shaft final drive instead of chain, ultimate handling or comfort as a priority, and of course how fast you want to go! The decision is yours.

## CATALYTIC CONVERTER

During the late 1980s, BMW became the first motorcycle manufacturer to offer customers the chance to own a machine with a fully controlled three-way 'cat' (on the K100 series); today, the company has extended this to include many of its products, including both 'K' and 'R' series bikes.

As in the automobile industry, BMW was quick to see the 'green' benefits of fitting a catalytic converter to ensure cleaner exhaust emissions. The cat works through the processes of conversion, reduction, and oxidation. The stochiometric ratio between the amount of fuel actually supplied and the amount of fuel theoretically required is based on an air/fuel mixture of 14:1. To maintain this mixture, regardless of running conditions, the oxygen sensor (sometimes also referred to as the Lambda probe) measures the amount of oxygen in the exhaust gas emitted by the engine.

In the three-way catalytic converter employed by BMW, the expensive metals required for oxidation

(platinum and palladium) and reduction (rhodium) are applied to a metal substrate. Oxidation converts carbon monoxide into carbon dioxide, and hydrocarbons into carbon dioxide and water. The withdrawal of oxygen then allows the breakdown of nitric oxides into nitrogen and carbon dioxide.

In comparison to a ceramic-based catalytic converter, the metallic converter offers advantages in terms of both space and time. Not only is it smaller, but it also responds more quickly, since the metal substrate is more efficient than a ceramic one in absorbing the heat from the exhaust gas.

At the end of its working life, the BMW-fitted catalytic converter is recyclable, again an important 'green' consideration. Other manufacturers have already begun to follow BMW's example. In the near future, bikes will no doubt follow the automobile industry's example of making a 'cat' standard fitment throughout the industry.

# CLASSIC BIKES

There has always been a fascination with motorcycles from a bygone era, a trend which has grown strongly since the late 1970s. What was once the preserve of the ultra-enthusiastic few has grown into a cult following of millions all around the world. And the most coveted of all classic bikes are the performance models, with famous names such as the postwar BSA Gold Star and Triumph Bonneville, and latter day classics including the Honda CB750, Kawasaki Z1, Moto Guzzi Le Mans, and Ducati 900SS.

Running parallel to the progression of modern motorcycle technology has been a growing fascination for bikes of previous generations. In the past two decades, however, the historic motorcycle market has seen a complete transformation. The classic bike movement has now grown to represent a whole new, flourishing industry. What was once the preserve of specialist engineers and amateurs lovingly rebuilding the dream bikes of their youth has developed into a worldwide phenomenon in countries as far apart as the USA, Japan, UK, Germany, Australia, and just about every other nation on earth. It has also been responsible for creating a market in which old motorcycles are often valued more highly than new motorcycles, bikes for the first time being

**The Kawasaki Z1 from 1973 established the Japanese company as builders of high performance motorcycles. The heart of the machine was a dohc air-cooled 4-cylinder engine producing 82 bhp and 210km/h (130mph).**

seen as a genuine investment. Luckily, most bikes are still owned by enthusiasts first, speculators second. Long may this state of play continue.

So what defines a classic motorcycle? In the context of this book and the industry itself, a classic bike is one built since the end of World War II, with the cut-off creeping in to include some early 1980s machines, before models such as the Suzuki GSX-R750, Kawasaki ZZ-R1100, and Honda CBR600 arrived. But who is to forecast what a classic may mean in the year 2020 – probably those three bikes to begin with!

Bikes built before World War II are referred to as either veteran or vintage, depending on age, which is generally defined by World War I. Veteran motorcycles (also known as pioneers) came before the conflict; vintage thereafter. It would be true to say that the classic scene arrived at the end of the 1970s. This came following a surge of interest in British machines from the 1940s, 1950s, and 1960s, in particular. In the 1970s, bikes of these eras were still available at very low prices. People who had been in their twenties during these

**One of the most famous model names in motorcycling history, Triumph's long-running Bonneville debuted in 1959. The first model was the 649cc T120. This featured twin Amal Monobloc carbs and 46bhp. A separate chrome Lucas headlamp and new chassis arrived in 1960 (shown).**

decades had money to spare to indulge the re-creation of their youth. Yet, as the decades roll on, more and more bikes fall into the classic category.

Two examples of what are generally seen as classics of their own eras are the BSA Gold Star and the Kawasaki GPZ900R, but this is only the tip of the iceberg. It is impossible, in a book aimed at the high-performance motorcycle of today and the immediate past, to do anything other than attempt to select the true classics from 1945 until the early 1980s.

### GREAT BRITAIN
In terms of motorcycling, there always used to be a 'Great' in front of Britain. This accolade was earnt over the first half century of the motorcycle's existence with some truly great achievements,

with great marques, great men (both designers and riders), and great bikes. Then, as Bert Hopwood's well-known book *Whatever happened to the British Motorcycle Industry?* recalls, things went wrong in a big way.

During the first half of the 20th century, Britain largely ruled the motorcycle industry, as it had done in the previous century with its Navy. World War II did not stop this trend, at least not in the early postwar years. When hostilities ended in 1945, the British economy was at a low ebb and virtually everything manufactured in the first four or five years of peacetime went for export, notably motor vehicles, which of course included motorcycles. By 1950, however, the tide had begun to turn and, for the first time since 1939, British motorcyclists were able to buy a new gleaming bike of their own.

In 1950, Britain had a thriving motorcycle industry with an almost never-ending list of manufacturers, including AMC (AJS and Matchless), the BSA Group (BSA, Triumph, Sunbeam, and Ariel), Douglas, Norton Panther, Royal Enfield, Velocette, and Vincent, not to mention scores of smaller marques such as Cotton, DMW, Dot, Excelsior, Francis Barnett, James New, Hudson, Scott, and Sun.

BSA not only controlled the most powerful grouping, but at that time the BSA was the best-selling motorcycle in the world. From BSA came not only Gold Star singles, but also pre-unit motorcycles (separate engine and transmission) in the shape of its 497cc A7 Star Twin and 646cc A10 Golden Flash. Later, the company developed higher performance versions, including the A7 Shooting Star, A10 Road Rocket, Super Rocket, and finally, in 1962, the Rocket Gold Star.

In September 1949, the first three production models of Triumph's new 649cc Thunderbird made headlines by each running at more than 148km/h (92mph) average for 800km (500 miles) and then doing a flying lap at more than 160km/h (100mph) at the Montlhéry circuit just outside Paris. The Thunderbird had been developed from Edward Turner's masterpiece, the

# TURBO-CHARGING

The purpose of a turbo-charger is to make use of the large amount of energy carried away by exhaust gases. This energy, readily available when an engine is under load and exhaust flow is high, is utilised to force a higher volume of air through the engine, increasing its effective displacement. Thus turbo-charging delivers extra power from an engine in the middle and high rpm ranges.

The general advantages of this are obvious in that a given amount of power can be extracted from a relatively small, light engine and, when extra power is not needed, it can be run economically at relatively low rpm. Except for prototypes and small batch productions, it was only the Japanese who attempted to exploit the turbo for standard production models. But the Japanese factories applied the technology in different ways from the simple to the ultra-complex, with mixed results.

Suzuki and Yamaha placed turbos behind their across-the-frame four-cylinder engines, which made routing of the exhaust pipes relatively easy, but had the disadvantage of increasing response time because the turbo was some considerable distance from the exhaust ports. Meanwhile, Honda placed the turbo near the exhaust ports of its CX V-twin models, but high in the frame, contributing to an already high centre of gravity.

To combat turbo lag, some manufacturers (including several in the automobile industry) have used reed intake valves to bypass the turbo until boost pressure surpasses atmospheric pressure. The intention is to let the engines run efficiently without boost; however, because of relatively low compression ratios, power output is still less than it would be with non–turbocharged engine.

Of the big four Japanese motorcycle marques, Kawasaki was to be the most successful – it took things a stage further. To eliminate the low-rpm bypass found on early prototypes, the

Kawasaki engineers shortened the induction path as much as possible by placing the air filter near the engine sprocket. The result was to show four positive outcomes: first, minimal lag between the time the exhaust gas leaves the ports and starts driving the turbine; second, minimal loss of heat energy in the turbo system; third, a relatively low centre of gravity; and, fourth, heat isolated from the rider.

The Kawasaki turbo-charging system was protected by a waste-gate which passed exhaust gas around the turbo if boost pressure reached 560mm (22.04in) Hg. As a further safety measure, the DFI (digital fuel injection) system cut off fuel supply to the engine if boost reached dangerous levels. The engine should run at tick-over for 30 seconds before switching off.

As a rider aid, Kawasaki fitted their production 750 Turbo of the mid-1980s with an LCD boost display.

**All four Japanese manufacturers – Honda, Yamaha, Suzuki, and Kawasaki – produced high-performance turbo bikes during the 1980s. Kawasaki's 750 was the best. Of vital importance on all turbo models is the need for regular oil changes.**

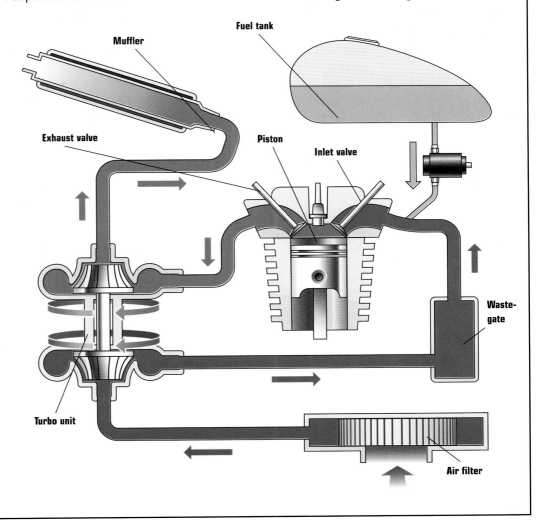

Speed Twin, which had first appeared in 1937 to such acclaim. Like their BSA counterparts, there were several high-performance versions of both the Speed Twin and Thunderbird developed during the 1950s and 1960s. These included the 500cc Tiger 100 (T100), the 650cc Tiger 110 (T110), and the most famous of them all, the T120 (Bonneville).

The Bonneville took its name from the Bonneville Salt Flats in Utah, a venue with a worldwide reputation for speed record attempts. First offered in 1959, the Bonneville is one of the all-time great performance bikes. From its launch until the end of 1962, it was built in pre-unit form; thereafter, the engine, gearbox, and clutch were housed in a common crankcase and known as the unit Bonneville. Very approximately, Triumph's 100, 110, and 120 prefixes referred to their maximum speeds in miles per hour. Later, during the 1970s and 1980s, the Bonneville was sold as the T140, but this did not relate to its maximum speed, which was little changed from the original.

The Bonneville was hugely popular in North America and was raced in the USA both on tarmac and dirt, and used as a record breaker and for endurance races. Meanwhile, in Europe, it was used in endurance events such as the Thruxton 500 race in Great Britain (which it won several times) and won

**The 1960 Triumph T120 Bonneville was the top twin-cylinder performance bike of its day, being able to reach 177km/h (110mph). Besides being an excellent choice for fast road work, the Bonneville was also successful in production-class racing, including the Thruxton 500-miler.**

the Production TT on a regular basis. It is also one of the longest-running bike models ever, with it being built at Triumph's Meridan plant from 1959 until its final closure in 1983 (by then the plant was run by a workers' cooperative). Production was then restarted at Newton Abbot, Devon (UK), thanks to Les Harris in 1985 and in 1989, before being 'relaunched' in 2001 in an updated, completely redesigned form by John Bloor's new Hinkley Triumph operation.

## THE NORTON FACTORY

Unlike its BSA and Triumph rivals, Norton was slow to develop new models after the war, even though on the Grand Prix race circuit it was often unbeatable during the same period. In fact, many questioned whether the company was neglecting its production side, in order to seek glories on the track. The first Norton twin, and in fact its first postwar new bike, was the Model 7 of 1948. This, like the later Dominator 88, used a 497cc pre-unit

engine. Next in 1956 came the 77 and 99, with a 596cc power plant.

The 88 and 99 were really sporting high-performance versions with the famous race-developed Featherbed frame (first used by the factory's team riders, including Geoff Duke and Artie Bell). In 1960, the engine grew even more to 646cc to become the 650 model. The more sporting twin-carb 650SS arrived together with a twin-carb 88SS the following year. Both these were, like their Triumph counterparts, very successful in both long-distance and sports-machine races of the day. A specially developed 88 – the Domiracer – finished third in the 1961 Senior Isle of Man TT and, in the process, lapped the famous 61km (37.73-mile) mountain circuit at more than 160km/h (100mph).

Later still came an even larger engined bike, the Atlas, which was built from 1962 to 1968 and introduced the 745cc engine (still pre-unit) employed on the 750 Commando from 1967 to 1973. Finally, there was the 850 Commando, with its 829cc engine size.

---

## OTHER BRITISH MANUFACTURERS

Turning away from the BSA group, AJS and Matchless – both part of the AMC (Associated Motor Cycles) empire – built a range of parallel twins from late 1948, coded Model 20 (AJS) and G9 (Matchless). AMC badly needed a twin-cylinder presence following the Triumph lead in 1937. BSA and Ariel had been quick to bring models out just after World War II and were followed in 1948 by Norton and Royal Enfield. The heart of the AMC 'modular' twin (essentially the Model 20 and G9 were the same except for badge engineering) was the basic layout of the British overhead-valve parallel twin, with both pistons moving together dictated by the magneto, then considered mandatory. The AMC variant was different in that it had a third, central main bearing between the two crankshaft throws. It also had separate heads and barrels, and gear-driven camshafts fore and aft.

The Model 20/G9 engine had a displacement of 498cc, which, as with its main rivals, saw steady enlargement over the life span of the AMC. The first increase came with a special 550cc model for the USA (1954–1955), before AMC engineers enlarged the motor to 593cc for the 1956 season. In 1958 came a bigger 646cc engine size, before the final incarnation of the AMC parallel-twin theme, the 745cc. The latter was something of a cheat, as in fact it was a Norton engine, AMC having swallowed up the Birmingham company during the 1950s, before moving Norton to

**Using the famous Featherbed frame developed from its racing models, Norton's 88 and 99 twins were not only fast, but also handled and braked better than most rival marques. Outwardly identical, the 88 displaced 497cc, the 99 597cc.**

**The Norton Commando ran for a decade from the late 1960s until the late 1970s. The first Commandos used a 745cc engine size, while the bike illustrated is a 1974 829cc 850 Roadster with Lockheed hydraulic disc front brake. Maximum speed was 200km/h (125mph).**

AMC's Plumstead headquarters in 1962. The performance version of the 'real' AMC engine was the 646cc AJS 31CSR/ Matchless G12CSR, which had a performance equalling that of the BSA Super Rocket, Triumph Bonneville and Norton 650SS.

The first Royal Enfield parallel twin of the postwar generation was the 495cc 500 twin, which was announced in late 1948. As with the other British parallel twins of the era, the crankcases split vertically and the valves were pushrod operated. The last of the 500cc Enfield twins was the Meteor Sports Twin, production of which finally ceased in 1963. The first of the performance twins from Royal Enfield, however, was the 692cc Constellation, which the company proudly boasted '700cc 50bhp'. This ran from 1958 to 1963. The second performance twin, the even bigger and more powerful 736cc Interceptor, was built between 1962 and the early 1970s. The Constellation and Interceptor were, together with Norton's Atlas, the largest capacity British twins of the 1960s.

Famous for its legendary Square Four Ariel was another UK manufac- turer to build a series of parallel twins. After the war, British firms such as Ariel needed a twin as a priority to compete with Triumph. In this, Ariel possessed a couple of advantages. First was the existence of cycle parts which could take the size, weight, and power of the four, which meant the company had the option of using single or four components for the chassis and knowing it would all work. Secondly, an initial design study by design chief Val Page had been carried out during the war so that Ariel had a running prototype as early as 1944.

Page had copied Triumph's capacity of 499cc and, when Ariel launched its 'new' bike in November 1947, there were actually two versions, the KG500 tourer and the more sporting KH500 Red Hunter. The Red Hunter was also later produced with an all-alloy engine, which could reach 145km/h (90mph) – for the period (1953), this matched all but Triumph's ultra-sporting Tiger 100. The year 1954 saw the introduction of the FH Huntmaster. The newcomer was able to use what amounted to a lightly re-engineered BSA A10 engine and thus shared the latter's 647cc.

Apart from the parallel twins, the majority of British postwar performance bikes were singles, the exceptions being the BSA and Triumph triples of the late 1960s and early 1970s, and the HRD Vincent V-twin. There is no doubt that the best – and fastest – big British singles (which actually meant 350 or 500cc)

were the BSA Gold Star; Norton International (the only one with an overhead camshaft engine, except purebred racing bikes); and Velocette Viper, Venom, and Thruxton. Others deserving an honourable mention are the Ariel Red Hunter, Royal Enfield Bullet, and the HRD Vincent Comet. The AMC singles from AJS and Matchless were also decent motorcycles, but with no real performance tendencies.

If we were to select just three, they would have to be the BSA DBD500 Gold Star Clubmans, the Norton Featherbed-framed 500 International, and the Velocette Thruxton. All three could touch, even exceed, 177km/h (110mph), which for a road-legal single-cylinder heavyweight was an excellent achievement. These three also had the advantage of a race-developed chassis, so it was not just speed, but also the overall package which made them such outstanding examples of their genre. As for power output figures, these differed between the three and, in some cases, from bike to bike. Yet 40bhp is a sensible figure for this trio of 500cc singles. In blueprinted, stripped, and tuned form, each was capable of exceeding the 40bhp output figure.

## BSA GOLD STAR

Of all the above motorbikes, one deserves special consideration. Few motorcycles can be everything to everyone, but the famous BSA Gold Star – the 'Goldie' to its legion of fans – came as close as it is possible to get. A 160km/h (100mph) lap at Brooklands, clubman's racing, scrambling (motor-cars), trials, street bike – the Goldie could cope with almost anything. Today, however, it is remembered most for its role as a café racer, an icon of 1960s youth, the ultimate performance machine of the rockers' era.

The Gold Star's original concept goes way back to 1937 when, on the final day of June, the famous TT rider Wal Handley won a coveted Brooklands Gold Star for lapping the legendary Surrey (UK) banked track at more than 160km/h (100mph) on a 500cc iron-engined BSA Empire Star, specially tuned for Jack Amott and Len Crisp to

# DESMODROMICS

Only Ducati and car giants Mercedes Benz have managed to exploit fully the desmodromic positive-valve system. Coined from two Greek words meaning 'controlled run', its mechanical principle is the concept of eliminating one of the chief dangers of valve operation at ultra-high engine revolutions – the phenomenon of valve float or 'bounce'. This occurs when the valve springs are unable to respond quickly enough to close the valves back onto their seats. The desmodromic principle replaces the springs with a mechanical closing system much like that employed to open them, thus providing a positive action.

Although this theory had been around since the pioneering days of the internal combustion engine, making it work successfully was an entirely different matter indeed. One of the first examples to be tested appeared at the French automobile Grand Prix of 1914, when the Delage concern fielded a form of positive valve operation, which the French referred to as *desmodromique*. Many others tried during the 1920s, including Norton, but without any real success.

Then came the 1950s, when Mercedes used the system in its W196 racing car and Ducati also applied the system via the genius of Ing. Fabio Taglioni. Taglioni had joined Ducati in the spring of 1954 and his first machine to use the desmodromic system (which Ducati has since shortened to Desmo) made a victorious debut in the now 124cc triple-camshaft single, which won first time out in the 1956 Swedish GP. In the late 1960s, Ducati became the only manufacturer of motorcycles (and for that matter cars) to put a Desmo engine into series production. At first, this was used in its existing range of bevel overhead-camshaft singles, but its use has slowly spread to include all Ducati's current range of production and racing models. This includes the factory World Superbike Championship winners, too.

**Only Ducati and car giants Mercedes Benz have successfully harnessed Desmodromic valve operation. This is a process in which the valves are both open and shut mechanically, using two rockers per valve. Today, all Ducati motorcycles are so equipped.**

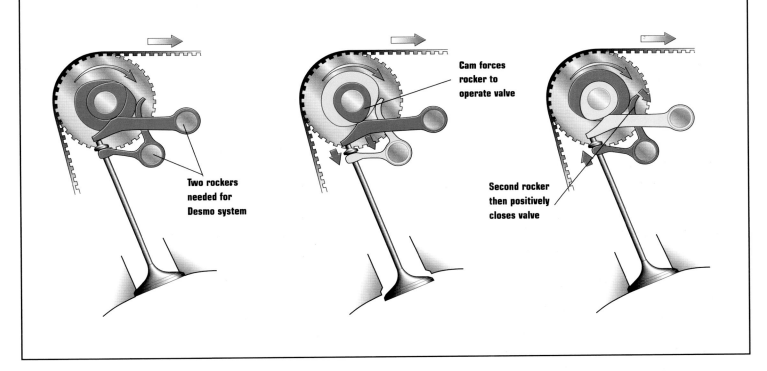

Cam forces rocker to operate valve

Two rockers needed for Desmo system

Second rocker then positively closes valve

run on methanol. In fact, Handley's race-winning average speed was 164.58km/h (102.27mph), with a best lap of 169.89km/h (105.57mph). This outstanding performance resulted in the Empire Star title being dropped in favour of Gold Star for the 1938 model year.

Three production versions were offered: standard, competition, and

pure racer. Light alloy was used for the cylinder barrel and head with screw-in valve seats, and the pushrod tower was an integral part of the castings. A racing-type Amal TT carburettor was standardised and, most surprising of all, the gearbox shell was cast in magnesium alloy. For the following year, the gearbox shell reverted to alu-

minium, but there was the advantage of an optional close-ratio cluster.

The 1939 Gold Star was the last for nine long years. The outbreak of World War II meant that production requirements were no longer for consumer use – not even such superb sportsters as the BSA single – but instead for military purposes. In BSA's case, this meant the

side-valve M20 model. After the war, in a transport-starved world, the factory concentrated on satisfying demand by building cheap-to-build, cheap-to-run B31 and B33 models, which benefited from the use of telescopic front forks, but still featured a rigid frame. A competition version, the B32, fitted with an iron engine, was offered for trials use.

The next development in the Gold Star evolution came in late 1948, when high-performance versions of the B31/33 range were announced, rather than direct descendants of the pre-war M24 Gold Star model. The 350 (348cc) version featured an alloy barrel and head; it was known as the ZB32. These engines were of the long-stroke type, with internal dimensions of 71 x 88mm (2.79 x 3.46in). At this stage, although a 500 was planned, it was not actually authorised for production. Based on the 350, but with a larger 85mm (3.34in) bore, the 500 (coded B34) finally entered production for the 1950 model year. Its power output of 33bhp gave a maximum speed of more than 144.8km/h (90mph) in full road trim. The 350 put out 25bhp and was good for around 136.79 (85mph).

It should be remembered that, in those days, 'pool' petrol was the norm, a fuel with a very low octane rating. The chassis had also received attention and, from the first production ZB32 of 1949, plunger rear suspension replaced the rigid frame of the early postwar standard models. Another improvement was in stopping power, thanks to a brand-new 200mm (8in) front brake. The 350s, in particular, had become successful not only in off-road sport, but also in clubman's racing, too; the Clubman's TT was organised to allow machines such as the Gold Star a chance to take Isle of Man glory. With supercharging banned by the sports governing body, the FIM production class racing was another option open to the Goldie. Strangely, the bike proved too successful for its own good, winning the Clubman's TT every year from 1949 until 1956, when the race was finally axed. Meanwhile, proving the versatility of the design, the BSA works scrambles and trials teams were also proving virtually unbeatable.

On the production front, the engines brought in detailed changes for 1951, including die-cast cylinder heads and

**The legendary BSA Gold Star Clubmans, with either a 348 or 499cc ohv single cylinder engine. During the 1950s, these dominated the Isle of Man Clubman's TT races to such an extent the class was axed. The model then became a café racer in the 1960s.**

barrels, and the introduction of bolt-on rocker boxes. The following year, 1952, saw the BB32 with several mechanical changes. Valve angles were changed from 37 to 33 degrees and both inlet and exhaust valve diameters were increased, and their ports opened up to match. To take advantage of this, a larger Amal TT9 carburettor was fitted. A test of the new BB32 in *Motor Cycling* magazine found the top speed to be an impressive 158km/h (98mph) and commented: 'The engine appeared to have no vices at all, beautifully smooth, it ran cleaning up from about 4300 rpm to over 7000 rpm.'

### SWINGING-ARM REAR SUSPENSION

When the 1953 model range was announced, BSA revealed that the Gold Star models were to be considerably revised. Under the B prefix, the new machines featured duplex cradle frames and swinging-arm rear suspension. Swinging-arm rear suspension was one of motorcycling's more significant technical advances. It is generally accepted that the Ulsterman (Northern Ireland) Rex MacCandless was responsible for inventing the swinging-arm form of rear suspension. Developed in Belfast during World War II, it was originally referred to as the 'spring heel'.

Prior to the arrival of swinging-arm twin-shock rear suspension, riders were forced to put up with either rigid frames with sprung saddles or plunger rear suspension, which was quite often completely undamped and hardly any improvement over the rigid set-up. With swinging arm and two hydraulically operated shock absorbers, the rider was not only given a much increased level of comfort, but also control of his machine.

The swinging arm worked on the principle of leverage. At the front, just after the engine assembly, was the pivot, usually a specially strengthened steel pin which passed from one side of the machine to the other and operated on a series (usually two) of bushes. These bushes were usually manufactured from phosphor bronze, but sometimes fibre or plastic was used. Additionally, silent-bloc (rubber/metal) bushes have been used, but these allow the pin and swinging arm a certain amount of flex, which is detrimental to the handling and road-holding of the motorcycle. From the early 1980s, the conventional two-shock swinging-arm set-up has been gradually supplanted by the more modern monoshock variety.

Returning to the Gold Star, in 1951, the CB arrived, distinguished by its massive engine finning. This motor had a shorter con-rod and oval flywheel to clear the piston. Valve adjustment was carried out by an eccentric rocker spindle to cut down on reciprocating weight and an Amal GP carb was

**BSA Gold Star engine with its massive, heavily finned aluminium cylinder head and barrel. The 499cc version was fitted with an Amal GP carburettor. Producing 40bhp at 7000rpm, it could achieve 180km/h (112mph) with a silencer, or 187km/h (116mph) with a racing megaphone.**

## 500 GOLD STAR (1956)

**Engine:** 4-stroke, vertical single, ohv, 2-valves-per-cylinder, air-cooled
**Bore & stroke:** 85 x 88mm (3.3 x 3.4in)
**Displacement:** 499cc
**Compression ratio:** 8:1
**Carburation:** Amal GP 1.5in
**Ignition:** Magneto
**Lubrication:** Dry sump
**Gearbox:** 4-speed close ratio (RRT2)
**Clutch:** Wet, multi-plate
**Frame:** Double cradle, all steel construction
**Suspension:**
  *Front:* telescopic, fully enclosed
  *Rear:* swinging arm, twin shock
**Brakes:**
  *Front:* 190mm (7.48in) full-width drum
  *Rear:* 177.8mm (7in), single-sided drum
**Tyres:** 482.6mm (19in) front and rear
**Dry weight:** 705.4kg (320lb)
**Power:** 40bhp at 7000 rpm (with megaphone 42bhp)
**Top speed:** 180km/h (112mph) silencer 187km/h (116 mph) megaphone

# THE WANKEL ENGINE

Felix Wankel is today credited with the invention of the Wankel engine; however, a similar unit had appeared as the British Beaumont as far back as 1938, although, with the onset of war, development of this particular project was shelved. Also, if you call the Wankel a revolving-piston engine – a rotary engine – then several others existed as prototypes as early as 1886. Whatever the arguments, it was Felix Wankel (together with his sponsor, the German NSU company) who achieved the first commercial application of the concept and therefore occupies an important place in motoring history.

NSU's first contact with Dr Wankel came in 1951 and, throughout the remainder of the 1950s, Wankel and NSU slowly developed the design. NSU built a number of cars, including the RO80 which ultimately caused the company's financial collapse, but, as far as two wheels go, Wankel and NSU sold patents for the design to other companies, notably Sachs (Hercules), Suzuki, and Norton. Although often referred to as a rotary engine, the Wankel had nothing in common with this engine type other than the process of internal combustion. This takes place in an epitrochoidal chamber.

By the time the final engine types were made by Hercules, Suzuki, and Norton from the mid-1970s, the rotor seals had embraced the advantages of ceramics technology. The revolving rotor performed all the usual four-stroke cycle of operations – induction, compression, expansion, exhaust – uncovering various ports as it rotated. In fact, each face of the rotor is simultaneously going through part of the operational cycle, with one face in the middle of compression while the next is beginning the exhaust

**The German inventor, Dr Felix Wankel, together with NSU, were responsible for the engine bearing his name. But the potential of the Wankel engine was never fully realised due to early rotor tip failure at high fuel consumption.**

phase and the one behind already beginning the intake of fresh gas. In a piston engine, separate phases of action take place sequentially on the piston's top.

In some respects, a Wankel engine is closer to a two-stroke. Here the designer has to compromise the port timing to achieve optimum results, but the Wankel has considerable overlap of the functions going on inside its working chamber at any time. Fresh gas enters at 2 o'clock, compression begins just before 12 and reaches its peak at 9 o'clock, combustion starts at 9 and continues between 5 and 4 o'clock when the rotor uncovers the exhaust port and the exhaust phase begins. Thus the Wankel should be correctly termed a rotary combustion engine.

Unfortunately, after all the high hopes, only two manufacturers were truly successful with the Wankel engine: Mazda on four wheels and Norton on two. Even they were unable to defeat the its biggest drawback – a thirst for fuel greater than the conventional internal engine – so the Wankel has slowly faded from the scene, a somewhat sad end to a concept which, in the 1950s and 1960s, seemed to promise so much.

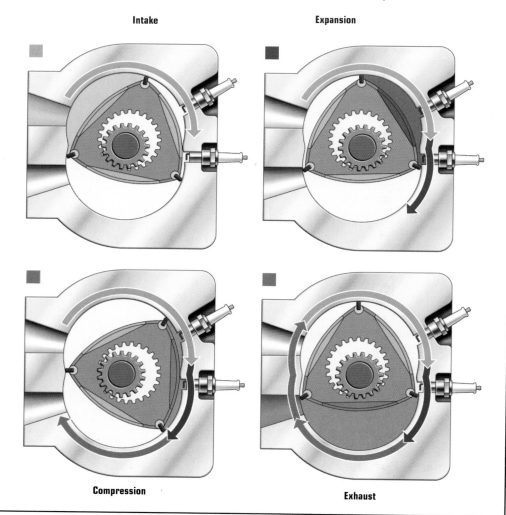

Intake

Expansion

Compression

Exhaust

specified for the first time. Power was increased to 30bhp at 6800 rpm on the 350, while the 500 kicked out 37bhp at 6600 rpm. Other changes included a timed engine breather, EN36 crankpin and Nimonic 80 exhaust valve, and, at last, for the first time, the Clubman version came with clip-on handlebars as standard equipment. The 1960s café racer's basic formula had arrived.

Under revised ACU regulations for the Clubman's TT, machines had to be equipped with lighting sets, speedometer and an efficient (!) silencer. The new DB Gold Star debuted for 1955 and utilised a standard Lucas Magdyno and battery, a larger Lucas headlamp, and a tubular silencer filled with glass wool; the latter item was manufactured for the Burgess concern.

Virtually the final stage of the Gold Star's development came in 1956 with the introduction of a 190mm (7.48in) front brake and a 1.5in GP carburettor for the 500, which pumped out 42bhp at 7000rpm. That year also saw a double Clubman's TT victory session, thanks to Lincolnshire rider Bernard Codd. Codd's average speed for the ultra-demanding 60.71km (37.73-mile) circuit was 138.93km/h (86.33mph), while he averaged 131.99km/h (82.02mph) on the 350. The following year, the 350 was axed, but track success came in the form of a win at Daytona in the 100-miler and at Thruxton in the nine-hour endurance event.

Former Army Captain Eddie Dow had made a name for himself racing the BSA singles, but was even more successful on the business front when his Banbury motorcycle emporium – known as 'Britain's Gold Star Shop' – sprang to fame and fortune selling go-faster accessories for Gold Star models. Besides a range of performance parts, Dow offered other items such as the Lyta polished alloy fuel tank, Taylor Dow front fork conversion, and a host of smaller components such as finned rocker covers and ball-end control levers. Perhaps the most well-known of all the individual Gold Star performance parts, however, was the RRT2 close ratio gearbox, which allowed an amazing 113km/h (70mph) in bottom gear!

With the looks, performance, and handling of a racing bike, the Gold Star went on to become the ultimate street racer. Clip-ons, swept-back exhaust, 'twittering' silencer, and its aggressive appearance all gave the image of a performance bike which other roadsters of the day simply could not hope to match. The poor handling of many of its twin-cylinder rivals helped foster this image.

Of the two engine sizes, the smaller 350 is the more reliable, smoother, and better handling option. However, the 500, in DBD guise, is the one every classic bike enthusiast wants, even though it vibrates and is less reliable. However, on a good day and on a clear, open road – its high first gear makes riding it in heavy traffic an absolute pain – it can still be a truly great performance motorcycle. For all its faults, a good 500 Goldie is still an exhilarating bike to ride and, more than any other bike, it gives a taste of the classic 1960s café racer.

Today, many of the above classic bikes – especially the BSA DBD500 Gold Star Clubmans, the Norton Featherbed-framed 500 International, and the Velocette Thruxton – are hard to find and expensive to buy as pristine,

**The Stevenage-based Vincent concern produced the fastest and most expensive roadgoing motorcycles of its era. This 1950 998cc Series C Rapide could reach 200km/h (125mph). The more highly tuned Black Shadow and Black Lightning versions were quicker still.**

original examples. Strangely, they are much more valuable than their twin-cylinder brothers – except, that is, for the HRD Vincent V-twin.

## HRD VINCENT

Of all the immediate postwar British performance bikes, or at least those that are road legal and thus covered by this book, there is one that stands head and shoulders above the rest and that is the mighty HRD Vincent V-twin.

The original HRD Motors company was set up by TT victor Howard Raymond Davies. HRD built high-quality, sporting motorcycles, using frames built in-house and JAP engines. The Model 90 featured a single-port, 499cc motor, while the more expensive Super Sport came with a twin-port racing unit which could achieve almost 160km/h (100mph). However, HRD could not match profit with the quality of its bikes and hit the financial rocks

Left: Honda's CB750 four, the bike which changed the face of motorcycling and ushered in the era of the modern-day superbike, went on sale in 1969. The original CB750 was powered by a single overhead cam 736.5cc unit construction engine with five-speed gearbox.

Below: The four-pipe CB750 engine produced 67bhp at 8000rpm, giving a top speed of 193km/h (120mph). Other features included horizontally split crankcases, wet multi-plate clutch, 12 volt electrics, and four-pipe exhaust.

during 1927, although the machines continued to be built until 1928. The name and assets were purchased by Ernie Humphries, who in turn sold them to a young Cambridge undergraduate, Philip C. Vincent. The latter had long been an enthusiast of the HRD brand and the bikes he went on to produce became known as HRD Vincents. They featured Vincent's own rear suspension, with a form of cantilever frame and a pair of almost vertically mounted shock absorbers, and were fitted with bought-in Rudge and JAP engines.

HRD Vincent continued to use proprietary engines until a disastrous showing at the 1934 Isle of Man TT, when its JAP motors proved unreliable. This prompted Vincent to seek the services of gifted Australian engineer Phil Irving, and together they designed the 499cc engine for the Series 'A' Vincent. From Vincent's collaboration with Irving came such classic postwar motorcycles as the 500cc Comet and Grey Flash singles and, most notably, the various models powered by the legendary 998cc V-twin engine, including the Rapide, Black Shadow, Black Lightning, and Black Prince. The Vincent V-twin was, in reality, the only true high-performance 'Superbike' of its era, as no other standard production road-legal motorcycle could match its 200-plus km/h (125-plus mph) maximum speed.

## NORTH AMERICA

Postwar motorcycles in the USA meant Harley-Davidson (as its deadly rival Indian was never to recover its pre-war eminence), imports from Europe

(largely meaning Britain, Germany, and Italy), and eventually the massive invasion of the USA by the Japanese steamroller in the 1960s.

Between 1939 and 1945, Harley-Davidson had produced some 88,000 motorcycles for military use. When peace came, just as in Britain, many of these were civilianised for sale to a transport-starved public. The most popular of the ex-military bikes was the WLA45, a 750cc side-valve V-twin featuring interchangeable front and rear wheels, together with footboards and deeply valanced mudguards. The WLA also came with the 'springer' front forks, which were finally discontinued in 1948,

## HONDA CB750 (1969)

**Engine:** 4-stroke across-the-frame four, sohc, 2-valves-per-cylinder, air-cooled
**Bore and stroke:** 61 x 63mm (2.4 x 2.5in)
**Displacement:** 736.5cc
**Compression ratio:** 9:1
**Carburation:** 4 x Keihin 28mm (1.1in)
**Ignition:** Battery/coil
**Lubrication:** Dry sump
**Gearbox:** 5-speed
**Clutch:** Wet, multi-plate
**Frame:** Rectangular section steel tubing, duplex

**Suspension:**
*Front:* telescopic forks with hydraulic damping, internal springs, and rubber gaiters
*Rear:* Twin shock, swinging arm
**Brakes:**
*Front:* Single 296mm (11.7in) hydraulically operated disc
*Rear:* 180mm (7.1in) drum
**Tyres:**
*Front:* 3.25 x 19
*Rear:* 4.00 x 18
**Dry weight:** 217.7kg (480lb)
**Power:** 67bhp at 8000 rpm
**Top speed:** 193km/h (120mph)

the same year that saw the introduction of the new 'panhead' engine.

In 1958, Harley-Davidson introduced the 1200cc Duo-Glide. This featured overhead valves, 12-volt electrics, swinging arm, and several modern

features – well, modern, at least, by Harley-Davidson standards. The Duo-Glide replaced the earlier Hydra-Glide, weighing in at 322kg (710lb) dry, and the newcomer was seen as the Cadillac of motorcycles. It was later developed into the Electra Glide (with electric starter) at the end of the 1960s. The same 1200cc ohv V-twin engine was used to power the more sporting Super Glide. These bikes, together with the 1000cc Sportster, formed the basis of the Milwaukee, Wisconsin, company's output until the late 1970s.

During the same period, Harley-Davidson also built and sold a range of smaller bikes produced at Varese, Italy, and sold in Europe under the Aermacchi brand name. But, as with the Europeans, the Japanese invasion and subsequent introduction of Honda's CB750 four in 1969 was as big a leap for the Americans and Europeans as going to the moon was

**Following Mike Hailwood's famous comeback victory on a Ducati 900 NCR in the 1978 Isle of Man TT, the Bologna factory built and sold the Mike Hailwood Replica from 1979 until 1985. It used an 864 bevel driven Desmo V-twin engine. The 1979 model is shown below.**

for the astronauts that same year. Today, Harley-Davidson builds cruiser and retro bikes, rather than trying to compete with the Japanese and European manufacturers.

## GERMANY

Although Germany, in both the West and the East, built vast numbers of motorcycles during the late 1940s and early 1950s, a major sales recession in West Germany during the late 1950s sounded the death knell for many formerly well-known brands such as Adler, Horex, TWN, and Victoria. Other companies, including Hercules, Keidler, NSU, and Zündapp, had to revert to building either mopeds and scooters, or cars as a means of staying in business. Even BMW was to be affected and, although it had made a speedy recovery with refinements to its range of 250 singles and 500/600cc horizontally opposed twins, it almost went bust in 1959, only being saved by the German banks and the Quandt

family. From that point onwards, BMW was to rely on its cars, rather than its two-wheelers.

Meanwhile, in the regulated East, there were no such problems; the state-owned MZ and Simson marques enjoyed stability for many decades, until the Berlin Wall came down in 1989, when they thereafter experienced a repeat of what happened in the West during the late 1960s. Also, it should be remembered that, although there were many German marques, the vast percentage built small capacity two-strokes. The performance bikes, unlike the British industry during the same period, were only represented by BMW, together with Horex, NSU, and Zündapp. By 1970, this was down to one: BMW. Highlights of that decade's models included the 898cc R90S, which debuted at the 1973 Paris Show exactly 50 years to the month from the launch of the company's first model, the R32, and the full-faired R100RS (980cc) emerged in 1977.

## ITALY

Although Italy had for many years built a succession of high-performance lightweights from the likes of Bianchi, Benelli, Aermacchi, Parilla, MV Agusta, Gilera, and Rumi, only Moto Guzzi and Gilera had built what could be called bigger motorcycles, and even these were 500cc singles such as the Guzzi Falcone and Gilera Saturno. Italy's first really big bike arrived in the mid-1960s in the shape of the Moto Guzzi V7. Few bikes can have had a stranger evolution, as it had its origins – or at least that of its 90-degree ohv engine – in a contract with the Italian army to supply the extraordinary 3 x 3 go-anywhere tractor.

The original 3 x 3 project began in the late 1950s, when the Italian Defence Ministry in Rome came up with a requirement for a go-anywhere, light-weight tractor to operate in virtually any conditions. It was the military authorities who were to play a vital role in transferring the same basic V-twin engine into a motorcycle, when the need arose in the early 1960s for a suitable replacement for its agency fleet of Guzzi flat-single Falcone models. Both the military and police authorities issued tenders.

Work on the original prototype of what was to emerge as the V7

The 1976 981cc dohc Laverda Jota featured an across-the-frame three-cylinder engine and was the first production motorcycle capable of reaching 225km/h (140mph). It had considerable racing success, winning the prestigious Avon Production series.

motorcycle began in 1964. Early the following year, the first examples were being presented for government approval. Even then the Moto Guzzi management and staff realised that here was a machine with a much wider clientele than originally envisaged. The first civilian prototype was displayed to the public during December 1965 at the Milan Show. Hailed immediately

by journalists and show-goers alike as the star exhibit, orders were soon winging their way from all over the world to Guzzi's Lakeside factory at Mandello del Lario in northern Italy.

The V7 took its title from the 703cc of the original series. Other features of the design included shaft final drive and twin-shock rear suspension. But, weighing in at 234kg (515.8lb) and producing only 40bhp, the V7 was no performance bike. Sporting enthusiasts had to wait for the subsequent V7 Sport before Guzzi rightfully claimed its own Superbike. Producing 53bhp at 6300rpm and 201km/h (125mph), the V7 Sport arrived in 1971.

## EARLY DISC BRAKES

The first use of disc brakes on a motorcycle came in 1957, when the famous Maserati automobile firm built an ohv 250cc sports single which utilised the system. This made sure that Maserati at least made it into the history books, even though it ultimately did not make the grade as a bike builder. Then, in 1961, the American Midget Motors Autocycle Co equipped one of their scooter-like machines with a disc brake as an optional extra.

It was to be the Italian Innocenti concern's Lambretta TV175 series 3 scooter, however, which was to be the first powered two-wheeler to be mass-produced with a disc brake. Operating on the front wheel only, this was a mechanically operated device which worked by being pressed onto a full-circle pad and against the rotor via a cable-operated front-brake lever. This rotor was prone to uneven wear or warping if heated by continual use.

Obviously, for higher performance, notably in relation to motorcycles, a fresh approach was needed. This came about in two ways. First, thanks to the Italian Campagnolo Company, a mechanically operated calliper type device was fitted in the mid-1960s to the MV Agusta 600 four and also, experimentally, to the Benelli 250 four-cylinder GP racer.

It was the second option, however, a disc (usually in cast iron) with a calliper which was hydraulically operated by a handlebar-mounted master cylinder, which won the day and is today standard fitment on virtually all motorcycles. At first, this employed two circular pistons mounted within the calliper and being pushed out by hydraulic pressure onto the brake disc. Over the years, the number of pistons has increased and now there are even pistons of different diameters in the same calliper.

By this time, the Italian industry had woken up to the incipient Superbike age, resulting in a string of new models, including the Ducati 750GT and Sport (748cc), MV Agusta 750S (743cc), Laverda 750SF/SFC (744cc), and Benelli 750 Sei (747cc). From these machines were to come some of the really classic Italian bikes – not just of the 1970s, but of any other decade – such as the Ducati 900SS and Mike Hailwood Replica (864cc), MV Agusta America (790cc), Benelli 900 Sei (906cc), Laverda Jota (981cc), and the Moto Guzzi 850 Le Mans (844cc). For many enthusiasts, the 1970s are Italy's golden years of motorcycling.

### JAPAN

Although Japan had produced motorcycles from almost the turn of the 20th century, it was not until the arrival of Soichiro Honda during the late 1940s that things really started to happen. Then, as far as Europe was concerned, it took Grand Prix racing success during the 1960s to show what deeply serious rivals the Japanese were – and by then it was too late.

First news of an impending Japanese onslaught on the position of the high-performance, sporting motorcycle – primarily held at that time by British singles and twins – came in 1964, when a journalist reported on an entirely new 500cc class parallel twin, which he had seen while visiting the Honda works. At that time, many had believed that the Japanese would leave the production of larger displacement bikes to other nations, such as Britain, and would totally limit their efforts to concentrate on the lightweight sector. The newcomer, later to be identified as the Honda CB450, was the very motorcycle the British industry had thought, hoped, and prayed the Japanese would never build. It was, in fact, only to be the start of what would turn out to be a whole series of up-to-the-minute big cube bikes from the Land of the Rising Sun.

By the end of the 1960s, the future was set, thanks very largely to a certain four-cylinder model from Honda, the CB750, which had stunned the world of motorcycling when it arrived in 1969. There was nothing new in an across-the-frame-four – the Italians had been winning races with exactly the same format, as indeed had Honda itself. What was new, and why the CB750 broke new ground, was the fact that it was the world's first mass-produced four-cylinder motorcycle.

The CB750 was powered by a single overhead camshaft 736.5cc unit construction engine, with five-speed gearbox and wet multi-plate clutch. There was also a single-disc hydraulically operated front brake, electric starter, and full instrumentation. In many ways, Honda had taken a huge gamble, but it paid off handsomely. It also coined an entirely new word in the bike world, 'Superbike'. Before the CB750, bikes were just bikes. Maximum power output of the CB750 was 67bhp at 8000rpm, giving a top speed of 185km/h (115mph).

There is no doubt that Honda not only caught out the Europeans and Americans, but also the remainder of its Japanese rivals. However, Kawasaki, Suzuki and Yamaha soon responded. At first this response came via two-stroke models, including Kawasaki's 500H1 (Mach III) triple, the Suzuki GT750 (another triple, but this time water-cooled), and Yamaha's YR3 twin. But in truth none of these really matched the Honda as an all-round performer. Yet it was Kawasaki who moved the

**Since World War II, Harley-Davidson has dominated the domestic motorcycle manufacturing industry in the USA. Its staple diet has been a never ending series of V-twin engines. In the early postwar period, the most popular was the 750cc side-valve WLA model.**

game on, when in 1973 it launched a highly impressive newcomer, the 903cc Z1, and in the process rewrote motorcycling parameters and established Kawasaki as builders of large displacement, high-performance motorcycles.

The Z1 sported a double overhead cam engine. Peak power was 82bhp at 8500rpm, giving a maximum speed of 210km/h (130mph). It also put a big spoke in Mr Honda's wheels, not only by putting the CB750 in its place for the first time, but by outselling it, too. During its four-year production life, the Z1 set new records wherever it went. For example, at Daytona Week in March 1973, a trio of Z1s claimed no fewer than 45 American and world speed and endurance records. Like the CB750, the Z1 came equipped as standard with a disc front brake, electric starter, five speeds, and full instrumentation.

The remaining pair of Japanese manufacturers was much slower getting off the mark with new four-strokes of

their own. Suzuki introduced its four cylinder GS750 (749cc) in 1977, while Yamaha launched its three-cylinder dohc XS750 (747cc) a year later still. By the end of the decade, all four

**During the 1970s, some of the most exotic of all classic bikes came from Italy. The 1976 Moto Guzzi Le Mans Mark I is just such a bike. It included ohv V-twin engine, shaft final drive, and triple disc brakes.**

# FUEL INJECTION - KAWASAKI

Although it was the Germans who largely pioneered the use of fuel injection in racing during the 1950s, Kawasaki was to be the first manufacturer to get the system into a standard production motorcycle: the air-cooled four-cylinder Z1000H of 1980. The Kawasaki Electronic Fuel Injection (KEFI) took the place of conventional carburettors and provided an electronically controlled fuel/air mixture to the engine.

The KEFI had three basic components: an air-intake system, a fuel-delivery system, and an electronic control system. Its benefits included cold start performance, improved fuel economy, lower exhaust emissions, and lower maintenance. Even though the system was basic in the extreme compared to today's sophisticated fuel injection set-ups, it nonetheless set the ball rolling.

Kawasaki then switched, in 1983 (on the GPZ1100), to a much superior system known as Digital Fuel Injection (DFI). In contrast to the more conventional electronic fuel injection (known in the car world as EFI), the DFI has no flaps or gate to measure the air flow, which leaves the intake passage completely unobstructed and thus free from the turbulence created by such sensors. Even more importantly, it eliminates the slight hesitation which occurs between the opening of the throttle and the response of the air

flap to the increased air flow. The DFI system eliminates the tendency for the air flap to 'bounce' when the throttle is closed and then immediately snapped open again – this can cause a sudden delay just when immediate acceleration is most required. Also, in place of the EFI's restrictive air sensor, the DFI reads the throttle opening, engine revolutions, and air and engine temperature, plus the atmospheric pressure. The system then instantaneously computes the appropriate fuel-injection rate for optimum performance.

The DFI also has a 'fail-safe' circuit which allows the motorcycle to be ridden even if the electrics fail. Other advantages include smoother and more immediate throttle response, easier starting (regardless of engine temperature), and significantly improved high-altitude performance (the altitude sensor can even register changes in the barometric pressure due to the weather). Also, as with all modern fuel-injection systems, fuel consumption and exhaust emissions are also improved over the conventional carburettor. Strangely, however, Kawasaki and the rest of the Japanese motorcycle industry did not follow up with the widespread use of fuel injection, instead leaving the field open to the Europeans.

Japanese marques had even bigger and faster bikes on the market. Honda now offered a new twin-cam 750 (introduced in 1976) and the CB900 followed soon after. In 1979 came the six-cylinder CBX (1047cc). Yamaha's response was to enlarge its XS triple to 844cc and bring out an all-new XS1100 (1097cc) the latter with shaft final drive.

By 1977, Kawasaki had increased its four to 1015cc, creating the Z1000. But, as with Honda, even this was not enough for Kawasaki, so, in 1978, it brought out the Z1300 (1286cc): a liquid-cooled 294kg (653lb) monster with shaft final drive, which was only beaten on the scales for bulk by Harley-Davidson's Electra Glide and Honda's Gold Wing touring bikes. At the end of 1977, Suzuki had also joined the muscle class with its GS1000 (997cc) – a bike viewed by many as the best handling of all Japanese bikes at that time. However, even this model was soon uprated, this time as the GSX1100 (1075cc).

As the 1980s dawned, it seemed that there was a runaway race where only engine size and power counted. Of course, this state of affairs could not last. First a recession came to slow things down, followed by a new breed of performance bike led by Kawasaki and its superb GPZ900R.

When Kawasaki launched its new GPZ900R to the world's press in December 1983, it became the first manufacturer to offer a truly revolutionary design since Honda had stunned the motorcycling world with the launch of the CB750 four back in 1969. Make no mistake, in terms of the high-performance, big-bore motorcycle, the GPZ900R was very much an innovative design. It boasted the world's first liquid-cooled 16-valve dohc across-the-frame four-cylinder motorcycle engine and was also the first machine to combine a lightweight diamond frame, aluminium rear frame section, and 406mm (16in) front wheel. Kawasaki claimed it was the first with forks that delivered truly progressive wheel travel, combined with the company-patented rising-rate Uni-Trak rear-suspension system.

The 908cc motor produced 114bhp and could achieve a genuine 252km/h (158mph), a phenomenal speed for the time. The GPZ900R was not just a straight-line missile, but handled just as well. If any proof of this statement is needed readers should recall that Geoff Johnson won the three-lap 182km (113-mile) 1984 Isle of Man Production TT at an average speed of 169.42km/h (105.28mph), the first of a Kawasaki first, second and third in the event.

At a time when computer analysis was still in the future, the streamlining was achieved by numerous wind-tunnel tests to improve aerodynamic characteristics – the resulting coefficient of drag was a surprisingly low 0.33. Kawasaki engineers had generally got things right straight away, as there

## GPZ900R (1984)

**Engine:** 4-stroke, across-the-frame four, dohc, 4-valves-per-cylinder, water-cooled
**Bore & stroke:** 72.5 x 55mm (2.8 x 2.2in)
**Displacement:** 908cc
**Compression ratio:** 11:1
**Carburation:** 4 x Keihin CVK34
**Ignition:** Electronic inductive
**Lubrication:** Wet sump
**Gearbox:** 6-speed
**Clutch:** Wet, multi-plate
**Frame:** Tubular steel spine-type, with alloy sub-frame
**Suspension:**
*Front:* 38mm (1.49in) telescopic with automatic anti-dive
*Rear:* Single shock, alloy swinging arm
**Brakes:**
*Front:* twin 280mm (11in), hydraulically operated discs
*Rear:* single 270mm (10.6in), hydraulically operated disc
**Tyres:**
*Front:* 120/80 V16
*Rear:* 130/80 V18
**Dry weight:** 228kg (502lb)
**Power:** 115bhp at 9500 rpm
**Top speed:** 254km/h (158 mph)

were no major design changes until 1990, when a mini-redesign took place. This redesign included larger diameter fork legs and a switch from a 406mm (16in) to a 432mm (17in) front wheel. At the same time, the anti-dive was removed and there were new floating discs with four-piston calipers. In addition, a modified airbox was

Kawasaki's GPZ900R of 1984 featured the world's first liquid-cooled 16-valve dohc across-the-frame four-cylinder motorcycle engine. It was also the first to combine a lightweight diamond frame, aluminium rear frame section and 406mm (16in) front wheel.

fitted which reduced both maximum power and top speed.

Even when held up in comparison to later machines, the reason that the GPZ900R was so good was because of its combination of key components, the most important of which was its use of liquid-cooling. This was necessary to enable the engine to produce a high specific power of 127bhp per litre (27.9bhp per gallon) and allow the cylinder block to be more compact. Water-cooling meant that the unit could run a higher compression ratio. It also allowed Kawasaki's engineering

team to position the cam–chain on the nearside of the crankshaft, rather than up the middle of the engine as it had appeared on its earlier air-cooled fours, including the Z1.

Another vital factor in the GPZ900R's success was the achievement of reduced friction losses by dispensing with one of the main bearings and making all four inlet tracts straight, rather than being kinked inwards as on the previous air-cooled cylinder heads; a narrower engine width helped in both respects. Finally, a crucial design feature – and one which makes the GPZ900R's

engine unique amongst four-cylinder bikes – was a double-engine-speed balancer shaft. This also gave the unit amazing smoothness for its type.

In some markets, notably the USA, the model was sold with the name Ninja, and the last GPZ900R rolled off Kawasaki's production line in 1996.

The GPZ900R awoke the Japanese, and the rest of the world, to the fact that there was much more to producing the ultimate performance bike than simply specifying a big engine. A new breed of high-performance motorcycles had been born.

# RETRO BIKES

Unheard of a decade ago, the Retro Bike is today one of the most vibrant and fastest growing sectors in the motorcycle industry. The market leader is the Suzuki Bandit in 600 and 1200 guises and the hugely popular Ducati Monster family. Other serious contenders include the Triumph Bonneville, Honda CB1200, Yamaha XJR1300 and the amazing American Buell Cyclone. The retro is really a combination of yesteryear looks, modern mechanics and a street fighter image.

Another new – but in many ways old – performance motorcycle sales sector was born in the late 1980s when the Italian Moto Guzzi marque played the nostalgia card by launching the 1000S. What made the newcomer different from other motorcycles was that it clearly aped the classic 750S3 model of the early 1970s, but with considerably more performance.

Possibly without realising it, the long-established Italian factory had put the wheels in motion for an entirely new category of motorcycle, the Retro. The English dictionary defines the word 'retrospect' as 'when you look back' – just as Guzzi had done, in fact. However, this simple statement does not fully tell the tale. To begin with, the motorcycle industry could hardly refer to this phenomenon

**The American Buell Cyclone uses a tuned Harley-Davidson V-twin engine and a purpose-built chassis by Erik Buell. Performance is enough to lift the front wheel in any gear.**

as Retrospect, thus it was shortened to Retro. Secondly, almost all Retro bikes built since have been performance oriented, not simply rehashes of old favourites. Even though the style is from the past, the engineering is usually bang up to date.

## KAWASAKI AND THE ZEPHYR

The Japanese Kawasaki firm was the first to appreciate truly the mass-market potential of the Retro and began in Japan with a Japanese-market-only 400 four, named Zephyr, during 1989. Then came a larger-engined model in 1990 – basically a Japanese-market 400 bored and stroked to 553cc. Rather than simply attempting to reinvent the past in contemporary form, Kawasaki reached back in history and re-created a piece of it. Sold in both Japan and the USA, the 1990 ZR550B1 Zephyr – to give the model its full title – played the nostalgia card to perfection.

Visually, the 550 Zephyr copied the hot-rodded Kawasaki street bikes of the previous two decades and specifically the 1000R Eddie Lawson Replica,

'arguably Kawasaki's ultimate hot rod', as the US *Cycle* magazine said in its 1990 test of the new Zephyr. From the subtle contours of the tank and tail section to the Kerker-like, four-into-one exhaust, the 550 Zephyr looked the business; in fact, Japanese after-market companies were soon selling lime-green bodywork to cement the connection. The irony was that the Zephyr's American styling was created by the Japanese themselves, and then exported back to the USA!

Although the original 550 Zephyr only produced some 46bhp, this only told half the story, as this extract from a *Cycle* test reveals: 'The Zephyr can hold its own in roll-ons against the bigger, more sophisticated and more powerful sporting 600s. That's partly because at 200kg (441.5lb), it's lighter, but more importantly it's geared significantly shorter and isn't afflicted with the Grand Canyon torque curves of the 600s. The 550 makes at least 83 per cent of its torque available from 3500rpm to redline. And it combines that strength with crisp throttle response, and reasonably well controlled driveline

lash. So although the Kawasaki doesn't pump out dyno-rocking horse power, it puts what it has right in your hand, right where you can use it, anywhere, any time'.

Unlike many later Retros, the 550 engine technology was not particularly modern and was able to trace its heritage back a full decade, to Kawasaki's original KZ550 of 1980. The torquey engine was backed up by a full-cradle, double-downtube, twin-shock steel chassis, with specifications and handling abilities closer to modern standards than the motor. This type of old engine/new chassis concept had already been used before, notably in the Suzuki GS500 twin, and it made good commercial sense. Put simply, it is cheaper to construct a new frame than a new engine. Of course, Kawasaki at

**The first-mass-produced retro bike was the Kawasaki 550 Zephyr of 1990. Its success ensured a bright future for the genre. Visually, the Zephyr series copied the hot-rodded Kawasaki street bikes of the previous two decades, specifically the 1000R Eddie Lawson Replica of the early 1980s.**

## EXOTIC MATERIALS

Stainless steel is being used more and more in the motorcycle industry. This trend began in the late 1970s, when owners of BMW twins despaired at their original-fit rot-prone silencers and bought stainless steel replacements. The motorcycle is unfortunately a prime target for corrosion.

The success of stainless steel for exhaust system components has led several manufacturers – including BMW, Ducati, Moto Guzzi, Suzuki, Yamaha, Kawasaki, and Honda – to enhance the quality of their products by using more and more stainless steel components. Whereas painted, plated (either chrome or cadmium), and even rubber parts can deteriorate, stainless is virtually indestructible. Even cost is not the barrier it once was, as today motorcycles are seen as luxury goods – in contrast to the attitude of the past, when they were seen primarily as a means of transport. And it is not just stainless steel.

In an increasingly larger number of the bigger, more expensive machines the likes of titanium, magnesium, and several special alloys such as avional and anticoradal are found. Some manufacturers build their frames from high-quality steel tubing, including chrome-molybdenum. Some marques such as Bimota even resort to oval instead of round or square section tubes. Then there are non-metallic materials such as carbon-fibre and kevlar, both of which are used for their combination of light weight and strength, as are an increasingly large amount of high-grade plastics.

In many ways, the materials of the modern high-performance motorcycle are often the same as that found in the automobile and bike racing world, on exotic cars (including Porsche, Ferrari, and Lamborghini), and in the aviation sector. This is set to continue as more high-grade materials are chosen as in the design of tomorrow's performance-motorcycle creations.

that time did not have the benefit of seeing into the future and thus the subsequent boom in Retro bikes. If it had, the original 550 Zephyr might well have had a more technically advanced engine.

Thanks to a strong demand for the model in both Japan and the USA, in September 1990, it was announced that the 550 Zephyr would be marketed on a worldwide basis in 1991 and at the same time a larger version, the Zephyr 750, would also be sold. Clearly based on the 550, the 750 Zephyr's most notable changes were: 738cc four-into-two exhaust, a five-speed gearbox, 41mm (1.61in) – 39mm (1.53in) on the 550 – and a dry weight of 201kg (443lb). Once again, Kawasaki recorded excellent sales.

A year on, in October 1991, Kawasaki took the whole Retro concept a stage further when it launched the 1100 version. It is also worth noting that Kawasaki obviously had at last embraced the Retro principle, as the company replaced the Zephyr tank badge with the Kawasaki one, making the series an integral part of Kawasaki's 1992 model year line-up worldwide. Following in the footsteps of the smaller Zephyrs, the new 1100 was to be the flagship of Kawasaki's

Retro range, at least for the time being; it would also play a significant part in other manufacturers ultimately taking a similar route.

The 1062cc air-cooled engine was unlike its smaller brothers in that it was largely a new unit, benefiting as it did from the company's latest big-bore four-cylinder engine technology. It featured a gear-driven balancer and was specially tuned to deliver strong torque in the low and mid ranges in a way that the smaller engines could not match, giving not only more top speed at 225km/h (140mph), but also a relaxed riding stance and more impressive roll-on performance, without the need for constant downshifting. Another feature of the 1100 Zephyr was its two small spark plugs per cylinder, which Kawasaki claimed provided superior propagation characteristics, with improved burn and enhanced fuel economy.

The details of the 1100's specification included: a pre-programmed digital ignition, a massive seven-row oil cooler (with 50 per cent greater radiation efficiency than the 750 Zephyr), a hydraulically operated clutch incorporating a Back-Torque Limiter for smoother downward gear changes, a stronger frame, and 43mm (1.69in) fork stanchions. Dry weight was up to

242kg (533lb). At that time, the dohc eight-valve engine featured the largest bore ever fitted in a Kawasaki air-cooled, across-the-frame, four-cylinder engine. Of course, Kawasaki's rival three Japanese manufacturers were somewhat upset that it was 'Big K' that had stolen a lead in this new market sector. Each was to respond in its own way.

### THE RESPONSE TO KAWASAKI

To cash in on the Retro craze, Honda re-created the CB750 ('Nighthawk' in the USA) in 1991. This 'back-to-basics' street bike epitomised the almost timeless qualities that had made Honda famous in the big bike arena. The 'new' CB750 had an air-cooled 747cc 16-valve engine based on the 1984 CBX750, with dohc, rather than the sohc of the original 'classic' 1969 CB750 four. Then, in 1992, Honda got far more serious and produced a real performance Retro of its own, the CB1000 Big One. This was much more hi-tech, using the liquid-cooled 998cc dohc 16-valve four from Honda's CBR1000F sports/tourer. Even though it was de-tuned to 100bhp for use in the unfaired CB1000, it still offered plenty of go – 225km/h (140mph) in fact. It was also the first liquid-cooled Retro bike to reach the market.

# NAKED BIKES

Retro – or retrospect – means, as defined by the dictionary, 'when you look back'. Owning and riding a Retro usually means an unfaired and thus 'naked' motorcycle. Some Retros do have a miniature screen, or in the case of, say, Suzuki's excellent Bandit series, you are given the option of either the naked (N) or faired (S) versions, the latter at a slightly higher cost.

Until the mid- to late 1970s, most bikes, even performance ones, lacked a fairing of any sort. Then BMW and Ducati introduced off-the-shelf models with weather protection, which started a changeover to bikes with the built-in weather protection found on most modern bikes (except Retros of course!). The main effect of riding a naked bike is wind buffeting at around 145km/h (90mph). Also, you are exposed to the elements: the cold as well as rain. However, in warmer climates, naked bikes come into their own.

Of course, at lower speeds, particularly around town, a naked bike is not such a drawback. Additionally, the faired retro versions do not look half as good as the naked examples, as evidenced by the two versions of the Bandit.

---

Not to be outdone, Yamaha joined in by introducing the XJR1200. This used the air-cooled 1168cc four-cylinder engine previously found in the company's long-running FJ1200 sports/tourer, itself derived from the even older FJ1100 of the mid-1980s. At the time of its introduction, many considered the XJR1200 to have the best engine – with loads of torque from tick-over upwards – but the handling did not match the Honda CB1000. On performance, the two bikes were virtually equal, both being able to reach 225km/h (140mph) – that is, if you were able to hang on at this speed without any form of wind-cheating fairing.

## ENTER THE SUZUKI BANDIT

So what of the fourth member of the Japanese Big Four manufacturers, Suzuki? Well, it took longer, but ultimately had a hit with its Bandit models. The first of these, launched in time for the 1995 season, came in the shape of a sensational 600cc bike. The GSF600 Bandit was a knockout, The press was ultra enthusiastic in its test reports, while the big-buying public voted the Suzuki entry number one with the best form of response – their cheque books. Many agreed that this was the best bike of 1995, irrespective of cubic capacity, cost, or model category. It was a Japanese bike with real character. It was a quick steering, well-balanced backlanes bike that would corner, wheelie, or eat the miles under its tyres with no problem. Even the pillion seat was comfortable! The key difference was the way in which it topped 193km/h (120mph) and still cost less than the opposition.

The top-selling *Motor Cycle News* even went as far as placing the new Bandit among the top five bikes of modern times (the others were the Honda C90, Honda CX500, Honda CBR600, and Suzuki GSX-R750). *Motor Cycle News* said: 'Of thousands of bikes on the roads, only a handful stand out as red-hot winners. They're the bikes that have got it all.'

Suzuki had achieved the seemingly impossible, an excellent performance bike at a knock-down price. The 599cc oil/air-cooled engine was borrowed from the GSX600 sports model and re-tuned for improved mid-range punch, which allowed the 600 Bandit to be hurried along far more quickly than anyone had thought possible. It was still keen to rev when necessary, and helped by an excellent gearbox, but the real pleasure was that you could still make rapid progress without having to scream the engine in the lower gears. *Motor Cycle News* commented: 'It's surprising what sort of sports bikes the Bandit can keep in its sights.'

The frame did not look anything special and was the basic steel-tube affair, but worked well and, unlike the first crop of Japanese Retros, the 600 Bandit scored well by having the more modern single-shock rear suspension (which Kawasaki, Yamaha, and Honda had not considered suitable, sticking to the old-fashioned 'classic' twin-shock arrangement for fear of spoiling the Retro image instead). The single rear shock improved both handling and comfort over the period twin shockers.

Suzuki claimed 76.4 bhp at 10,500 rpm and the 600 Bandit sported four-valves-per-cylinder and a six-speed gearbox to complete its impressive credentials. Yet Suzuki was not content to sit back by simply producing the top middleweight performance Retro; a year on, it made another truly inspired move when, in early 1996, it launched the GSF1200 Bandit.

The 1200 Suzuki Bandit took the market by storm in 1996. It was a great bike. The combination of a 1157cc four-cylinder engine coupled with a lithe chassis and a dry weight of just 464lb (211kg) – much lighter than either the Yamaha XJR or Honda CB Retros – made it easy to see why the big Suzuki had so much going for it. Also, unlike its revvy 600 brother, the 1200 had an engine blessed with a truly heavyweight punch. The bigger Bandit had real heritage, too, being based around the power plant of Suzuki's original modern muscle bike, the infamous GSX-R1100, whereas the Honda had its origins in the CBR1000 and the Yamaha the FJ1200. These were great bikes, but not quite with the same image as the big, bad GSX-R. So, Suzuki had the opposition licked on image and street credibility.

Then came the riding part. Sling a leg over the Suzuki's wide saddle and the first thing that you noticed was the Bandit's size. It was more compact than the Yamaha and positively tiny in comparison to the Honda. Despite a flat, wide and, it must be said, comfortable seat, most riders were still able to plant both feet flat on the ground. The wide handlebars were not only comfortable, but offered plenty of leverage for low-speed work. The whole bike also felt light and thus manoeuvrable – much easier to ride than any GSX-R1100, in fact! A key to this compactness came from Suzuki doing an excellent job of replicating the 600 formula so that the two bikes shared almost identical proportions. It is not until the clutch is let out that the difference between the 600 and 1200 becomes apparent.

But what a difference there is in the two Bandits' performances. The 1200's oil/air-cooled, dohc, across-the-frame, 16-valve four was basically a bored-out GSX-R lump, re-tuned for superior mid-range and bottom-end power. With the engine putting out its maximum torque at 4000rpm and

100bhp at 8500rpm, the 1996 GSF1200 Bandit was pretty potent as it left the factory. It was, of course, wholly possible to tune the motor with features from the GSX-R options list, but it might have put the steel chassis under pressure to cope with a full-power GSX-R specification.

The short-throw gearbox was easy to use and the balance of the transmission was also well up to Suzuki's usual high standard. Set up very much for acceleration and low-down punch, the five-speed gearbox could have easily pulled a higher gear, or even a sixth ratio. Top was in fact too low, making the engine feel somewhat busy at motorway cruising speeds. However, as you could purchase either a naked bike (N) or the version with a small fairing (S), potential owners wishing to do a lot of motorway riding or to use their bike during the winter months could choose the faired option, even if it did lack the unfaired bike's cool, street-fighter style.

Where the 1200 Bandit really scored was in the way in which its smooth delivery of power and excellent suspension made it extremely user-friendly and almost as easy to ride as the 600. Handling and road-holding were almost up to Racer Replica standards. Having done around 150 laps of Cadwell Park (UK) race circuit on my own 1200 Bandit, I can honestly say that the only limiting factor was the standard-fit Michelin Macadam tyres.

The wide 432mm (17in) cast-alloy wheels came straight off the GSX-R. The brakes again were from the GSX-R parts bin, the four-piston Nissin calipers biting into a pair of 310mm

**Honda's first retro was the 998cc liquid-cooled dohc CBR-engined CB1000 Big One of 1992. The arrival of bikes such as the XJR1200 Yamaha and 1200 Bandit Suzuki forced Honda to up their game; the result was the CB1200, which arrived in 2000.**

**Suzuki's GSF1200 Bandit was introduced at the beginning of 1996. Its combination of retro looks and massive roll-on power from its GSX-R-derived power plant made it an instant best seller. The Bandit's handling and road-holding abilities also put many of its rivals in the shade.**

(12.2in) discs. A four-header exhaust system benefited from its construction from stainless steel, whilst the vast aluminium silencer was conveniently chamfered to allow additional ground clearance. As for performance, the 1996 1200 Bandit could easily top 209km/h (130mph), whilst it despatched the standing 0.4km (0.25-mile) sprint in 11.2 seconds, a terminal speed of 195km/h (121mph).

Other features included chromed clock housing (for speedometer and tachometer), grab handles either side of the seat for the pillion passenger, centre and side stands, 43mm (1.69in) telescopic front forks, and monoshock rear suspension with rising-rate linkage. As if to emphasise the talents of the Suzuki Bandit family, a 1-model race series for the 1200 version has proved a major success story in Great Britain. Modifications on the Bandit are limited to exhaust, suspension and tyres. This new racing category allows riders to take to the track without breaking their bank balance due to its low running costs.

The formula remained so good that, except for a few additional colours, the 1200 Bandit remained the same until the 2001 model year. As *Which Bike?* had to say in its Autumn/Winter 2000 edition: 'There are more than 60,000 big Bandit owners out there now, many of them distinguishable by broad smiles and distinctly stretched arms. They make a useful bunch for obtaining feedback, and whaddya know? Suzuki has done some serious listening, and given the Bandit a thorough revamp as a result.' Yes, the Bandit 1200 had changed, but its basic formula and simple, rugged appeal have survived intact. This was important, as quite often these exercises rob a bike of its original

**Engine:** Oil/air-cooled, dohc, 16-valve, across-the-frame, 4-cylinder, 4-stroke.
**Bore and stroke:** 79 x 59mm (3.1 x 2.3in)
**Displacement:** 1157cc
**Compression ratio:** 9.5:1
**Fuel system:** 4 x Mikuni 36mm (1.41in) CV carbs
**Ignition:** Electronic
**Gearbox:** 5-speed
**Frame:** Tubular steel, double cradle
**Suspension:**
  *Front:* 43mm (1.69in) telescopic forks
  *Rear:* monoshock with rising-rate linkage
**Brakes:**
  *Front:* 2 x 310mm (12.2in) discs, with 6-piston calipers
  *Rear:* single 240mm (9.44in) disc, with 2-piston caliper
**Wheels:** 432mm (17in), aluminium
**Tyres:**
  *Front:* 120/70 ZR17
  *Rear:* 180/55 ZR17
**Dry weight:** 'N' naked 214kg (471lb) 'S' faired 221kg (487lb)
**Power:** 100bhp at 8500rpm
**Top speed:** 'N' 212.4km/h (132mph); 'S' 217km/h (135mph)

character in the search for so-called 'improvements'.

Top of the original model owners list had come a larger fuel capacity, followed by greater seat comfort and wind protection. Thus the 2001-model 1200 Bandit got a bigger fuel tank – although capacity had only gone up by 1 litre (0.21 gallons) from 19 to 20 litres (4.1 to 4.4 gallons). The seat was also revised with a low seat height and the addition of a non-slip surface at the rear of the saddle to assist the pillion passenger. The issue of wind protection was addressed by the 'S' model's more

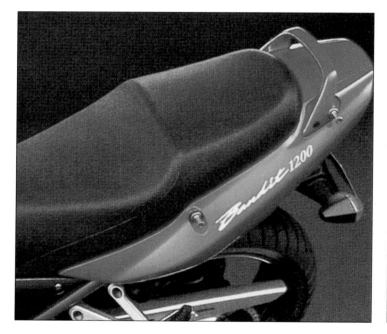

comprehensive and stylish fairing, which supports powerful new twin projector-beam headlamps. Suzuki's engineering team also spent time on the engine, fitting a new exhaust camshaft providing the oil/air-cooled 16-valve engine with reduced valve overlap to increase torque at low engine revolutions. At the same time, the ignition timing was revised, as were the 36mm (1.41in) Keihin carbs. Peak power was still around 100bhp. Other engine-related improvements included a beefed-up clutch and larger oil cooler.

The chassis also came in for change, with a slightly reworked steel frame,

although the latest version's straighter top tubes were more for comfort and cosmetic reasons, rather than to improve handling. The steering angle was slightly revised by making it steeper; trail and wheelbase were thus reduced by a few millimetres. Front and rear suspension were now stiffened up marginally. Front and rear damping rates were also increased slightly, the overall effect making the 1200 Bandit stick to the road even better than before. The front brakes were given six-piston Tokico calipers, replacing the original four-pot devices; the result is best described as akin to hitting a brick wall!

**A quartet of views showing features of Suzuki's best-selling 1200 Bandit, including fuel tank, instrumentation, dual seat, headlamp, matching chromed speedo and tacho pods, twin horns, and direction indicators. The Bandit, in both 600 and 1200 guises, outsells every other retro.**

All-in-all, the changes, although relatively minor, add up to an even better machine and the original was not half bad. The new model is probably best summed up as more comfortable, cleaner running, and better equipped. The 2001 1200 Bandit has only made the opposition's job of competing more difficult. Appearance wise, it was difficult to tell the 600 and 1200 Bandits apart; in fact, the newer, bigger version boasted the same sharp handling and aggressive looks. But, unlike its more revvy smaller brother, the 1200 packed a massive punch. The era of the high performance Retro had really arrived.

## THE EUROPEANS RESPOND

Although Moto Guzzi had almost unwittingly begun the Retro movement, it was to be the Japanese who were the first commercially to embrace the Retro theme. However, although the Japanese companies had exploited – fostered even – the Retro craze, the European factories had also seen the vast sales potential of combining classic 'yesteryear' styling with modern–day motorcycle technology. Triumph, Ducati, Laverda, and even BMW soon were all producing creditable Retros – and high-performance ones at that – to tempt enthusiasts.

Over the past decade, the British fighting spirit has been reborn, thanks almost solely to the efforts of John Bloor and that great British marque, Triumph, which has made a comeback. For decades, with bikes such as

**The road-holding abilities of both the 1200 Bandit (seen here) and its smaller 600 brother have made the Bandit series a pleasure to ride on major roads and country lanes alike. The steel tubular full-cradle frame is massively strong.**

# LUBRICATION

Without any form of lubrication, even the most basic engine will simply grind to a halt. In the earliest motorcyles, the delivery of oil was as much by accident as by design, on the basis that, if the oil was splashed around inside the crankcase, some of it at least might arrive at the correct place. It might fall there through gravity from a container above the engine, usually in a separate compartment integral to the fuel tank, its descent assisted by gravity and impeded by an adjustable metering valve that graduated its flow to a periodically repeated drip. Alternatively, it might be delivered via a hand-operated plunger pump. In either case, the oil was not recovered, being known as the total loss system.

The next phase came with a pump mounted within the engine and a circulation system, so the lubricant could be reused. The most popular forms of oil pump in the era of the British bike (up to the end of the 1950s) were the plunger, rotary, and gear pumps. None of these is really suitable for use in the high-performance, high-revving engines of today. Instead, the most popular is the trochoidal rotor pump, in which two lobed rotors of different diameters suck oil in through one port and squeeze it out through another, as it rotates.

There are also either wet- or dry-sump lubrication systems. In the former, the oil is stored in a sump in the base of the engine, whereas the dry-sump type does not allow the oil to collect in the crankcase, but is instead pumped away to a separate tank which can often allow a larger volume of oil to be carried and circulated (and cooled). However, in this case, two separate pumping circuits are needed. One pumps oil out of the crankcase and into the storage tank, and is called the 'scavenge' pump; the other draws oil from the tank and delivers it under pressure to the engine bearings and oilways, and is thus called the 'feed' or 'pressure' pump. To ensure continuous evacuation of the crankcase, it is necessary for the scavenge pump to be of greater capacity than the pressure pump, but it is not always necessary for two separate pumps to perform these duties – quite often, especially in the case of gear pumps, a single unit can be internally subdivided to serve as two.

Finally, in engines featuring an oil cooler as standard equipment, there is occasionally another safety valve built into the oil-pressure regulator. This ensures a bypass and thus, in an emergency, can deliver oil directly to the engine. Many pumps also incorporate an oil-pressure warning switch.

**Above: The new Bonneville is not the first Hinkley Triumph retro machine; this honour went to the Thunderbird (2000 model shown here), or the naked Trident in 1992. The John Bloor Triumph enterprise certainly cashes in on famous names from the past.**

**Below: A 2000 model year Thunderbird sport. Earlier versions featured a three-into-two crossover exhaust system; this was later rationalised into a conventional system with twin silencers, as shown. Either way, it is an attractive piece of kit.**

best received, having as they did a character all their own. The best of these new three-cylinder models was the 885cc Trident. It was not trying to be a sports bike, so it did not matter that it was on the top-heavy side, while the relatively soft suspension did not impede its cornering potential. It was just a well-balanced, capable, everyday bike with enough force from its lovely 98bhp three-cylinder dohc across-the-frame engine to provide performance and pleasure for most people. There was also a smaller 749cc 90bhp version, but it lacked the low-down torque compared to its bigger brother.

Almost unconsciously, Triumph had created its own Retro. The re-born British marque had considerable success during the early to mid-1990s selling the unfaired 900 Trident, which weighed in (dry) at 212kg (467lb) and could top 298km/h (135mph). One UK magazine said: '[the Trident handles like a GPZ900 and wheelies like a LC Yamaha'.

The success of the Trident saw Triumph embrace the Retro image

the Speed Twin, Tiger 100, Bonneville, Daytona, and Trident, the old Meriden-based Triumph company built inspirational performance bikes which became legends on both side of the Atlantic. In fact, it would be true to say that the Americans loved Triumph more than the British themselves. Then, at the beginning of the 1970s, came the BSA group's demise, which first dragged down Triumph, then NVT (Norton Villers Triumph). Finally, after much political wrangling, there was the creation of the infamous Triumph Workers' cooperative, which itself floundered at the beginning of the 1980s. Nobody, however, had reckoned on John Bloor, a successful Midlands builder, who bought the legendary name in 1983. He spent the next seven years re-creating an entirely new Triumph factory at Hinckley in Leicestershire. As the 1990s dawned, the first of the new models arrived. Eventually these included 750, 900, and 1200 class machines, with either three or four cylinders.

Of all those original 'new' Triumphs, the 900 triples were the ones that were

## TRIUMPH BONNEVILLE (2001)

**Engine:** Air-cooled, dohc, 8-valve, parallel twin, 4-stroke
**Bore and stroke:** 86 x 68mm (3.38 x 2.67in)
**Displacement:** 790cc
**Compression ratio:** 9.2:1
**Fuel system:** 2 x 36mm (1.41in) Keihin carbs
**Ignition:** Electronic
**Gearbox:** 5-speed
**Frame:** Duplex steel cradle
**Suspension:**
*Front:* 41mm (1.61in) telescopic fork
*Rear:* swinging arm, twin shock
**Brakes:**
*Front:* 2 x 310mm (12.2in) disc, with 2-piston calipers
*Rear:* single 255mm (10.03in) disc, 2-piston calliper
**Wheels:** 483mm (19in) front, 432mm (17in) rear, wire spokes with chrome-plated rims
**Tyres:**
*Front:* 100/90-19
*Rear:* 130/80-17
**Dry weight:** 205kg (451.94lb)
**Power:** 61bhp at 7400rpm
**Top speed:** 185km/h (115mph)

with a performance version, the Speed Triple, which could achieve almost 241km/h (150mph) still unfaired; and which saw its own race series for a couple of seasons at British championship level. Then came the Thunderbird, which *Bike* magazine hailed, in 1996, as 'the most stylish Retro by far, which not only faithfully apes the original but handles, steers and brakes better than its locks'. But, in many ways, stylish as it might have been, the new T-bird was not really a performance Retro, thanks to its hi-bars and de-tuned 70bhp engine (still three-cylinder, 885cc). The real Triumph Retro bike was still some time in the future, arriving in 2001.

### TRIUMPH BONNEVILLE – ORIGINS TO 2001

The first Bonneville arrived as part of Triumph's 1959 model range, almost as an afterthought, being in effect a twin-carb version of the existing Tiger 110. Even so, it soon became a model with its own identity from the 1960 year onwards. For many years thereafter, it was the bike everyone aspired to own.

The Bonneville name stemmed from the 344km/h (214mph) twin-carb T110 with which the American rider Johnny Allen sped across the Bonneville Salt Flats, Utah, in September 1956. Unfortunately, FIM, the international

**Compared to the original Bonneville, Triumph's new 2001 version sports a dohc eight-valve engine, short stroke 86 x 68mm (3.4 x 2.7in) dimensions, 790cc, Japanese Keihin carbs, 61bhp at 7400rpm, and a top speed of 185km/h (115mph).**

governing body of motorcycle sport, subsequently failed to ratify the speed as a world record on a technicality, but even so everyone else knew that the streamlined machine had achieved the then fastest two-wheel speed. The record bid and the row which ensued between Triumph and the FIM brought tremendous publicity to the company based in Meriden, Coventry, enhancing the widespread demand for a more powerful version of the Tiger 110. The Bonneville, coded T120, could trace its engine ancestry way back to Edward Turner's Speed Twin of 1937 and the family look showed not only in its general style, but also its engine unit.

The Bonneville displaced 649cc from engine dimensions of 71 x 82mm (2.79 x 3.22in) and was a 360-degree parallel twin with equal firing intervals: the norm for the British industry. Construction of the engine was based on a vertically split crankcase cast in aluminium and separate from the gearbox. The split was on the engine centre-line and the case halves had an identical ball-race main bearing on

each side, plus a pair of bronze bushes. The crankshaft was a forged one-piece affair, while the cylinder block was held down by eight studs. The cylinder head was an aluminium casting. It had splayed inlet ports that were threaded for the inlet tracts which screwed into place and each was then locked by a large nut. Twin Amal 26.9mm (1.06in) carburettors were employed – and these were 'chopped' so that the float section was deleted. This function was carried out by a circular Amal Grand Prix racing–type chamber clamped to the seat tube with a rubber strip to reduce the effects of vibration.

For the first year's production (1959), the bike was simply a stock Tiger 110 with the twin-carb engine and higher specification. But its tremendous sales demand that year ensured a dedicated

Bonneville came along for the 1960 model year. This example, with its powder blue and silver finish, is now seen as a classic and somehow, hard as they tried, subsequent versions never quite recaptured the spirit of that 1960 bike. With its flat bars, chrome Lucas headlamp, narrow section mudguards, dual (grey/black) seat, parcel grid atop the tank, and purposeful lines, it still looks breathtaking today. It was also able to reach 177km/h (110mph) – more with tuning items such as E3134 cams – and it was capable of matching anything on two wheels, except for the now out-of-production 998cc Vincent V-twin. The next major update came for the 1963 model year, with a new nine-stud, unit-construction engine, points in the timing cover, coil ignition, and revised chassis.

## BONNEVILLE EVOLUTION

**1959** T120 Bonneville launched as a result of demand for a high-performance version of the 649cc pre-unit version of single-carb Thunderbird/T110 models. Featured dynamo, splayed alloy head, iron barrel, twin Amal Monobloc 376 carbs, headlamp nacelle; 46bhp at 6500rpm, 177km/h (110mph).

**1960** Revised Bonneville introduced with new duplex frame, new swinging arm, new front forks, alternator, more sporting mudguards, separate chrome Lucas headlamp and revised styling.

**1961** Rev counter drive on timing cover.

**1963** Unit construction engine, nine-stud head, points in timing cover, coil ignition, revised frame.

**1964** Induction balance pipe.

**1965** New front forks, modified rear brake.

**1966** New-style tank badges, frame changes, oil supply to exhaust tappets.

**1967** Improved oil pump.

**1968** Modified front brake and forks; separate contact breaker points.

**1969** Modified silencers, exposed rear springs, exhaust balance pipe.

**1970** Minor changes to carb settings, ignition coil, engine breather and suspension units.

**1971** New frame housing engine oil, new forks, brakes, conical brake hubs, indicators.

**1972** Five-speed gearbox available as an option.

**1975** T120 discontinued.

**1976** T140V 744cc, left-hand gear change.

**1977** Silver Jubilee Bonneville produced. Special finish.

**1978** Halogen headlamp, new cylinder head, Amal Mark 2 Concentric carbs. Electric starter available as an option.

**1979** Electronic ignition. Some bikes produced with cast alloy wheels and two-into-one exhaust.

**1980** Electric starter available as standard; model coded T140ES. Executive model introduced.

**1981** Limited edition Royal model, with German Bing carbs.

**1982** TSS model introduced with eight-valve engine and all-alloy top end, new stiffer crankshaft with larger diameter big-ends. 2 x 34mm (1.33in) Amal Concentric Mk2 carbs, 9.5:1 compression ratio. A second new model, the TSX was a custom styled bike based on stock T140. The engine was standard two valves per cylinder, with Bing carbs and megaphone-type silencers. Cast alloy wheels, 483mm (19in) front and 406mm (16in) rear. Twin front brake discs optional. Two-level dual seat.

**1983** Production at Meriden ends.

**1985** Production resumed in Newton Abbot, Devon, UK, thanks to spares specialist Les Harris. Limited number of 744cc-engined Bonnevilles produced over next four years using a mixture of British and Italian component suppliers. Thus the brakes were Brembo, forks Paioli, and instruments Veglia.

**1989** Production at Newton Abbot ends.

**2001** New John Bloor, Hinkley Triumph company launches brand-new Retro-styled model with 790cc eight-valve dohc engine, 2 x 36mm (1.41in) Keihin carbs, 483mm (19in) front and 432mm (17in) rear wheels, both with disc brakes. 61bhp at 7400rpm, 185km/h (115mph).

A popular role for the Bonneville was racing. There was even a special limited-run Thruxton Bonneville named after the famous Hampshire (UK) airfield circuit which had witnessed many of the Triumph's race wins. Riders such as Malcolm Uphill from Wales, UK, also won the coveted Isle of Man TT on Bonnevilles. In the USA, a special Bonneville TT was sold, but this machine had no connection with the Isle of Man or even European racing. Instead it was a dirt-track racing motorcycle.

As for the standard production Bonneville, this saw small changes virtually every year throughout the remainder of the 1960s. Another major update came in 1971, when a new oil-bearing frame was introduced, together with new front forks, conical brake hubs, and indicators as standard fitment. In 1972, the first Bonneville to sport a five-speed gearbox went on sale. By the mid-1970s, in an attempt to counter the growing opposition from bikes such as the Norton Commando, Ducati 900, and Laverda Jota, Triumph finally enlarged the

## LCD DISPLAYS

LCD (liquid crystal display) technology really began in the 1980s. It was slower to arrive in the motorcycle world than in the car world. However, it is here, it is going to stay, and several firms, including the Italian pace-setter Aprilia, are championing its cause. When Aprilia launched its all-new RSV Mille Super Bike at the Milan Show towards the end of 1997, one of its most talked about features was its dashboard. According to the American specialist journal *Sport Rider*, the RSV was something to get excited about: 'If you're one of those techno-gadget freaks, you'll definitely like the Aprilia's dashboard.' This was in reference to the mass of information accessible via its two LCD panels, which are mounted on either side of a large analogue tachometer.

On the left, a digital speedometer is accompanied by an odometer/trip meter, but that is only the start. The rider can access the average and maximum speeds attained on any outing; there is also a lap timer (actuated by the hi-beam flash switch on the left clip-on handlebar, which can store up to 40 laps, a digital clock, a coolant temperature and battery voltmeter display, as well as an engine diagnostics and periodic maintenance function. The tachometer also has a gear shifter (red) warning light that allows the

rider to programme the required rpm change point. The Aprilia lead will no doubt be standard issue throughout the performance bike industry before long.

**The latest generation of motorcycles often use LCD (Liquid Crystal Display). All but the tachometer are thus calibrated, including speed, fuel, distance and engine temperature.**

engine to 744cc, at the same time transferring the gear-change from the right to the left. A special edition to celebrate the Queen's Silver Jubilee in 1977 was built, dressed out in a blue and chrome finish.

By this time, the workers' cooperative had taken over the Meriden plant and, although it subsequently built an eight-valve all-alloy Bonneville-engined bike, the TSS, things went from bad to worse. The cooperative finally went bankrupt in 1983. But still the Bonneville did not die. Instead, from 1985 until 1989, it was built in Devon by Les Harris, using a mixture of British and Italian components. However, it was John Bloor, not Harris, who had purchased the rights to the Triumph name when the cooperative floundered in 1983. From the early 1990s, a new

breed of Triumphs – without the venerable Bonneville – was built at a new greenfield complex in Hinkley, Leicestershire, in the UK.

That was, until the year 2001, when the John Bloor Triumph enterprise sprung one of motorcycling's biggest ever surprises by launching a new Bonneville. This machine is an exceedingly clever design, echoing as it does the original, but with an all-new 790cc short-stroke engine sporting twin overhead camshafts and twin balancer shafts, and developing 61bhp at 7400rpm. *Bike* magazine, in its January 2001 issue, asked the question: 'What's in a name?'. As it answered itself: 'Well in this case, plenty. When you're talking about genuinely world famous motorcycle tags, ones which might even be recognised by your

middle-aged woman down the precinct, you'll struggle to reach a handful. Electra Glide? Possibly. Gold Wing? Maybe. Bonneville? Surely.'

Yet, despite having the power of that name at his disposal, owner John Bloor resisted the temptation to cash in until certain of making the right move. Although the new 'Bonnie' looks similar to the original, it is actually virtually a new bike in all but name and tank badge style. Yes, it does have a parallel twin engine, two wheels, and a frame, but start digging deeper and you begin to discover a wide range of differences. Major changes include the disc brakes on both wheels (the 1959 original had drums on both wheels), the kinked exhaust, the double overhead cams instead of pushrods, the Japanese-made Keihin carbs (instead

**Ducati's Monster (900 shown) has been a tremendous sales success. The work of designer Miguel Angel Galluzzi, it was called the 'Monster' after an unnamed factory worker dubbed the prototype *Il Monstro* after seeing it for the first time.**

Designed by Mignel Angel Galluzzi, the first the world saw of this inspired creation was at the German Cologne Show in September 1992, when an original pre-production prototype was displayed. The Monster name came about after a factory worker dubbed the prototype the 'Monster' after seeing it for the first time. The label stuck.

The M900 Monster, which entered production in mid-1993, was in reality a simple marriage of two prime constituents, the chassis from an 888 SP4 and the engine from the existing 900SS. The 904cc oil/air-cooled sohc Desmo two-valves-per-cylinder 90-degree V-twin, with belt-driven cams, was exactly the same unit found on the 900SS sportster. Chassis-wise, things were slightly more varied, although not radically so. The basic frame, as already stated, was taken from the 888 SP4, with the 41mm (1.61in) Showa-made inverted front forks coming from the 1993 888 Strada. Up front, the braking was taken care of by a pair of floating 320mm (12.59in) discs and Brembo four-piston goldline calipers, while at the rear there was a single 245mm (9.64in) disc with two-piston calliper.

Besides its excellent styling job and all-round ability, the most striking

of the British Amal originals), and the short-stroke engine dimensions, not to mention the larger 790cc displacement.

Having said all that, however, the new Bonneville looks right, goes right, and will probably be a huge commercial success for the reborn Triumph marque. Like other Retros, it also benefits from modern technology advancements made since the original was first sold in the 1960s.

## THE DUCATI MONSTER SERIES

Best described as the radical end of the Retro scene, Ducati's Monster series has become one of the real sales successes of recent years, outselling all other versions of the Italian company's V-twin family. Just what an impact the M900 made when it was launched back in 1993 is best illustrated by this extract from a *Motor Cycle News* test of April 1994: 'Twice in succession, Ducati has created the most talked about bikes of the year. Right now the number 916 is on everyone's lips, usually while they're wondering when it will arrive. And last year people were muttering the same question about the Monster, desperate even to see one of the radically-styled machines.'

**Above: Much of the success garnered by Ducati's Monster series has been down to its excellent combination of torquey V-twin engine, flex-free steel trellis frame, and low weight. Actually, the Monster tab is hardly accurate, as the bike is nearer flyweight than heavyweight.**

**Below: Introduced in 2000, the Italian Cagiva Raptor uses the powerful 996cc Suzuki TL1000 V-twin engine.**

Moto Guzzi's V11 Sport uses the 1064cc two-valves-per-cylinder ohv 90 degree V-twin fuel-injected engine similar to that found in the latest California tourer, but suitably tuned and joined to an entirely new six-speed transmission.

and absolutely loads of carbon-fibre extras, plus racing quality brakes, wheels, and engine tuning.

Ducati gave the 900 Monster fuel injection for the 2000 model year by utilising the same engine specification as the latest 900SS. Even this was dwarfed, however, by the advent of the 916-engined Monster S4, which arrived for 2001 and at last put the Italian V-twin on par with anything the remaining Retros could offer.

### OTHER ITALIAN STALLIONS

Like Triumph, the Italian Laverda marque was reborn in the early 1990s and, in answer to Ducati's Monster, Laverda introduced the Ghost in 1996. It, too, sported a steel trellis frame, inverted forks, single rear shock, and triple Brembo hydraulically operated disc brakes. What was different was the 668cc dohc 180-degree parallel twin engine, with four valves per cylinder,

aspect of the M900, or any Monster for that matter, is size, or lack of it. It is hardly a 'Monster' at all really, with even the most short-legged amongst the riding fraternity being able to put both feet firmly on the floor, the seat height being a super-low 770mm (30.3in). Other specification details included a pair of 38mm (1.49in) Japanese Mikuni carbs, a six-speed gearbox, and a dry weight of 184kg (405lb). Like all other Ducatis of recent times (post-1985), it featured single-shock rear suspension.

A 583cc '600' arrived in 1994, with much less power (53bhp) and a host of cost-cutting measures, including a single-disc front brake, no oil cooler, a mechanical clutch, and plastic instead of carbon-fibre side panels. A 750 (748cc) version followed in 1996. For 1998. a higher per-formance 900S version was introduced. But of course the factory, small after-market firms, and even

private owners have built many special editions. Probably the fastest Monster on earth was the PCS Turbo version of the 900, while the trickiest was that from CH Racing, which constructed a batch of 20 special Azzalini Monsters in 1996–97.

It used many one-off components, including an oval-section frame in high-grade chrome-molybdenum tubing

**The Guzzi V11 Sport entered production during 1999 (2001 model shown) and boasts an impressive specification, including inverted forks, monoshock rear suspension, three-spoke wheels, oil cooler, and Brembo Goldline brakes with floating front discs.**

# ELECTRICAL EQUIPMENT

Modern motorcycles have made truly great strides with regard to electrical equipment. During the early 1960s, before the Japanese arrived in Europe and North America, virtually all motorcycles had weak six-volt electrical systems, often with equally poor electrical equipment. Present-day motorcycles, however, including the Retro, have generally efficient, reliable and power-ful electrical components. Currently, most items are electronic and thus sealed for life, a trend first begun during the 1970s. Whereas, on older motorcycles, it was often possible to repair components, on today's models replacement is often the only option.

Besides the electrical components themselves, wiring has also seen major improvements, with current bikes using far less of the stuff, which in turn, means there is far less to go wrong in a bike's electrical circuit. It is also worth explaining that ,whereas most classic bikes will have either a magneto/dynamo or alternator, and coil ignition (with points and condenser), new bikes almost universally have an alternator (for charging) and electronic ignition. However, there are variations of each of these three main types.

Modern-day electrics mean servicing work is best left to a main dealer for your brand of motorcycle. This is because today the various systems need to be diagnostically checked with sensitive and expensive equipment, which is not only of a complex nature, but also extremely costly to purchase. The old days of consulting your workshop manual and getting out your tools are now almost a thing of the past. Motorcycles, like cars, are now best left to the main dealer servicing regime.

---

mixed air-oil cooling, and chain-driven camshafts. It also featured fuel injection and a six-speed gearbox.

But even if the original Ghost did not quite match the Monster in the styling stakes, the new-for-1997 Ghost Strike certainly did, with a bold yellow and black paint job, aluminium-beam frame borrowed from the company's 668 sports bike, and mini fairing. When it came to performance, the Ghost, even with 236cc less cubic capacity, was the equal of the original carb-version of Ducati's M900 Monster. At first, the Ghost Strike shared the same 668cc displacement as the standard Ghost, but later it benefited from the more powerful 747cc 82bhp motor from the 750S sports model.

It could almost be argued that all Moto Guzzi bikes are in the Retro tradition, but it is probably the V10 Centauro (which used the four-valves-per-cylinder ohc engine from the Daytona sportster) and the six-speed two-valves-per-cylinder V11 that came the closest. The latter, introduced in 1999, can polish off the standing 0.4km (0.25-mile) sprint in 12.71 seconds and achieve 212.4km/h (132mph). This is from 82bhp at 7600 rpm and claimed torque figures of 9.26kg/m (67lb/ft). All Guzzi V-twins feature shaft final drive, making them an acquired taste for the performance buff.

Introduced in the year 2000, the Cagiva Raptor and V-Raptor both use Suzuki's powerful TL1000 V-twin engine. Displacing 996cc, the dohc 90-degree, four-valves-per-cylinder liquid-cooled 90-degree V-twin provides the new Cagiva entries with a 229km/h (142mph) top speed and the ability to

Harley-Davidson's performance arm, Buell, is now largely responsible for promoting a more sporting image for the manufacturer. Erik Buell built his reputation by tuning Harley-Davidson's V-twins, before the two companies joined forces to sell Buells together through the Harley-Davidson dealer network.

**The top Buell is the X1 Lightning, with its 1203cc two-valves-per-cylinder 45-degree V-twin engine putting out 95bhp at 6200rpm. Out on the street, this gives a maximum speed of 219km/h (136mph).**

match virtually any motorcycle on acceleration, as *Bike* pointed out in its December 2000 issue: 'On a track day at Snetterton everyone in the office was having a go. There were no complaints – except from R1 and Blade riders it nicked past driving hard out of bends.'

## THE GERMAN RETROS

The German connection is made by BMW, in the shape of a couple of oddball Retros, which, on the face of it, would appear to be for BMW traditionalists, but actually have a potentially wider audience. If you can live with the weird styling, that is.

The R1100R and R850R were both introduced in autumn 1994 and were the German marque's first all-new machines for years to have no form of fairing. At the heart of both bikes was the essentially same fuel-injected, shaft drive R259 air/oil-cooled four-valve-per-cylinder flat twin engine series that had made its debut on the R1100RS in 1992. Both machines also employed the pioneering telelever front suspension system, paralever rear suspension and digital electronic/Bosch Motronic fuel injection, BMW's adjustable riding position, and optional catalytic converter. ABS brakes were optional on the 850 and standard on the 1100.

The R1100R's engine, displacing 1085cc, was most closely related to that of the R1100GS trail bike. Like the GS, the R's engine had its emphasis on strong mid-range and low-down torque, rather than pure maximum speed – which with lack of a fairing made sense. At first sight, the two bikes looked identical, except for engine size.

In fact, in the author's opinion, smaller is better, as the R850R offers the best balance of performance and pleasure from the flat-twin configuration. Although its top speed is lower, at 189km/h (118mph) compared with the bigger bike's theoretical 200km/h

(125mph), the rider is hard pressed to spot the difference.

As *Motor Cycle News* discovered in its December 1994 test, the R850R put out a genuine 75bhp, seven up on the manufacturer's claimed figure and only 5bhp less than its larger-engined brother. At the test track, *Motor Cycle News* proved that the 0–97km/h (0–60mph) time was only 0.2 seconds slower than the 1100 (4.1 seconds compared with 3.9 seconds).

To rework the R as an 850 BMW, engineers reduced bore size (which meant lighter pistons), and gave the machine slightly lower gearing. *Motor Cycle News* ended its test by saying: 'The R850R undercuts its big brother by £1000 exactly – without any significant disadvantages. The handling agility of the 1100 is retained, the performance loss is barely noticeable in everyday riding, and the engine runs more sweetly. The bike doesn't look pretty, but is distinctive, important when so many modern machines are getting so bland'.

Except for minor styling changes over the years, this pair of BMW Retro bikes keeps finding a steady stream of buyers, proving that, as an overall package, the company got things right first time around – even with those somewhat unusual looks.

## STATESIDE RETROS

Harley-Davidson is the big-name biking marque in the USA, but it is largely left to Harley-Davidson's performance arm, Buell, to provide speed machines. Erik Buell built his reputation by tuning Harley-Davidson V-twins and now, in conjunction with the Harley-Davidson company, markets

Buell bikes via the official Harley dealer network. This means that, in effect, Buell is the performance arm of Harley-Davidson.

The top Buell is the X1 Lightning, its 1203cc two-valves-per-cylinder 45-degree air-cooled V-twin engine putting out 95bhp at 6200 rpm and delivering 11.89kg/m (86lb/ft) of torque. Out on the street, this relates to a maximum speed of 219km/h (136mph). At 200kg (440.9lb), the X1 Lighting is 8kg (17.6lb) heavier than the bike Buell sees as its closest competitor, Cagiva's TL1000-engined Raptor. And, as *Bike* magazine commented in its December 1999 issue: 'Those bags of sugar count when you're cranked into a tightening bend and you want to lose speed.'

Compared with other Harley-engined bikes, however, the Buell is definitely a sporting package. The specially tuned engine fits into a chrome-molybdenum tube frame with inverted Showa front forks and a cunningly slung shock underneath the motor. The X1 Lightning is a highly

individual bike and it gives a unique experience – perhaps the best expression is that it is the ultimate straight-out-of-the-crate street fighter. That mighty V-twin engine with its digital fuel injection and the narrow angle of the cylinders allow the Buell to be both quick and sharp handing, certainly compared to any other Harley V-twin ever made. *Bike* again: 'The motor invades your senses – whether its pile-driving down the high street or romping down a fast A-road in a blizzard of booming exhaust, induction and engine noise, you're constantly aware of the lumpen ironmongery at work below. If only because you have to change gear so often. You'd think a 1203cc V-twin would be flexible, but the X1 is not.' This obviously will come as a big surprise to many readers, but it

is true. Even so, the X1 Lightning offers a unique slice of Retro fun, with enough go to keep most people satisfied. It is also possible to buy the cheaper M2 Cyclone. Basically, this is a budget version of the same bike, but with less zest, a 40mm (1.57in) carb instead of fuel injection, a huge 'lunchbox' airbox on the offside of the engine, conventional telescopic forks with only preload and rebound adjustment, slower steering, and revised bodywork. But it is still a Buell with attitude.

For riders who must have a Harley-Davidson sticker on the tank, there is much to choose from in the Harley-Davidson catalogue, but none of them is a real performance bike.

All these bikes illustrate how far Retros have come in little over a decade, to a point where they now provide a whole new sector of the performance bike, with all the major manufacturers showing a real interest. What is likely in the future is a trend towards even bigger cubic capacities and even higher performance.

**It could be argued that all Harley-Davidsons are retros, as the stateside brand leans heavily on nostalgia. The 2001 FXSTD model features some nice touches, including tank-top instruments, curved saddle, stacked mufflers, wire front wheel, and pullback bars.**

## PICTURE CREDITS

**Action Plus**: 26-27, 58-59, 73 (Phil Masters), 102-103. **Aerospace Publishing**: 34-35, 35, 49, 69, 93, 94, 97 (b), 110, 112, 122, 163. **Roy Bacon**: 31. **BMW**: 126, 128 (t). **Roland Brown**: 9, 14 (t), 28, 33, 37 (b), 97 (t), 100, 151 (Oli Tennant). **Buell**: 154-155. **Harley Davidson**: 172-173. **Ducati**: 45. **Patrick Gosling** 60-61. **Mac McDiarmid**: 16 (b), 18, 20, 32, 36, 37 (t), 39, 42, 43 (b), 48-49, 62 (t), 65, 68-69, 70 (t), 72 (b), 76-77, 91, 95, 114, 124, 125, 128 (b), 130, 132, 134-135, 138-139, 140, 145, 146 (t), 148, 149, 165, 167 (b), 171, 172. **Andrew Morland**: 14 (b), 17. **Don Morley**: 6-7, 10. **John Tipler**: 30, 75, 120-121, 129, 164 (both), 167 (t). **TRH Pictures**: 12, 13, 16 (t), 22, 64 (b), 88, 89, 101, 111, 112-113, 133, 136, 138, 142, 143, 146 (b), 150, 168, 169 (t).

**Mick Walker**: 41, 43 (t), 50, 54, 55, 56, 57, 62 (b), 64 (t), 66, 67, 70-71 (b), 72 (t), 78, 83, 84, 85, 86, 92, 104, 106, 107, 109, 115, 116, 117, 118-119, 131, 156, 162 (all), 169 (b), 170 (both). **WMCNA (Doug Jackson)**: 52, 108, 159.

## ILLUSTRATIONS:

De Agostini UK: 80-81, 152-153.
Aerospace Publishing: 11, 141.
Richard Burgess: 25, 40.
Mark Franklin: 22-23, 147, 160-161.
Kevin Jones Associates: 15, 24, 38, 46-47, 52-53, 74, 82, 90, 98-99, 105, 123, 127, 137, 144.